THE LEADERSHIP MYSTIQUE

FT Prentice Hall
FINANCIAL TIMES

In an increasingly competitive world, we believe it's quality of thinking that will give you the edge – an idea that opens new doors, a technique that solves a problem, or an insight that simply makes sense of it all. The more you know, the smarter and faster you can go.

That's why we work with the best minds in business and finance to bring cutting-edge thinking and best learning practice to a global market.

Under a range of leading imprints, including *Financial Times Prentice Hall*, we create world-class print publications and electronic products bringing our readers knowledge, skills and understanding which can be applied whether studying or at work.

To find out more about our business publications, or tell us about the books you'd like to find, you can visit us at **www.pearsoned.co.uk**

PEARSON
Education

THE LEADERSHIP MYSTIQUE

LEADING BEHAVIOR IN THE HUMAN ENTERPRISE

Second Edition

Manfred F. R. Kets de Vries

Prentice Hall
FINANCIAL TIMES

An imprint of **Pearson Education**

Harlow, England • London • New York • Boston • San Francisco • Toronto
Sydney • Tokyo • Singapore • Hong Kong • Seoul • Taipei • New Delhi
Cape Town • Madrid • Mexico City • Amsterdam • Munich • Paris • Milan

PEARSON EDUCATION LIMITED

Edinburgh Gate
Harlow CM20 2JE
Tel: +44 (0)1279 623623
Fax: +44 (0)1279 431059
Website: www.pearsoned.co.uk

First published 2001
Second edition published in Great Britain in 2006

ISBN-13: 978-1-4058-4019-4
ISBN-10: 1-4058-4019-6

British Library Cataloguing-in-Publication Data
A catalogue record for this book is available from the British Library.

Library of Congress Cataloging-in-Publication Data
A catalog record for this book is available from the Library of Congress.

10 9 8 7 6 5 4 3 2 1
10 09 08 07 06

Typeset in 10.5pt Scala by 70
Printed and bound in Great Britain by Bell & Bain Ltd, Glasgow

The publisher's policy is to use paper manufactured from sustainable forests.

To the memory of my grandfather, Florian Houtman,
who showed me the way.

About the author

Manfred F. R. Kets de Vries brings a different view to the much-studied subjects of leadership and the dynamics of individual and organizational change. Bringing to bear his knowledge and experience of economics (Econ. Drs., University of Amsterdam), management (ITP, MBA, and DBA, Harvard Business School), and psychoanalysis (Canadian Psychoanalytic Society and the International Psychoanalytic Association), he probes the interface between international management, psychoanalysis, psychotherapy, cognitive theory, and dynamic psychiatry. His specific areas of interest are leadership, career dynamics, executive stress, entrepreneurship, family business, succession planning, cross-cultural management, and the dynamics of organizational intervention and change.

A clinical professor of leadership development, he holds the Raoul de Vitry d'Avaucourt Chair of Leadership Development at INSEAD, Fontainebleau, France (and has five times received INSEAD's distinguished teacher award). He is director of INSEAD's Global Leadership Center and program director of INSEAD's top management program, "The Challenge of Leadership: Creating Reflective Leaders." Furthermore, he is scientific director of the program "Coaching and Consulting for Change." He has held professorships at McGill University, the École des Hautes Études Commerciales, Montreal, and the Harvard Business School, and he has lectured at management institutions around the world. He is a member of 17 editorial boards and a founding member of the International Society for the Psychoanalytic

Study of Organizations. He has been elected a Fellow of the Academy of Management. The *Financial Times, Le Capital, Wirtschaftswoche*, and *The Economist* have called Manfred Kets de Vries one of the world's leading management thinkers. In 2005, he received the International Leadership Award for his contribution to leadership research and practice.

Kets de Vries is the author, co-author, or editor of 21 books, including *Power and the Corporate Mind* (1975, new edition 1985, with Abraham Zaleznik), *Organizational Paradoxes: Clinical Approaches to Management* (1980, new edition 1994), *The Irrational Executive: Psychoanalytic Explorations in Management* (1984, editor), *The Neurotic Organization: Diagnosing and Changing Counter-Productive Styles of Management* (1984, new edition 1990, with Danny Miller), *Unstable at the Top* (1988, with Danny Miller), *Prisoners of Leadership* (1989), *Handbook of Character Studies* (1991, with Sidney Perzow), *Organizations on the Couch* (1991), *Leaders, Fools, and Impostors* (1993), the prize-winning *Life and Death in the Executive Fast Lane: Essays on Irrational Organizations and their Leaders* (1995, winner of the Critics' Choice Award 1995–96), *Family Business: Human Dilemmas in the Family Firm* (1996), *The New Global Leaders: Percy Barnevik, Richard Branson, and David Simon* (1999, with Elizabeth Florent-Treacy), *Struggling with the Demon: Perspectives on Individual and Organizational Irrationality* (2001), *Meditations on Happiness* (2001), *The New Russian Business Leaders* (2004), *Are Leaders Born or Are They Made? The Case of Alexander the Great* (2004), *Lessons on Leadership by Terror: Finding Shaka Zulu in the Attic* (2004) and *Leaders on the Couch* (2006). He has also developed a number of multi-rater feedback instruments: *The Personality Audit* and the *Global Executive Leadership Inventory* (2004).

In addition, Kets de Vries has published over 200 scientific papers as chapters in books and as articles. He has also written over 100 case studies, including eight that received the Best Case of the Year award. He is a regular writer for a number of magazines. His work has been featured in such publications as *The New York Times, The Wall Street Journal,* the *Los Angeles Times, Fortune, Business Week, The Economist,* the

Financial Times, and the *International Herald Tribune*. His books and articles have been translated into more than 20 languages.

Kets de Vries is a consultant on organizational design/transformation and strategic human resource management to leading U.S., Canadian, European, African, and Asian companies. As a global consultant in executive development his clients have included ABB, Aegon, Air Liquide, Alcan, Alcatel, Accenture, Bain Consulting, Bang & Olufsen, Bonnier, BP, E.ON, Ericsson, GE Capital, Goldman Sachs, Investec, KPMG, Liberty Life, Lego, Lufthansa, Lundbeck, McKinsey, Novartis, Nokia, NovoNordisk, Rank Xerox, Shell, SHV, SABMiller, Standard Bank of South Africa, Troika Dialogue, Unilever, and Volvo Car Corporation. As an educator and consultant he has worked in more than 40 countries.

The Dutch government has made him an Officer in the Order of Oranje Nassau. He was the first fly fisherman in Outer Mongolia and is a member of New York's Explorers Club. In his spare time he can be found in the rainforests or savannas of Central Africa, the Siberian taiga, the Pamir mountains, Arnhemland, or within the Arctic Circle.

Contents

List of Tables

List of Figures

List of Boxes

Acknowledgments

I would like to thank the group of people who have helped me the most to achieve clarity in the confusing topic that is leadership: my students in my leadership programs at INSEAD. Without their willingness to talk frankly about very personal issues of concern, this book would never have been written. Through the years, they've kept me on target, offering their lives as case studies as we've talked about substantive issues in leadership.

As always, I would like to express my gratitude to INSEAD's R&D department – in particular, Anil Gaba, and the always helpful Alison James. Whatever strange road I've taken – and there have been a few – they've always been cheerleaders, encouraging me in my research endeavors.

Special thanks go to my assistant, Sheila Loxham, who with her good humor is always able to show me the positive side of things. Moreover, her role as a constructive Cerberus, freeing me from day-to-day administrative hassles, is very much valued. I would also like to express my appreciation to my research project manager, Elizabeth Florent-Treacy, who is always prepared to go out of her way to help me solve ongoing research issues. Last, but certainly not least, I would like to express my gratitude to my editors, Kathy Reigstad and Sally Simmons, both of whom I consider to be great text magicians. They cheerfully transform my business vernacular and psychobabble that I include into more palatable material.

PARIS, FRANCE
February 2006

Preface

The most difficult thing in life is to know yourself. THALES

I've learned one thing – people who know the least anyways seem to know it the loudest. ANDY CAPP

You can observe a lot by just watching. YOGI BERRA

I would like to begin this book on leadership with an anecdote, one that's most likely apocryphal. It's about Wilfred Bion, a psychiatrist and psychoanalyst who has greatly influenced my thinking. During World War I, Bion was a tank commander. For those of you who have never been in a tank, it's a very small "working environment" indeed. Bion learned a considerable amount about small-group behavior while serving in such a machine. One world war later, when he was the director of a mental hospital dealing with people suffering from war neuroses, Bion was able to apply some of the concepts he had learned in his military career.

Although Bion had acquired considerable insight into the dynamics of war neuroses by this time, many questions remained. What factors contributed to the problems that the patients in his mental hospital faced, for example? What led to their neurotic symptoms? Why did they suffer from combat fatigue? More important at that moment, what could he do to help them? Bion worked with his patients in small-group settings and wrote about the psychological processes he observed. His work intrigued many people, but his writing style was dense and his conceptualizations complex.

Many years ago – he's been dead quite some time now – there was a conference in London at which Bion was to be a featured speaker. There was a lot of excitement about his presenting; people were interested to hear what he had to say, expecting him to clarify some of his complicated ideas. According to the story, when Bion walked onto the podium, he looked out at the packed auditorium and said, "Here we are!" And having uttered these words, he walked away. That was it.

At lunchtime that day, one of the organizers of the conference went to Bion and said diplomatically, "Dr. Bion, many people have commented on your speech and told me how fascinated they were with your ideas. But they found the presentation somewhat short. Would it be possible for you to elaborate? Could you say something more? Would you mind if we organized a special session this afternoon?" Bion agreed, so a special afternoon session was scheduled. Again, the auditorium was packed. Bion walked to the podium, looked around, and said (or so the story goes), "Here we are again!" And off he marched.

When I'm scheduled to give a presentation, I'm often tempted to act in a similar manner. As must have been the case with Bion, many thoughts cross my mind just before I step up to the podium. I ask myself: Can I articulate my ideas clearly? Will I remember everything that I want to say? Can I meet the audience's expectations? And I'm realistic enough to realize that in each case the answer is probably no, given my own human failings and the audience's range of personal agendas. No wonder that every time I make a presentation I'm very curious to hear what I have to say!

I teach at the most global business school in the world – an institute called INSEAD, which is located in France and Singapore. The main campus is situated in the forest of Fontainebleau, not far from Paris. What once used to be the hunting grounds of the French kings now is the gathering place of probably the most geographically diverse student group in the world. Most of these students – as I tend to say facetiously – walk around with their head tilted slightly to the left (a behavior that they share with the faculty, for the most part). And that tendency inclines them to walk in circles.

Most of my students are "rational" engineers and economists, "logical" thinkers whose left brain appears to be overdeveloped. Preoccupied with rationality and objectivity, they seem to be interested only in "hard" data to analyze complex business situations. They tend to perceive intuition, emotion, and subjectivity as being somewhere on the continuum between rather wishy-washy and dangerously soft, not realizing that "soft" matters can actually be very "hard." Because soft matters can kill a career, I frequently give my students (and colleagues) a slight knock on the head to get the brain back into equilibrium, to help them deal with *both* sides of that vital organ. But my efforts last only briefly. After a short time, most left-brainers go back to "normal," walking once more in circles.

In my academic work, I make an effort to merge two major disciplines. As I sometimes like to say, I try to combine what John Maynard Keynes called "the dismal science" (once upon a time I was an economist) with what Sigmund Freud called "the impossible profession" (I'm also trained as a psychoanalyst). Thus my interest lies in the interface between management and clinical psychology.

In this book, I'll address a number of themes that touch upon leadership, using the clinical paradigm as my microscope for looking at the world. (By *clinical paradigm* I mean the particular perspective that underlies psychoanalysis and related fields – but more on that later.) Unlike many of my organizational colleagues, I'm not interested just in organizational structures and systems. Although I certainly put these variables into the equation when I look at an organization, I'm more interested in the people who make up that organization.

My main objective in studying leadership is *to bring the person back into the organization*. Obvious as the need for the human factor may seem, a considerable body of research in organizations stands out for its conspicuous neglect of the people who are the principal actors in these organizations. Far too many organizational specialists give structures and systems precedence over people. In general, positivism and objectivity prevail in the world of organizations. The credo is that what you can't see doesn't exist. One of the explanations for this outlook is that it's much easier to deal with structures and systems than with people. People are much more complex. Furthermore, people are much harder to change. (As I sometimes like to say, it's easier to change *people* than to *change* people.)

My clinical orientation to management comes at a price. While my interest in the stories people have to tell makes my observations richer, it also makes my life more complicated. After all, structures and procedures are so much more tangible than personality and biography. Furthermore, my focus on the human factor has caused some students of organizations to denigrate my work. For a large number of organizational researchers, storytelling isn't serious business. They see real life as consisting of "rats and stats;" according to their view, only controlled experiments that center on subjects evoking no empathic reactions and that generate unambiguous statistics make phenomena real. Granted, this outlook makes both business and life simpler. The internal, subjective world of the individual – indeed, the whole process of inter-subjectivity (that is, the constellation of effects of one person on the other) – is much harder to control.

In my work, I pay considerable attention to the internal world of people, one person at a time. I ask myself questions such as: What are the focal problems that preoccupy this individual? What has emotional resonance for him or her? What are the script and setting of this person's internal theater? But it's not only the *internal* world of the individual that's important. A person is also part of a *social* setting. We can talk meaningfully about a person only in the context of others. Nobody is an island unto him- or herself (much as some people would like to think so); people function in relationship to others. Thus I also pay attention to the interpersonal dimension. I'm interested in the chemistry of one person with another, especially in the ways that leaders affect the lives of those working (and living) with them.

As I try to get to know individuals in the workplace, looking to both personal and social issues as I deal with people within the context of their organization, I always keep a basic rule of journalists in mind: I focus on the five W's. When interacting with people, I ask the following questions: Who? What? Where? When? Why?

This book on leadership is based on a series of lectures I've been giving on the topic to many different audiences in more countries than I care to recall over a period of many years. Although the comments and conclusions contained herein are based on a large body of research on leadership, it's not my intention to write a highly theoretical book. This is meant to be a *workbook*, a volume that uses practical exercises to actively engage practicing executives who want to learn more about leadership and its vicissitudes – individuals who want to increase their leadership effectiveness.

In spite of the practical slant of this book, however, it's not a simple "how to" presentation. It's also an attempt to reflect on what leadership is all about. Many of the observations to be found in this book are based on research contributions I've made over many years in the study of organizations and their leadership. Readers who are interested in further developing their understanding of the clinical approach to organizational analysis may want to read some of the original source material. (I've included at the end of the book a list of some of my research contributions and those of others on which this book is based.)

I'd like to caution readers that many of the things I say in this book aren't new; some of the ideas I present have been around for a long time. Furthermore, many of those ideas may seem quite obvious. But ideas that lack the sheen of novelty shouldn't be ignored on that ground alone. Ideas that have a long history aren't necessarily worse than a trendy set of new ideas. (Neither, I should add, are they necessarily better.) What matters is how these ideas play out in the workplace, in the lives of real leaders and followers. So I encourage you to look at my observations in light of your own experience, and to evaluate that experience critically. Ask yourself what *you're* doing about the leadership factor. How do *you* execute your *own* leadership style? Whether you work on the shop floor or have a corner office on the top floor of a shimmering skyscraper, what have *you* done today to be more effective as a leader? Do you walk the talk? Are you making an effort to be as effective as you can be?

There's a story of a frog that was lying on a log in a river. Because the log was surrounded by alligators, the frog was at a loss as to how he could cross the river unharmed. At one point, he looked up at a tree and saw an owl sitting on a nearby branch. He said, "Wise owl, please help me. How can I cross this river without being eaten by the alligators?" The owl said, "That's very simple. Just flap your legs as much as you can. That should do it. That will make you fly, help you cross the river, and keep you out of reach of the alligators." The frog did as suggested, and just before he fell into the water, to be snapped up by one of the alligators, he asked the owl, "Why, *why* did you give me this advice? I'm going to be eaten." To which the owl responded, "My apologies. I'm only into concepts. Implementation of the concepts is not my cup of tea."

As the story suggests, only a fraction of the strategies that are formulated in organizations are effectively executed. Most people aren't very good at synchronizing vision and action, at aligning ideas and execution. Anyone dealing in ideas needs to take into consideration people's abilities to implement those ideas. Navel gazing alone doesn't take visionaries past the drawing board. Leaders, to be successful, must understand *action* as well as *theory*.

This book hopes to help leaders shape their action effectively. It does so by addressing the following leadership themes:

- ❖ Chapter 1, "Decoding the human mystique," first looks at what leadership is and does and then introduces the clinical paradigm (which, as I noted earlier, governs my approach to organizational theory and action).

- ❖ Chapter 2, "Emotional intelligence in the world of work," focuses on emotional intelligence, identifying ways that it can enrich both a leader's self-understanding and his or her ability to understand, motivate, and support followers.

- ❖ Chapter 3, "The mussel syndrome," looks at the natural human tendency to resist change – a tendency that can bring down leaders and organizations alike. It also takes stock of the changes occurring in the world of organizations.

- ❖ Chapter 4, "The failure factor in leadership," dissects the interplay of rational and irrational forces behind executive behavior, examining how such issues as transference and narcissism affect leadership and offering ways to offset their power.

❖ Chapter 5, "The Dilbert phenomenon," looks at how organizations suck the life out of their people and offers ways to resuscitate lifeless employees.

❖ Chapter 6, "The rot at the top," introduces specific "neurotic" leadership styles – styles that originate with the leader but eventually have a "toxic" effect on the entire organization – and then offers suggestions for rebalancing these neurotic styles.

❖ Chapter 7, "Achieving personal and organizational change," probes the dynamics of the change process as it applies to individuals and the organizations they inhabit.

❖ Chapter 8, "Characteristics of effective leadership," looks at what leadership demands and outlines some of the competencies that distinguish effective leaders from those who are ineffective.

❖ Chapter 9, "Leadership in a global context," looks at cultural differences and their impact on business, reviews the special demands of global leadership, and highlights ways that organizations can select and develop leaders who work well in the global context.

❖ Chapter 10, "Roles leaders play," focuses on two dichotomies – leadership versus management and charismatic leadership versus architectural leadership – and suggests how leaders can balance these contrasting but necessary strengths.

❖ Chapter 11, "The dynamics of succession," presents the life-cycle of the CEO and reviews some of the dilemmas that make planning for leadership succession so difficult.

❖ Chapter 12, "Leadership development," deals with how organizations can assess leadership ability in potential candidates and develop leadership skills in those already within the fold.

❖ Chapter 13, "Best places to work," defines a new sort of workplace and challenges organizations to adopt that new model.

❖ Chapter 14, "Final thoughts," makes a case for the "fool" in organizations and presents some final thoughts on the subject of leadership.

As I indicated earlier, this book is intended to be somewhat interactive. To that end, it contains a large number of quizzes, self-assessment exercises, and questions. It's my hope that these exercises will facilitate the process of self-reflection in readers. Please note, however, that although many of these exercises are based on a robust body of research, neither the questions nor the measurement of responses have been validated. For that reason, the results of these exercises should never be the sole basis for making a decision. Rather, they should be looked at as guidelines to help readers reflect on and improve their leadership capabilities. These results need to be seen as part of a total package that includes the individual's experience, present life circumstances, and other factors. Our behavior is far too complex to be reduced to a set of simple questions in a self-assessment exercise. Exercises are valuable, but they're only a piece of the puzzle. The results should be seen as indicators, not as absolutes.

To simplify the reading, I've abstained from including source notes and references in this book. If you're interested in pursuing my research findings, or the research findings of others, please see the "Suggested further reading" at the end of the book.

1 Decoding the human mystique

Using the prism of the clinical paradigm

When you discover you are riding a dead horse, the best strategy is to dismount. SIOUX INDIAN SAYING

Nothing ages people like not thinking. CHRISTOPHER MORLEY

The sweaty players in the game of life always have more fun than the supercilious spectators. WILLIAM FEATHER

Organizations are like automobiles. They don't run themselves, except downhill. They need people to make them work. And not just *any* people, but the *right* people. The effectiveness of an organization's employees – particularly individuals in leadership positions – determines how the organizational "machine" will perform.

Some people are so effective at their job that a leader can do very little to make them better; others are so hopeless that almost nothing can be done to improve their effectiveness. The majority of the population, however, falls somewhere in between these two extremes. These people do their job adequately and go with the flow, looking to their leader to set the course, speed, and duration of that flow. They want some guidance, some suggestions about where to go and how to get there. Ethological studies of the animal kingdom also suggest that people have an actual *need* for leadership. Zoologists have written extensively about the complex leadership structures of the great apes – our direct ancestors – which serve as a good illustration of that need.

the effectiveness of an organization's employees determines how the organizational "machine" will perform

The Anglo-Saxon etymological root of the words *lead, leader,* and *leadership* is *laed,* which means "path" or "road." The verb *laeden* means "to travel." Thus a leader is one who shows fellow travelers the way by walking ahead. This metaphor of the leader as helmsman is still applicable today, although there are differences of opinion about the exact role leaders play. What we might call the "helmsman school" can be divided into two sub-groups: those who view leaders as movers of life-size chess pieces and those who look at leaders as individuals who speak to the collective imagination of their people, thereby co-opting them to join in the journey. While leaders of the first type are generally able to get people into motion, it is leaders of the latter type who are able to motivate workers to full commitment and extra effort.

In addition to the two-pronged "helmsman school," there is a third perspective on leadership. People who hold to this final view regard leaders as figureheads – puppets manipulated by forces of the environment. Those who belong to this camp claim that it makes little difference who is in charge; societal forces alone are responsible for what people do. People who hold this view believe that leaders have very little (if any) control over where they themselves are going, much less their followers; and thus leadership is mere illusion.

As a firm believer in the power of human will and action, I must reject the leadership-as-illusion position wholeheartedly. But while leadership isn't *nothing,* neither is it *everything.* Effective business leadership is never limited to the acts of one "heroic" individual; rather, it operates in a context of employees and of the business, industry, and larger social environment. Leaders who recognize the nuances of that context and guide their followers accordingly provide their organization with an extra stimulus. And leaders *do* make a difference, as a wide array of studies on organizations has demonstrated. Even the stock market pays close attention to corporate leadership, with share prices of any given organization influenced by the perceived effectiveness of the leader and the leadership team in charge.

It's clear, then, that anyone wanting to create or lead an effective organization needs to understand the dynamics of leadership. This is not to minimize such factors as economies of scale or scope, the company's market position, and its technological capabilities. These factors are important, to be sure – but they're not as important as leadership. If the leadership dimension isn't properly in place, a company simply can't be successful. A company can have all the advantages in the world – strong financial resources, enviable market position, and state-of-the-art technology – but if leadership fails, all these advantages melt away and the organization – like the driverless car – runs downhill.

If we're to understand leadership, we have to be willing to go beyond the directly observable. We have to pay attention to the presenting internal and social dynamics; to the intricate playing field between leaders and followers; and to unconscious and invisible psychodynamic processes and structures that influence the behavior of individuals, dyads, and groups in organizations. People who dismiss the complex clinical dimension in organizational analysis can't hope to move beyond an impoverished understanding of what life in organizations is all about.

if the leadership dimension isn't properly in place, a company simply can't be successful

Put another way, if we're to understand leadership, we have to choose a three-dimensional (rather than two-dimensional) outlook toward organizational life – a perspective that probes beneath the surface to discern unconscious fears, hopes, and motivations. And while some people may dismiss the kind of work I do in the daytime (to paraphrase Freud) – declaring that attending to people's needs, impulses, desires, wishes, fantasies, and dreams is not scientific – they may dream about me at night. Unconsciously, these factors become part of the equation (Box 1.1).

BOX 1.1

How do you view leadership?

Study the following statements and label them either TRUE or FALSE.

	TRUE	FALSE

1   Effective leaders are rational decision makers
2   Only highly competent people make it to leadership
    positions
3   Once a leader, always a leader
4   In the contemporary organization, leadership is of little
    importance
5   Good leaders have a balanced lifestyle
6   Nowadays we need managers, not leaders
7   Leaders are born, not made

These statements offer a preview of a number of the themes I'll discuss in this book. If you labeled all of them true, I've got some convincing to do!

Introducing key issues

In this book I plan to focus on three issues:

1   I'll argue that "irrational" behavior is a common pattern in organizational life and demonstrate that such behavior has a "rationale" to it. This "rationale" is critical in understanding a person's inner theater – those core themes that affect an individual's personality and leadership style.

2   I'll provide a number of insights into the darker side of leadership, highlighting some of the common behavior patterns that contribute to the derailment of leaders.

3   I'll address what's needed to become an effective leader, identifying what effective leaders do to create high-performance organizations and profiling what such organizations look like.

The rationale of irrationality

Like it or not, executives aren't always paragons of rationality. (They are, after all, people.) However, I'll demonstrate that behind their irrationality lies a rationale. And this rationale needs to be acknowledged and dealt with. Well-intentioned and well-thought-out plans derail daily in offices around the world because of out-of-awareness forces that influence behavior. The boiling cauldron of diverse motivational needs that is the human unconscious takes whatever outlet it can find – even if that means sabotaging a presentation or a promotion or a year-in-the-making plan for globalization.

Although our brains are genetically hardwired with certain instinctual behavior patterns, this wiring isn't irrevocably fixed. Especially over the crucial first months and years of our life (although in later years as well, to a lesser extent), rewiring occurs in response to developmental factors that we're exposed to. The **executives aren't always paragons of rationality** interface of our motivational needs with environmental factors (especially human factors, in the form of caretakers, siblings, teachers, and other important figures) defines our essential uniqueness. These elements work together to set the stage and draft the script for our inner theater.

For each one of us, our unique mixture of motivational needs determines our character and creates the triangle of our mental life – a tightly interlocked triangle consisting of cognition, affect, and behavior. No one of these dimensions of the triangle can be seen as separate from the others. The configuration is what matters. Cognition (that part of the mind that has to do with thinking, reasoning, and intellect) is essential, but so is affect, whose various emotional flavors give us our uniqueness; and cognition and affect jointly determine our behavior and action.

"Emotional intelligence" is the label we give to an understanding of the motivational forces of self and others. Given the importance of each individual's internal theater to cognition, affect, and behavior, emotional intelligence plays a vital role in the leadership equation. It comes down to this: people who are emotionally intelligent are more likely to be effective as leaders. Unfortunately, emotional intelligence isn't something that can be gleaned from a self-help book. On the contrary, becoming more emotionally intelligent is an *experiential* process. Furthermore, it's a learning activity best done with the assistance of a spouse, friend, colleague, leadership coach, therapist or other professional who can help make us aware of our blind spots and see how we interact with others. (See Chapter 2 for more on this subject.)

Leadership's shadow

Most of the literature on leadership depicts the leader as a paragon of virtue and speaks in glowing terms of the attributes that constitute leadership. I would like to remind readers that there's another side to the coin. We can all name at least a handful of political leaders tainted by the darker side of leadership. Adolf Hitler, Idi Amin, Joseph Stalin, Pol Pot, Saddam Hussein, Slobodan Milosevic, and Kim Jong Il all come readily to mind. We're far less likely to recognize leadership's shadow when it falls on the workplace, even though that shadow can darken the lives of many.

The second part of my agenda, then, is to provide insights into the darker, shadow side of leadership. Although it could be argued that ineffective leadership is a contradiction in terms – that the only *true* leadership is *effective* leadership – many organizational leaders derail. The questions we need to ask ourselves are: What makes them do so? What can be said about the failure factor in leadership? Can we identify specific warning signs? What effect is failed leadership likely to have on corporate culture, organizational structure, and patterns of decision making? In the chapters that follow, I'll offer some explanations for leadership derailment, address the psychological pressures that often lead to dysfunctional behavior, and discuss the interrelationship between personality, leadership style, corporate culture, and organizational decision making.

it could be argued that ineffective leadership is a contradiction in terms

The failure factor in leadership isn't a comfortable topic. Not everyone will like what I have to say, especially when I take aim at certain myths about leadership and point out the human limitations of becoming a leader. I'm not nearly as optimistic as all the self-help books on leadership, which suggest that everyone has leadership potential in abundance. My years of experience have taught me that, like it or not, not everyone has any such potential; that, like it or not, leadership failure is a reality – and a common one at that.

Clearly, talking about leadership failure is painful to someone who wants to become a leader but recognizes personal drawbacks or even pathology. It's hard to give up a dream. But it's also hard to talk about leadership failure if we're reluctant to see that our "heroic" leaders have feet of clay.

Seeking the essence of effective leadership

The third theme concerns what's needed to become an effective leader. In this context, I'll address a number of related questions: What are charisma and transformational leadership all about? What characterizes charismatic leaders? What competencies, practices, and roles distinguish effective from ineffective leaders? And what can be done to develop effective leadership qualities? I'll also comment on the psychodynamics of personal and organizational change, dealing with such issues as: What are some of the levers that make for successful change? What are the characteristics of high-performance organizations?

In discussing these issues, I'll demonstrate that an individual's leadership style – a synthesis of the various roles that he or she chooses to adopt – is a complex outcome of the interplay of that person's inner theater, as expressed in core issues (which are influenced by traits and temperament), the competencies that the person develops over the course of the lifespan, and the context in which the person is operating.

The centrality of the clinical paradigm

My work in organizations is grounded in the clinical paradigm. This means that I use concepts from psychoanalysis, psychotherapy, developmental psychology, family systems theory, and cognition to understand the behavior of people in organizations. The clinical paradigm is based on the following three premises:

1   What you see isn't necessarily what you get.

2   All human behavior, no matter how irrational it appears, has a rationale.

3   We're all products of our past.

The meta-force that underpins these three premises is the vast unconscious. A considerable part of our motivation and behavior takes place outside conscious awareness.

Premise #1: Perception isn't reality

The first premise of the clinical paradigm is that what you see isn't necessarily what you get. The world around us is much more complex than it looks to be on the surface. Much of what happens is beyond conscious awareness and we don't have complete control over our perceptual processes. Certain unconscious cognitive rules are in operation when we engage in seeing, and those rules affect what it is we perceive, often bringing us to false conclusions about what we actually see. Mired in our imagined perceptions, we perceive things incorrectly. And this is only *cognitive* distortions we're talking about. If we add in *emotional* distortions, we have a mix that all but repudiates the phrase "rational decision making," giving intuition pride of place.

We're so used to seeing issues as either/or – as polarities – that paradoxical situations confuse us. But paradox is a wonderful instructor: it teaches us to go beyond our customary ways of looking at things – a lesson that pays big dividends in organizational life. The most effective leaders are those who can reframe complex situations. By changing how they *perceive* a problem, they alter what they *see*.

Why is reframing so important? There are three kinds of leaders in this world: the rule takers, the rule makers, and the rule breakers. And it's the last group – those who are able to step outside the existing rules, reframing each problem as it comes up – that gets extraordinary results in the workplace. Richard Branson of the Virgin Group is that last sort of leader. A master of reframing, he's very effective at taking situations where the customer has had a bad deal and turning them into something positive. He's done it in the airline business and in entertainment, to give just a couple of illustrations. Reframers like Branson always ask, *What if? What next?* They know how to play competitive jiujutsu, and they enjoy the game. At the other end of the spectrum, the rule followers watch from the sidelines, unable to recognize an opportunity until it appears in a competitor's business.

Reframing sometimes produces some real surprises. Take the case of an executive who was chafing under an unpleasant, almost abusive boss. After several years of stress, she decided that she'd had enough. Although she liked the organization she worked for, she wasn't willing to throw her life away for someone she neither liked nor respected. When she went home that evening, she told her husband that she wanted to look for another job. He urged her to stay put, pointing out that a new job might mean a new city. He reminded her that his own job was both satisfying and lucrative and that the children liked their school.

In spite of her husband's concerns, this executive went to see a headhunter to find out what other opportunities were available. As she talked to him, she realized in a flash of inspiration that she could reframe her predicament in a way that might bring a solution pleasing to all. She changed tack immediately: instead of highlighting her own virtues, she emphasized the fantastic qualities of her boss. She praised her boss's capabilities; she elaborated on his talents in running the department; she talked about what a magnificent leader he was. The headhunter, intrigued by this profile, contacted her boss and offered him an opportunity to work for another company. Her boss accepted the offer. With him gone, this executive got a nice promotion. By successfully reframing her problem, she not only got rid of her unpleasant boss but she also got his job. She'd clearly used both sides of her brain.

Unfortunately, too many of us have been told by people important to us that it is dangerous to think outside the box and we've paid too much attention to them. As a result, we rarely think outside the box. If we hear that advice as we're growing up – if our outside-the-box thinking is stifled, our creative spark smothered – we begin to see innovation as transgression and end up spouting the same advice ourselves. Worse yet, we stick to that advice even when we hope to see a difference in outcome. In other words, we try to achieve change without changing anything. The challenge of effective leadership is to break out of the box.

the challenge of effective leadership is to break out of the box

Premise #2: Irrationality is grounded in rationality

The first premise of the clinical paradigm, as we just saw, is what you see isn't necessarily what you get. The second premise is that all human behavior, no matter how irrational it appears, has a rationale. A marriage of the two results in the fact that all human behavior – including our uniquely individual cognitive and emotional perceptual distortions – has a rationale.

Acknowledging this rationale helps us to understand all forms of behavior, even that which appears irrational. If we don't understand a particular behavior pattern in ourselves or others, we can try to determine its origins. If we can gather enough background and contextual information, even the most incomprehensible behavior makes sense. I'm the ultimate rationalist: I believe that there's a rationale for everything each of us does (or thinks or says). *Finding* the rationale is rarely easy, however. In corporate life, one has to be something of an organizational detective to tease out what's going on behind this manager's quirky behavior and that manager's insolence.

But given a perceptive eye and a healthy dose of perseverance, anyone who is emotionally literate can do the deconstruction. Generally, irrational behavior is connected to transferential reactions – reactions that involve a confusion in time and place – a process I'll describe in greater detail in Chapter 4. As an example, a CEO who needs to solve a difficult problem at short notice might hesitate to confront one of his executives about her lack of performance in executing the project because as a child that CEO faced unpleasant consequences whenever he confronted his mother.

Suffice to say, for now, that transferential reactions are a form of *unconscious motivation*. Many of our wishes and fantasies and fears are unconscious. But even lurking beneath the surface, they can motivate us. Indeed, the catalyst of much of our behavior lies beneath consciousness. Most people don't like to hear this observation, because they see bowing to unconscious motivation as a sign of weakness. That reaction is understandable. It's downright disconcerting to be under the sway of parts of our personality that we're not even aware of. Most of us would prefer to be in complete control over what we're doing. But like it or not, we all have "blind spots," and our challenge is to find out what they're all about.

Poets, novelists, and philosophers have written extensively about the importance of unconscious processes. Sigmund Freud, however, was the first to build a systematic psychological theory around the concept of unconsciousness. Freud pointed out that unconscious fantasies – images that have emotions attached to them – play a central role in human behavior. According to his theory, conscious motives guide consciously chosen behavior, while unconscious motives guide behavior over the long run. Thus many of our associations about people and events are developed outside our awareness.

Even aspects of our character – good as well as bad – can exist outside our awareness. Because we're equipped with a defensive structure that controls impulsive thoughts and ideas, we may not recognize our true character. We may not be aware of the fact that something we routinely do rubs people up the wrong way, for example – even if we leave burning heaps of irritation behind. When our blindness in this regard is extreme, psychiatrists say we have a "character disorder." One might say that a character disorder is a secret you don't know you're keeping. It's an operation outside consciousness.

Character is a form of memory. It's a person's crystalization of his or her inner theater, a configuration of central issues in his or her personality. As with a healthy person, a person with a character disorder reflects all that he or she has heard and seen and been and done. While each person is unique in character, and in character disorders, there are also similarities across the population. The similarities in disorders are chronicled in the handbook of psychiatrists, *The Diagnostic and Statistical Manual of Mental Disorders* (DSM-IV-Tr), published by the American Psychiatric Association, which lists ten personality types. Other specialists go even further and list additional types. These classifications are used to make assessments, diagnoses, and recommendations for dealing with the vicissitudes of life. Let's look at some of the types commonly named, all of which can be found in the workplace:

❖ **The narcissistic personality type** People of this type are characterized by a sense of grandiosity, a need for admiration, and a tendency toward interpersonal exploitation. Many leaders – including many excellent leaders – have a good bit of the narcissist in them.

❖ **The paranoid personality type** People of this type are hypervigilant, distrustful, apprehensive, concerned about hidden motives, prudent, and alert. They're constantly concerned that someone else will pull a fast one on them.

❖ **The obsessive-compulsive personality type** People of this type are very conscientious; they're preoccupied with orderliness, perfectionism, control, and conformity. They're interpersonally respectful, but they can also be rigid and dogmatic.

❖ **The histrionic personality type** People of this type are very gregarious. They engage in dramatic behavior, are attention seeking, demonstrate excessive emotions, have a fleeting attention span, connect easily to other people, and have a warm interpersonal style. They can be self-centered and sexually seductive.

❖ **The dependent personality type** People of this type are submissive, self-effacing, docile, ingratiating, and constantly in search of approval from others. Fearing abandonment and feeling helpless when alone, they like to be taken care of, often flocking to organizations dominated by a patriarchal leader. They're also common in family businesses.

❖ **The depressive personality type** People of this type have an unusually pessimistic outlook on life, suffer from feelings of worthlessness and self-denigration, and typically exhibit a rather joyless mood.

❖ **The schizotypical personality type** People of this type find interpersonal relationships difficult. Appearing "eccentric" or peculiar to others (because of their suspicion, unusual ways of thinking, odd speech, and inappropriate emotion), they're uncomfortable in social situations.

❖ **The borderline personality type** People of this type are impulsive and unstable in affect, sometimes making recurrent suicide threats or attempts. They typically feel empty or bored, fear abandonment, and are unsure who they are. Tending to be solitary, they avoid close relationships (including those of a sexual nature). They have a rather restricted range of emotional expression and appear indifferent to criticism or praise, although they often show inappropriate anger.

❖ **The avoidant personality type** People of this type demonstrate behavior similar to that of the borderline personality type, but in a less extreme form. Somewhat socially inhibited, they like to get close to others but have difficulty doing so. They suffer from feelings of inadequacy, are very timid, and are hypersensitive to negative evaluation.

❖ **The schizoid personality type** In contrast to people of the avoidant personality type, schizoid individuals have no desire to get closer to others. These people are aloof, introverted, and of a reclusive nature. They have difficulties in establishing friendships, prefer distant or limited involvement with others, and seem to be averse to social activities.

❖ **The antisocial personality type** People of this type, characterized by a low level of frustration, tend to be rather unreliable, irresponsible, and untrustworthy. They like to flout authority and rules and sometimes engage in criminal behavior.

❖ **The sadistic personality type** People of this type often engage in intimidating, abrasive behavior. They are power oriented, opinionated, and combative and abusive in their dealings with others.

❖ **The masochistic (self-defeating) personality type** People of this type act perpetually aggrieved. They tend to be self-effacing and self-denigrating, showing deferential and self-sacrificing behavior that reveals a deep sense of undeservedness.

❖ **The passive-aggressive personality type** People of this type have trouble saying no even when they mean no; they say yes and then fail to act. Because of their frustrating behavior, these people usually don't last long in organizations.

❖ **The cyclothymic personality type** People of this type can be recognized by their fluctuating mood state (thus this type is classified under mood disorders rather than personality disorders). The excitement that their behavior generates can be contagious.

So is everyone who falls within one of these types locked up in the loony bin? Absolutely not. Each type is well represented in workplaces around the globe (and, truth be told, in each of us at times). And all are capable of wreaking havoc. But, as noted earlier, because these character disorders are egosyntonic (that is, part of a person's character, and thus below the level of awareness), they're hard to change.

The first step toward change is awareness of dysfunctional behavior. That means feedback is essential. But even when people gain insight into their dysfunctional behavior patterns, change can't happen overnight. People are armed with sturdy defenses that, having developed over years or decades, are hard to budge. These defenses are another way in which a person's inner theater is enacted.

the first step toward change is awareness of dysfunctional behavior

Defensive reactions vary widely, from the primitive to the sophisticated. Some are quite harmless. The Ottoman Sultan Abdülaziz, for example, had a rather endearing defensive reaction: every morning he reflected his 350-pound bulk in a special mirror that had a slimming effect. Others can be destructive to both self and others.

Most defensive reactions fall into a few basic categories. In the following list, they are ranged from the most primitive to the least primitive:

❖ **Splitting** Some people engage in us-versus-them thinking. They see people as either for them or against them; there's no middle ground.

❖ **Projection** In projection, people falsely attribute their own unacknowledged feelings, impulses, or thoughts to others. Children often assume that others must feel as they do. Carrying that reaction into adulthood, many people project the condemnation of their conscience onto another person.

❖ **Undoing** In this process, people engage in behavior designed to symbolically ward off negative thoughts, feelings, or desires. Expiatory acts or compulsive ceremonials are the most common expressions of undoing. Lady Macbeth's compulsive hand washing after the murder of King Duncan is a great example.

❖ **Denial** People who resort to denial fail to accept some aspect of external reality that's obvious to others. Denial is a defense mechanism frequently used by children to ward off feelings of helplessness: they fantasize that they're strong and powerful.

❖ **Displacement** In displacement, people redirect their feelings toward a person who's less "dangerous" than the one the aggression is really aimed at.

❖ **Regression** If current conflict and tension are too stressful, people regress, returning to earlier patterns of behavior that previously had been given up as ineffective or immature.

❖ **Repression** People who employ repression experience seemingly inexplicable memory lapses. They "forget" to do things that they have no interest in doing.

❖ **Isolation** People who separate ideas from emotions resort to isolation. They break up disturbing ideas into different components, keeping concepts clearly segregated from feelings (which as a result become blunted).

❖ **Reaction formation** In reaction formation, people substitute behavior, thoughts, or feelings that are diametrically opposed to their own unacceptable ones (repeatedly saying, for example, how much they like a boss they despise).

❖ **Conversion** Conversion is the process of transforming psychic conflict into somatic symptoms. Some people show signs of physical illness in situations of stress, for example. Sometimes this process results in "secondary gains," as when a man with a nagging wife suddenly experiences deafness for which doctors can find no organic cause. (Although it's not pleasant to be deaf, the man no longer has to listen to his wife's complaints.)

❖ **Suppression** In suppression, people consciously avoid thinking about disturbing problems, desires, feelings, or experiences. If, for example, a person is angry at someone, she may not show that anger.

❖ **Rationalization** Rationalization involves the elaborate construction of self-serving but incorrect explanations for one's own (and others') behavior.

❖ **Altruism** Some people address their own problems by giving constructive service to others. For example, a person who was resilient enough to overcome a very troubled childhood may spend all his energy trying to help disadvantaged children.

❖ **Humor** Humor results in a playful approach to overcoming difficult issues. It can be seen as an overt expression of feelings without unpleasant effects on others.

Premise #3: People are products of their past

The third premise of the clinical paradigm has to do with the content of inter- and intra-personal processes: We're all products of our past. As the saying goes, "The hand that rocks the cradle rules the world." All of us are nothing more than a developmental outcome of our early (and later) environment modified by our genetic endowment. And because of the heavy imprinting that takes place at earlier stages of life, we tend to repeat certain behavior patterns. And yet, as the Danish philosopher Søren Kierkegaard once said, "The tragedy of life is that you can only understand it backward but you have to live it forward." Like it or not, there's a continuity between past and present. Scratch a man or woman and you find a child. As a Japanese proverb goes, "The soul of a three-year-old stays with a man until he is a hundred." We can't live in the present without paying attention to the past.

all of us are nothing more than a developmental outcome of our early environment modified by our genetic endowment

So why apply the clinical paradigm? Because in doing so we'll better understand what leadership is all about. We'll be more cognizant of things happening around us and more aware of the constant interface of past and present. Furthermore, we'll be cloaked in an extra layer of intelligence: as we apply the clinical paradigm, we'll become more emotionally intelligent. And people who possess emotional intelligence are more effective at motivating themselves and others. Such individuals also do better when placed in a leadership position, because they're better equipped to track down the rationality behind irrational behavior.

2 Emotional intelligence in the world of work

Mistrust first impulses; they are nearly always good.

CHARLES MAURICE DE TALLEYRAND

Ahab never thinks, he just feels, feels, feels. HERMAN MELVILLE

As you pass from the tender years of youth into harsh and embittered manhood, make sure you take with you on your journey all the human emotions! Don't leave them on the road, for you will not pick them up afterwards! NIKOLAI GOGOL

Researchers interested in the brain have found that the left hemisphere deals with speech, language, writing, logic, math, science, and right-hand touch, while the right hemisphere keeps busy with spatial construction, creative thinking, fantasy, art and music appreciation, and left-hand touch. In other words, the two hemispheres are responsible for different ways of thinking (Box 2.1).

Generally speaking, left-brainers tend toward a more cognitive style of thinking, while right-brainers tend toward a more emotional style:

❖ **Cognitive left-brainers** People who think more comfortably with the left hemisphere tend to be analytical and logical. They focus on dealing with what's sensible; they use abstract symbols, words, and numbers, and they favor specific statements over generalizations. They tend to be slower at information processing than right-brainers are.

❖ **Emotional right-brainers** Individuals who exhibit the more emotional right-brain style tend to be somewhat holistic and impressionistic. They assign feelings a major role in decision making; they rely heavily on metaphors, images, and narratives; they engage in sweeping statements (meaning that information processing tends to be much faster); and because they pay close attention to elusive signals, they do well at processing nonverbal communication.

Right-brain communication is what we all first learned; it's what we used as very small children to connect with our parents, communicating through (and being responded to with) very subtle signals. Unfortunately, in the process of growing up, we unlearned many of our right-brain skills. As a result, for most of us this form of thinking and communicating has atrophied. (See Figure 2.1 for an overview of different styles of thinking.)

in the process of growing up, we unlearned many of our right-brain skills

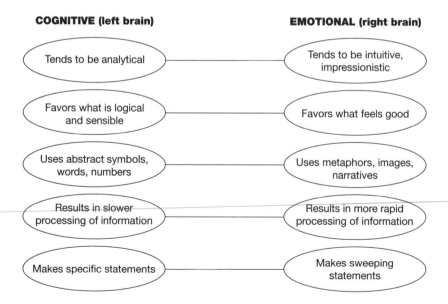

COGNITIVE (left brain)   **EMOTIONAL (right brain)**

Tends to be analytical	Tends to be intuitive, impressionistic
Favors what is logical and sensible	Favors what feels good
Uses abstract symbols, words, numbers	Uses metaphors, images, narratives
Results in slower processing of information	Results in more rapid processing of information
Makes specific statements	Makes sweeping statements

Figure 2.1 Styles of thinking

BOX 2.1

Which brain style do you favor?

Read each of the following statements and decide whether, as applied to you, it's TRUE or FALSE. Check your response.

TRUE   FALSE

1 I'm a great believer in using my intuition when making decisions
2 I analyze problems thoroughly before deciding on a plan of action
3 In making a point, I use my hands and the rest of my body quite
   actively
4 I rely on facts before feelings in making decisions
5 I like to present ideas in the form of visual images
6 Other people consider me a bit of a dreamer
7 I've always been very good with numbers
8 I like to organize my life in considerable detail so as to prevent
   unpleasant surprises
9 I frequently have vivid dreams at night, and I have a tendency to
   daydream as well
10 Math and science have always been my strong points
11 People tell me that I have a very controlled body posture
12 I really enjoy reading fiction and poetry
13 I'm very good at expressing my ideas in words
14 I like to do things on impulse rather than go through a great
    deal of planning

If you checked TRUE for statements 1, 3, 5, 6, 9, 12, and 14, the right hemisphere dominates your way of thinking. If you checked TRUE for statements 2, 4, 7, 8, 10, 11, and 13, you're more of a left-brainer. If your scores are equally divided, neither side of the brain dominates.

Intelligence as a multifaceted attribute

Not only are there different styles of thinking, there are also different styles of intelligence. According to Harvard educational psychologist Howard Gardner, intelligence comes in seven flavors: spatial, bodily kinesthetic, musical, linguistic, logical-mathematical, interpersonal, and intrapersonal (Box 2.2). Let's take a look at each:

❖ People with *spatial intelligence* are able to see patterns and forms quickly; they think in images and pictures. They're likely to express their ideas in drawings, photographs, and sculptures. Quite a few artists, computer graphics designers, and architects have this form of intelligence.

❖ People with *physical* (or *bodily kinesthetic*) *intelligence* know how to use their bodies with precision. They have very good motor coordination and understand the nuances of movement. They're also very good at mimicry, easily imitating other people's gestures and body movements.

❖ People with *musical intelligence* are very good with their ears; they can quickly identify a composer's style and recognize musical compositions. Music is an important part of their lives.

❖ People with *linguistic intelligence* have a great sensitivity to the meaning of words. They enjoy playing with language, learn foreign languages very quickly, and readily identify different intonations.

❖ People with *logical-mathematical intelligence* know how to solve logical puzzles and deal with numerical problems. These are the people who usually do very well on traditional IQ tests.

❖ People with *interpersonal intelligence* are able to empathize with others, understand how somebody else feels, get along well with other people, and get things done with and through others.

❖ People with *intrapersonal intelligence* have a good understanding of their own feelings. They typically have an intense emotional life, and they have a good understanding of their motivation and behavior. They can also be very intuitive.

Which of the many faces of intelligence do you wear?

What's the nature of your intelligence? How would you rate yourself on each of Gardner's seven forms of intelligence?

	Low	High
	1 2 3 4 5 6 7 8 9 10	

Spatial

Linguistic

Musical

Bodily kinesthetic

Logical-mathematical

Interpersonal

Intrapersonal

The higher you score on each dimension, the more versatile your intelligence is in that domain. These questions are merely diagnostic, however, and shouldn't be seen as absolute. Be aware that the last two dimensions are hard to measure through simple paper-and-pencil tests.

Despite this wealth of intelligence around us, most of us focus on the logical-mathematical component – the form of intelligence that's measured by an IQ test. That's what we value individually and as a society, and that's what we seek to instill in ourselves and others.

But IQ isn't everything. A person who breezes through college with straight A's can still flunk life. Some researchers of human development have argued that a high IQ contributes no more than 20 percent to a person's success in life. There are many other factors involved in success, including luck and serendipity, along with the other forms of intelligence.

a person who breezes through college with straight A's can still flunk life

Especially when it comes to organizational leadership, IQ is no predictor of success. First, people with a high IQ don't necessarily make good decisions. In fact, IQ and leadership qualities such as decision making are only weakly correlated. Second, people with a high IQ often fall into the intelligence trap, "intellectualizing" their wrong decisions. Third, people with a high IQ are often so talented at criticizing others that they focus on that rather than on arriving at constructive solutions.

In the world of business, emotional intelligence – an amalgam of Gardner's interpersonal and intrapersonal intelligences – is at least as important as logical-mathematical intelligence. A high IQ (or "intelligence quotient") can be trumped by a high EQ ("emotional quotient") (Box 2.3).

BOX 2.3

What's your EQ (or "emotional quotient")?

For each of the following scenarios, choose the response that most closely matches what you think you would do.

1 During a week when you feel stretched almost to breaking point trying to meet a number of critical deadlines, one of your two bosses comes into your office and asks you to take on yet another project. You know that his input is important for an expected promotion. What do you do?

A You agree to take on the new project and plan to cut corners on the already-in-the-works projects assigned to you by his colleague.

B You tell him that you're overstretched and ask him which project he feels you should drop.

C You organize a meeting with your two bosses to set priorities.

D You criticize his colleague for giving you too many emergency assignments and tell him that you can't do this additional one.

2 You're running a meeting with the members of your team to work out details of the launch of a new program – one that's been the subject of a lot of controversy. An exchange between two members of your team becomes so intense that one of them turns to you and says, "I've had it with this asshole." What do you do?

▶

BOX 2.3 continued

A You ignore the statement, accepting it as an inevitable part of so heated an exchange, and carry on.

B You ask for a break and take the angry team member aside to talk to him about his feelings.

C You stop the discussion of the project and explore the feelings of the members of the group.

D You tell the angry team member that his behavior is inappropriate and won't be tolerated.

3 You've been invited to a meeting with your boss, a man who has an overbearing personality. You know that the meeting concerns your next assignment and realize that there's a good chance you'll be asked to take on a position in Tokyo. Your children are at a critical phase at school, your spouse has an interesting job – and yet you know that a refusal to take an overseas assignment wouldn't be good for your career. What do you do?

A You refuse the job outright and hope for the best.

B You explain to him your family situation and solicit his understanding.

C Believing that it would be hopeless to try to convince your boss that you should stay put, you give your resumé to a headhunter.

D You initiate the interview by telling him about a project at the head office that urgently needs to be done and for which you're the most suitable person in the company.

Answers

1 The work scheduling problem
For question 1 the answer with the most emotional intelligence is C. You're obviously in a difficult situation, and setting some general rules would make your workflow more manageable. By asking for a meeting to deal with your scheduling problem, you're working to solve your predicament. Answer B also has its merits, in that you'd be making one of your superiors aware of the difficulties in managing your workload. While answer D has the advantage of being a straight response, it's a poor choice. It would be unwise to criticize your other boss in front of his colleague, since the latter may then wonder who you'll blame next and what you say about him when he's not there. Answer A, which reflects a pattern of conflict avoidance, is likely to make your other boss unhappy.

▶

BOX 2.3 continued

2 The explosive employee

For question 2 the most emotionally intelligent answer is C, because there may be more going on in the group than you're aware of. By exploring this issue you'll gain greater clarity about the situation. Both B and D are possibilities, but they don't go far enough; they simply make it clear (either privately or publicly) that the behavior of the explosive member of the team is inappropriate. Answer A might be your gut reaction, even if it's not how you'd cast your formal vote. Unfortunately, it invites disaster. Ignoring what happened won't make the problem go away. You've got an 800-pound gorilla on your hands, and if you don't deal with it, sooner or later it will make its presence felt again.

3 The Tokyo assignment

It's difficult to assign a value to the various responses in this case. Option B is probably the most obvious choice. However, its chance of success depends on the corporate culture and on your boss's outlook toward career management. Option D is also workable, despite its Machiavellian slant. By reframing the situation, you may convince your boss that you'd be best used at home. Option A is potentially risky. In some companies, refusing an assignment of this sort brings a person's career to an abrupt halt. Option C, which gives no hope to alternatives, is a very defeatist strategy.

A closer look at emotional intelligence

The word *emotion* comes from the Latin word *motere,* which means "to move," and emotion certainly does move people in various ways, in the workplace just as in all other spheres of life. Many organizations have come to realize that an ounce of emotion can be more effective than a ton of facts.

The three primary components of emotional intelligence are:

1   getting to know our own emotions

2   learning to manage those emotions

3   learning to recognize and deal with the emotions of others.

Getting to know our own emotions

Self-knowledge is the first step toward emotional intelligence. Since people who don't know themselves get locked unwittingly into dysfunctional behavior patterns (and furthermore are poor judges of other people), it's also the first step toward leadership effectiveness.

Once a year I run a seminar for top executives called "The Challenge of Leadership: Creating Reflective Leaders." Twenty top executives (most of them men) participate for three periods of five days, and one period of three days over a year. Frequently there are one or more follow-up sessions in the years afterwards. Given the duration of the seminar, and the opportunity cost of participants' time, no one feels much like talking about the weather or sports; instead, participants deal with issues that really matter to them.

The focus of each seminar is the "life" case study – that is, the life that each participant brings to the discussion. As we talk during the opening part of the seminar about feelings, some participants utter words to this effect, "I don't know how I feel. My wife [or son or assistant] tells me how I feel!" It's not a bit unusual for some participants to be this out of touch with their feelings. Their many years of conformity on the corporate path have blurred the distinction between their own feelings and the feelings that are expected of them. When the latter win out, a "false self" takes over, a caricature of the "good executive." This false self is like the man who, out shopping with his wife, tries on a new suit and asks, "Do you think I'd like this, dear?" Because the real human being is diminished as the false self gains prominence, one of the objectives of the seminar is to help participants eliminate cognitive and emotional distortions, freeing them to interpret the world accurately and helping them to recognize their feelings (and use them more effectively) – in short, to heighten their emotional intelligence. Thus the words that were written above the door of the temple of Apollo in Delphi – "Know thyself" – are the red thread of my leadership seminar.

Learning to manage our emotions

The next step in developing emotional intelligence is learning to manage our emotions – that is, learning how to acknowledge and deal with the whole spectrum of feelings we have (even when we don't like what certain feelings say about us). If we have a handle on those processes, we can learn to use emotions in the service of a goal – in other words, to motivate ourselves.

Learning to recognize and deal with the emotions of others

The next phase in the development of emotional intelligence is learning to recognize and deal with the emotions of others. The skill of empathy – of understanding how others feel – can be both taught and learned. Executives who are very self-centered have, however, a hard time putting themselves in another person's shoes. They can't imagine how the world looks through someone else's eyes. Once they have mastered that skill, however, leaders can begin to manage emotions in others, influencing co-workers via emotional means.

Honing the sub-skills of emotional intelligence

Three of the most crucial sub-skills that make up emotional intelligence are listening actively, picking up on nonverbal communication, and keying into the wide spectrum of emotions.

Active listening

This kind of listening is far more than simply waiting quietly for your turn to speak. It's the kind of listening that's an important part of the repertoire of psychotherapists – listening with complete attention and attempting to determine the full meaning of what a person has to say (as well as what he or she chooses *not* to say).

This is not the sort of listening most of us do, either at home or in the workplace. Students of communication suggest that most people talk at 125 to 150 words a minute, while they have the mental capability to receive and process 750 to 1,200 words a minute. Perhaps it's this imbalance that makes us such poor listeners. Our minds use the spare time between words to wander off.

Mental wandering is one of the least offensive of the poor listening habits I can name. Some people try to do one or more other tasks while listening – perhaps send an e-mail or an SMS message, finish some paperwork, or take calls that could just as easily be dealt with later. Other people engage in "pseudo-listening;" they pretend to listen, making eye contact and nodding appropriately, but they're thinking about other things. They're hearing, yes, but they're not *listening*; they're taking in facts, but (absorbed in their own agenda) they're not attending to the underlying meaning of what's being said. Still other people, unwilling to wait while the other person is thinking and speaking, interrupt whenever a thought crosses their mind. And another group are so involved in their own thought processes that they hear only what they want to hear, a form of listening that results in self-fulfilling prophecies.

Active listeners, by way of contrast, do one thing only: they participate fully in what's being said. That doesn't mean that they're necessarily silent, however. They paraphrase periodically to make sure that the message they heard was the message that was sent, using words such as "As I understand it, what you're telling me is . . .," or "If I could run down what you're saying . . ." Furthermore, good listeners reflect on the implications of what's being said. They make comments like, "What do you mean by . . .?" or "Are you making that statement because of . . .?" They also invite further contributions from the speaker, saying, for example, "What happened then – can you tell me more about it?" or "Tell me more about the predicament you found yourself in." They make an attempt to reflect on the underlying feelings as well, prompting feedback with statements such as, "If that happened to me, I'd be upset," or "What were your feelings at the time?" or "You must have been very pleased to have been told that" (Box 2.4).

Are you an active listener?

Respond to the following questions with YES or NO.

                                                                    YES   NO

- Are you able to let others finish what they have to say without interrupting?
- Do you ask questions if what's being said is unclear?
- Do you pay attention to what's being said and maintain eye contact?
- Do you keep an open mind to what's being said?
- Do you pay attention to nonverbal communication?
- Do you paraphrase back what you've heard, to make sure you've understood the speaker?
- Do you consider the implications of what's being said and confirm your understanding with the speaker?
- Do you attempt to get at the feelings that lie behind the words?

If you had difficulty answering these questions affirmatively, you may have listening problems. Regardless of whether you answered affirmatively or negatively, you might want to check your responses with other people who are close to you to see how your listening is perceived by others.

Listening with the eyes

Good listeners also use appropriate body language and pay attention to the body language of others, remembering that what's "appropriate" is determined by the context. In Western cultures, for example, good listeners make an effort to look the speaker in the eyes. In countries such as Japan, Korea, Taiwan, India, and the nations of the Middle East, however, making eye contact may be seen as an aggressive act. Other Western listening habits include nodding approvingly at intervals and leaning toward the speaker.

paying attention to nonverbal communication is an important part of the emotional intelligence equation

Paying attention to nonverbal communication is an important part of the emotional intelligence equation. Facial expressions, gestures, slips of the tongue – all these play a part in the process of communication. Subtle movements are interpreted almost unconsciously. Imagine, for example, that you have dinner with a friend who, during the course of the evening, gets some food stuck at the corner of her mouth. You could tell her so, of course. But a more tactful way of communicating the problem is to take your own napkin and wipe the corner of *your* mouth, looking at your friend as you do so. It's very likely that your friend will wipe her mouth as well. The cue and response are so subtle that if you ask her why she wiped her mouth, she probably won't be able to give you a sensible answer.

Keying into the emotional spectrum in self and others

While active listening and tuning in to body language are important elements in the repertoire of emotionally intelligent people, another major dimension has to do with the understanding and management of feelings. Although one might think it would be easy to distinguish, say, anger from sorrow or anxiety, there are some people who are absolutely colorblind with respect to their feelings. They're completely out of touch with what's inside them (Box 2.5).

BOX 2.5

How broad is the spectrum of your emotions?

1 What makes you angry? Reflect on the last time you got mad. How did you deal with the situation? Could you have handled it in a different way, perhaps a *better* way?

2 What makes you sad? Can you describe a number of incidents of sadness? How did you manage these situations?

3 What makes you feel ashamed? Describe a number of situations in which you've felt shame.

4 What makes you happy? Can you describe a number of incidents of happiness?

▶

BOX 2.5 continued

Write down your responses and reflect on them. They should tell you something about how attuned you are to your emotions and help you better understand your emotional life.

There are both positive and negative sides to all emotional states. Let's look at anger, for example – one of the so-called negative emotions. While anger often alienates others, prevents self-questioning, and puts a strain on the body, it also serves a protective function vis-à-vis self-esteem: it creates a feeling of righteousness and motivates a person to action. Sadness, likewise, has two sides. Although it makes a person feel awful, prevents realistic and effective action, and leads to greater susceptibility to illness, it also generally prompts a state of withdrawal that leads to a reevaluation of life. Feeling ashamed – whatever the emotion that triggers it – may force a person to stop procrastinating and do things that have been postponed for a long time. It may create the momentum to take action. Unfortunately, it can also lead to a state of passivity and self-pity.

in order to maximize the positive effects and minimize the negative effects of emotions, we need to become adept at recognizing emotions and fluent at expressing them constructively

The so-called positive emotions also have both a good side and a bad side. They feel pleasant, they promote positive relationships with others, and they encourage an adventurousness that creates the motivation to explore new boundaries – consequences that are well and good. But there's a negative side as well: with the positive emotions come decreased caution in regard to risk taking and unrealistic expectations that can lead to disappointment.

In order to maximize the positive effects and minimize the negative effects of emotions, we need to become adept at recognizing emotions and fluent at expressing them constructively. And as leaders, we need to be able to help our people do the same.

Benefiting from the sub-skills of emotional intelligence

In my experience, people who have high emotional intelligence:

- ❖ create stronger interpersonal relationships
- ❖ are better at motivating themselves and others
- ❖ are more proactive, innovative, and creative
- ❖ lead more effectively
- ❖ function better under pressure
- ❖ cope better with change
- ❖ are more at peace with themselves.

The higher up a person is in an organization, the more important emotional intelligence becomes (and the less important technical skills become). Although people usually get hired initially because of a specific technical skill set, once they've climbed the ladder to more senior levels in the organization it's emotional intelligence that makes the difference between a successful career and career stagnation. Derailment near the top of an organization is most often caused by a lack of emotional intelligence. Empathy and self-awareness are major career-enhancing factors. Soft skills can be very hard. There is nothing soft about learning how to communicate, how to give constructive feedback, or how to negotiate with a union, employees, or customers (Box 2.6).

BOX 2.6

How would you rate your emotional intelligence?

Ask yourself the following questions, assigning a rating from POOR to VERY GOOD. If possible, ask someone close to you to answer the questions too, on your behalf. That external perspective will help prevent self-reporting biases.

	POOR							VERY GOOD	
1	2	3	4	5	6	7	8	9	10

- How good are you at understanding others from their perspective?
- How sensitive are you about the feelings of others?
- Do you make friends easily?
- Are you willing to express your emotions to others?
- Are you good at solving conflicts?
- Can you easily adapt your behavior to changing circumstances?
- Does your behavior invite other people's expression of warmth toward you?
- Do you perceive the impact you have on others (even if no reaction is expressed)?
- When you're confronted with a perplexing situation, are you able to handle it?
- Can you easily deal with people who ask you questions about your personal life?
- Are you good at seeking out others to help you when the need arises?
- Do you routinely reflect on your actions?

If you (and others) consistently rate you on the high end of this scale, you're lucky: it sounds as if you have a high EQ. If not, you should put some effort into the further development of this crucial part of human functioning. (Pay special attention to differences between your own ratings and the ratings others give you. If there's a great variance, you may be engaged in self-deception or confuse others in your self-presentation.)[1]

As this discussion shows, having a high EQ doesn't mean just being nice. Neither does it mean giving free rein to emotions. It means being realistic about self and others, accepting humanity with all its varied dimensions, and using emotions appropriately. And the rewards for emotional intelligence are great: having a high EQ leads to more appropriate decision making, contributes to greater realism in interactions with others, and prevents disappointment in relationships.

A mood too far: managing emotional extremes

Emotional management is a critical ability in leaders. Ironically, the demonstration of too few emotions is just as problematic as the demonstration of too many. Interacting with a dead fish is just as unpleasant as dealing with a raging tiger. And yet many people are prone to one or both of these extremes. The impact that extremes of mood, or wild mood swings from one extreme to the other, has on others is enormous.

emotional management is a critical ability in leaders

Think for a moment about the following people. What did they have in common (apart from the fact that they were all leaders, were all men, and are all now dead)?

- ❖ King Saul
- ❖ Martin Luther
- ❖ Teddy Roosevelt
- ❖ Benito Mussolini
- ❖ Winston Churchill
- ❖ General George Patton

All of them had a tendency toward excessive emotional expressiveness. Clinically speaking, they all had symptoms of bipolar disorder, a mood disorder that varies widely in severity (as do the corresponding behaviors and their consequences). This mood disorder, which often goes undiagnosed – a troubling fact given its high suicide rate – is well represented in the workplace, especially in a mild form such as hypomania or cyclothymia (more on those terms later).

Roughly 25 percent of the population will suffer from a mood disorder at some point during their lifespan. Depression (which is a mood disorder but not a bipolar disorder) is the most common complaint. Among bipolar disorders, cyclothymia occurs in 4 or 5 people out of 100, while manic-depressive disorder occurs in 1 out of 100. The latter mood disorder is the most dangerous: 15 percent of people with full-blown manic depression kill themselves in the course of their illness.

The label *bipolar disorder* encompasses a wide range of mood disorders varying in severity from hypomania (or "mild" mania: the overactive phase of the mood disorder) to cyclothymia (characterized by noticeable but not debilitating changes in mood, behavior, and thinking) to life-threatening, full-blown manic depression. What makes people suffering from bipolar disorder of any kind unique is the cyclical nature of their mood: such people are as often depressed and irritable as they are elated.

People with bipolar disorder represent a strange mixture of feelings: a well-being characterized by sparkle and exhilaration juxtaposed against emptiness and loneliness. During the frequent upswings, their behavior possesses a larger-than-life quality. It's characterized by abundant energy, unbridled enthusiasm, thirsty gregariousness, intensity of emotion, a compelling sense of destiny, a strong belief in themselves and their ideas (bordering on the grandiose), persuasiveness in convincing others of their point of view, a willingness to go where others dare not go, optimism verging on exaltation, heightened alertness and observational ability, courage, a willingness to take risks (bordering on the imprudent), unpredictable and subtle changes in mood, impatience, and shortened attention span (Box 2.7).

BOX 2.7

How's your mood state?

Answer the following questions YES or NO. Be honest with yourself.

YES   NO

- Do you have a tendency to talk too much?
- Do you aggressively seek out other people in such a way that they feel intruded upon?
- Has anyone ever told you that you make inappropriate jokes and laugh at the wrong times?
- Do you tell everyone how great you feel when you're "up?"
- Have other people told you that you're "full of yourself?"
- Have you ever been accused of having grandiose ideas?
- Do others feel that your plans are unrealistic?
- Do others accuse you of having poor judgment?
- Are you highly distractible, jumping quickly from one subject to the next?
- Are you often physically restless?
- Do you get irritated when things don't go your way?
- Do you tend to be combative and argumentative?
- Do you try to do too many things at the same time?
- Do you feel that you have unlimited energy?
- Do you need very little sleep?
- Are you lacking in impulse control?
- Do you frequently engage in sexual indiscretions?
- Do you have a tendency to overspend or to engage in unwise investments?

If you answered YES to many of these questions (and your responses have been confirmed by people close to you), you may have hypomanic tendencies. If you feel that you have a problem, it might be useful to ask for professional help in stabilizing your mood state.

Predictably, the elevated mood state of people with bipolar disorder, with its enthusiasm and emotional intensity, can be intoxicating. Bipolars on the upswing are charisma personified: they inspire and motivate, drawing other people to them. Thus bipolar disorder actually helps those who possess it (or are possessed by it) to reach positions of leadership. The enhanced liveliness of bipolars in their elevated mood state, their uninhibited gregariousness, their interpersonal charm, their ability to find vulnerable spots in others and make use of them, their perceptiveness at the subconscious or unconscious level, and their social ease create an interpersonal and group dynamic that can positively affect organizational performance, eliciting exceptional efforts from those affected. However, like the Pied Piper, they may use their leadership to direct people astray, onto paths that are ultimately very costly to both leader and organization.

our moods give the world a glimpse of the person within

The home life of bipolars is rarely less tumultuous than their work life. Heightened sexuality is characteristic of this disorder. Normal sexual inhibitions may disappear; sexual thoughts, fantasies, and adventures may become an obsession; and sexual indiscretions may occur. Not surprisingly, then, the marriages of hypomanically inclined people are often turbulent, and many end in divorce. Financial extravagances are also common, as are drug and alcohol abuse, exacerbating interpersonal problems. Furthermore, when bipolars are in an extremely manic phase, they're prone to angry, explosive outbursts that alienate the people close to them. Finally, the threat of an upcoming depression – with its accompanying hopelessness, tearfulness, suicidal thoughts, melancholic feelings, and self-deprecatory and self-accusatory behavior – is ever present.

Our moods – good or bad, extreme or moderate – give the world a glimpse of the person within. But there's a great deal that remains hidden, even from ourselves. The inner imagery that motivates much of our behavior is revealed only if we're patient and persistent. So how can we go about identifying this inner imagery and figuring out what it's all about? What can we do to deconstruct its major theme?

The core conflictual relationship theme

A number of conflicting forces – primitive impulses and defenses that combat our "rational" being – make up our inner emotional life. In fact, all of us are engaged in an almost perpetual inner dialog – sometimes pleasant, sometimes painful. That dialog is part of our humanness. We have to reconcile the inner forces that test us, that tempt us. The challenge we all have is to understand these forces. For leaders, that challenge is especially critical.

Let's compare organizations to an iceberg for a moment. Most of my management colleagues, in looking at an organization, focus on what happens at the top of the iceberg (see Figure 2.2). They pay little attention to the struggles that take place in the depths, preferring to look only at what's readily visible. They study manifest phenomena such as mission, vision, goals, strategies, operations, job descriptions, tasks, roles, selection processes, control and reward systems, and spans of control. In short, they concentrate on the more rational dimensions of organizational life.

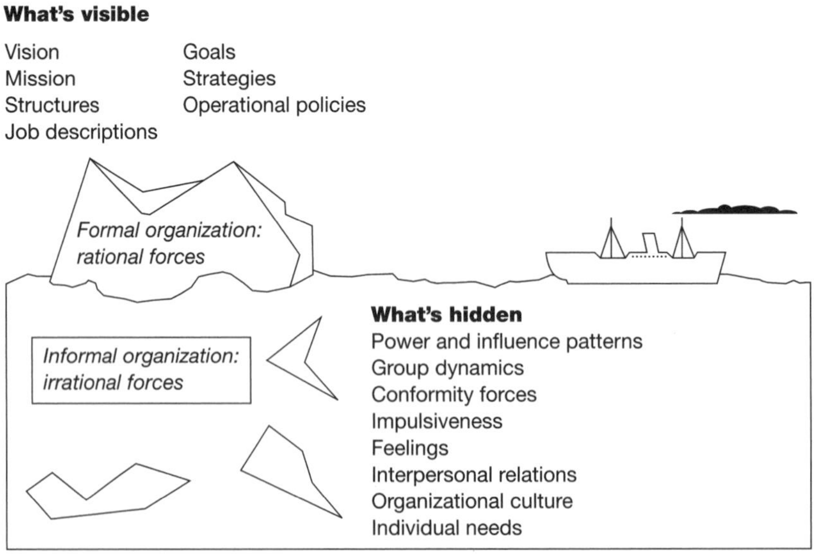

What's visible

Vision	Goals
Mission	Strategies
Structures	Operational policies
Job descriptions	

Formal organization: rational forces

Informal organization: irrational forces

What's hidden
Power and influence patterns
Group dynamics
Conformity forces
Impulsiveness
Feelings
Interpersonal relations
Organizational culture
Individual needs

Figure 2.2 Organizational processes

Without question, these factors are important. I too pay attention to them. But I'm also interested – in fact, I'm *more* interested – in what happens at those levels of the iceberg that lie deeply submerged. What kinds of informal processes take place there? What are the underlying dynamics? In other words, what are the "irrational" variables that make up the organizational culture? How are decisions really made? These variables include such factors as the underlying values of a corporate culture, power and influence patterns, group dynamics, interpersonal relations, stress reactions, and what some psychiatrists call the "core conflictual relationship theme" (CCRT – a way of studying people developed by the psychoanalytic researcher Lester Luborsky) of the key powerholders.

The core conflictual relationship theme permeates our personal life and is at the heart of all our repetitive relationship difficulties. It also colors everything we do in the workplace. For those in positions of leadership, its effects are far reaching: the CCRT of key powerholders determines the organizational culture and the decision-making processes of the organization.

Clearly, then, identifying the CCRT of a leader – isolating that person's central theme – provides insight into not only personality but also work style. But how do we go about that task? Let's begin by dissecting the CCRT itself. Each person's CCRT has the following three components:

- ❖ A wish in the context of a relationship.
- ❖ Our anticipation of how others will react to us in the context of this wish.
- ❖ Our own reaction to this response, be it behavioral or affective.

Sounds simple, right? It's not, primarily because the past taints the present. Our expectations of others' responses in the present are colored by our feelings, attitudes, and behaviors toward significant people from the past. (This issue, known as *transference*, is discussed in more detail in Chapter 4.) As if our distorted expectations weren't bad enough, we sometimes unconsciously entice people in the present to respond in ways that we expect from them. In other words, we help to create what we most fear, our expectations becoming self-fulfilling prophecies.

We can't apply the three CCRT components to a single relational episode and expect to come up with the definitive CCRT. Quite a few episodes need to be studied before a pattern can be identified. If we're trying to isolate our own CCRT we need to bring to mind between five and seven relational episodes of significance – episodes that ended either especially well or especially badly. Then we have to ask ourselves some penetrating questions:

❖ To get at the first component of the CCRT – a wish in the context of a relationship – we need to ask, What were our intents and wishes as we dealt with the other actor in each of these episodes? What core beliefs came into play? What were our expectations? What did we hope to see happen?

❖ To get at the second component of the CCRT – our anticipation of how others will react to us in the context of this wish – we need to ask, How did we expect the other party to respond in the context of our wishes? How did we *fear* the other person would respond? Did we expect the other person to be friendly, hostile, closed, detached? (Whatever the reality of the situation may be, it's the *expectation* that's important here. That expectation of others determines our outlook on life – determines whether in general we're trusting or suspicious, whether we like being controlled or fear it, and so on.)

❖ To get at the third component of the CCRT – our own reaction to this response, be it affective or behavioral – we have to appraise our feelings and actions honestly. We also have to examine whether we're reacting to the *actual* response or to the *expected* response of the other person (and if the former, whether we helped to bring about that response).

Although the existence of these three components is universal, crossing gender and race and age, their *content* is not. Everyone's CCRT is unique. Our central wish, and what we do and feel in response to that wish, is what makes us the person we are, makes us special. Often, though, the CCRT revolves around common issues – for example, the wish to be loved and understood, the wish to be distant and avoid conflict, the wish to hurt others, the wish to achieve, the wish to help other people, the wish to oppose and control, the wish to be controlled and not held responsible, the wish to assert oneself and be independent, and the wish to feel good and comfortable (Box 2.8).

BOX 2.8

What's your CCRT?

Two self-assessments

Getting at your own CCRT requires a number of self-assessment exercises. The first one focuses on your strengths and weaknesses; the second one focuses more directly on the CCRT.

Part I: Assessing your personality

A List the aspects of your personality that you're most satisfied with.

B List the aspects of your personality that you're most dissatisfied with.

C What aspects of your personality cause you most distress? What would you like to change about your personality? How does your assessment fit with the complaints people close to you have about your behavior?

D How do you plan to make these changes? Draft an action plan that includes a timeframe. To help you in this process, the following contains a list of factors that may affect your well-being.

My action plan includes:

1 To develop a more satisfactory relationship with my partner.

2 To become a more effective parent.

3 To resolve unfinished business with other family members.

4 To be more proactive in my career development.

5 To find ways to solve financial difficulties.

6 To become more socially engaged.

▶

BOX 2.8 continued

7 To develop new and further develop existing friendships.

8 To actively search out activities that I enjoy.

9 To pay attention to my physical health.

10 To take steps to acquire a better understanding of my inner world.

11 To find ways to make a contribution to society.

After you've gone through this exercise, you'll be better prepared to assess your CCRT. You may want to use the insights from the last exercise to modify your action plan.

Part II: Determining your core conflictual relationship theme

Reflect on a number of episodes during which you dealt with another person. (Five to seven episodes are recommended.) Look for overriding patterns in your own wishes, the responses you anticipated from others, and your reactions to those responses. Because we all have an intricate defensive structure, test your findings with someone who's familiar with your behavior.

First, for every relational episode you review, ask yourself what you really wanted from the interaction. What was your intent – your desire? What did you want to see happen?

Next, what kind of response did you expect from the other person, given your wish? What was your greatest fear about the other person's response?

How did you respond to the other person? What did you say or do? How did you feel while responding?

Deepening our understanding of our inner theater

Although the CCRT approach is one way to deepen our understanding of ourselves (and the effect we have on others), there are many other ways to get a better grip on this inner theater. We'll look at two here: tests (of various sorts) and dreams.

Testing to reveal the inner theater

Psychologists use a variety of means, from paper-and-pencil tests to projective tests, to reveal the script of a person's inner theater. In many instances, taking a whole battery of tests is the best way to deepen insight (in large part because the discussion of the various test results turns into a discussion of life themes). Tests aren't the definitive answer, however; they're just the beginning of a dialog that develops insights about our inner motivations, needs, wishes, and fantasies.

All tests have their shortcomings. As indicated earlier, paper-and-pencil tests are particularly susceptible to the so-called social desirability factor – that is, the tendency of people to distort the outcome of a test in an effort to present themselves in a good light. While this is often done unconsciously, some people are good at "psyching out" tests and choose false responses very deliberately. Other people answer inappropriately due to an unusual mood state, the issues going through their mind at the time of the test, or a limited understanding of their own feelings and behavior. The effectiveness of paper-and-pencil tests is also limited by their simplicity: certain complex behavioral responses are difficult to summarize in a brief test response, and efforts to do so may result in inaccuracy.

Tests that rely not on true–false or multiple-choice formats but on the interpretation of pictures or inkblots are called projective tests. The theory behind these tests is that what people see in a picture or inkblot reflects unconscious as well as conscious thoughts, needs, fears, conflicts, desires, and beliefs; and specific themes often arise as they interpret multiple images. Often, the stories people tell on the basis of these tests contain these specific themes.

Although less easily open to manipulation by the test taker, projective tests are subject to distortions on the part of the test giver. That person may project his or her own fantasies on the interpretation he or she hears, thus allowing personal biases to color the results. From a clinical point of view, however, the latter type is more interesting, since projective tests are more likely to tap the inner world of the individual.

The role of dreams

Another way of gaining insight into one's inner theater is through dreams and daydreams. Freud, who characterized dreams as the "royal road to the unconscious," felt that dreams offered a shortcut into the inner world. Even without interpretation of any kind, dreams reveal the issues that preoccupy us. And all of us dream. In fact, we sleep approximately one-third and dream approximately one-twelfth of our lives. For most of us, that translates to four to six dreams every night, or roughly 1,500 to 2,000 dreams every year. Dreams occur during what's called REM sleep. This stands for "rapid eye movement," a process that takes place during dreaming.

even without interpretation of any kind, dreams reveal the issues that preoccupy us

Not everybody gives much credence to dreams. Some people see them as random "noise" in the neurological system. But is this really true? Could the content of dreams be just nonsense? Apparently not. According to studies carried out in sleep laboratories, the cerebral cortex (or frontal lobes) – that part of the brain that's concerned with language, thinking, planning, organizing, and consciousness – is involved in the dreaming process. This implies that there's more to dreaming than random noise. Furthermore, dreams have a restorative function: they help us clear up the baggage that we accumulate during the daytime.

If we want to make sense out of our dreams, we have to look for patterns. Do we have nightmares, for example? Do we have repetitive dreams? In most nightmares, the dream imagery is so compelling, so frightening, that it wakes us up. Thus nightmares interrupt the function of sleep, which is to give the body rest. Repetitive dreams, by the same token, may be seen as attempts at mastery, attempts at conflict resolution, or urgent reminders of something we refuse to acknowledge in the buzz of daily life. Those repetitive dreams that are nightmares often have to do with the reliving of traumatic episodes – episodes that we go through again and again in an effort to change or deal with the outcome.

Dreams can also be aids in the creative process, because they put us in another world – a world where insights are distinct from reason. We dream in wildly surrealistic images; people and events from different times and places merge together, forming a second life in which the most fantastic things occur. And we all have these creative sparks every night! The fantastic content of dreams demonstrates that we all have a healthy dose of creativity in us. The question is, Do we pay attention to these creative sparks? Many of us just ignore our dream world. Some creative artists, however, take note of the fantastic imagery they find in their dreams and make use of it. A considerable amount of their inspiration is derived from the imagery that emerges during the night.

Unfortunately, many people don't remember their dreams (although they do dream, of course). This is true of many executives, who as a group have what are sometimes called "thick boundaries." That is, they possess such a strong defensive structure that much of the dream imagery doesn't surface; instead, it "melts" away and is quickly forgotten. By the same token, many artists have "thin boundaries;" they not only remember their dreams but actively use dream imagery in their work. For example, William Styron based his book *Sophie's Choice* on a dream; Robert Louis Stevenson wrote his famous story of Dr. Jekyll and Mr. Hyde as the result of a dream; and Isabel Allende bases all her stories on her dreams. Painters often portray their dreams in their work. Examples include Salvador Dali, Max Ernst, and René Magritte. Dali, in fact, referred to his work as hand-painted dream photographs. Likewise, all the films of the Swedish director Ingmar Bergman were influenced by his dreams, and Richard Wagner's *Rheingold* was based on a dream. Many scientific inventions have also had their origins in dreams or daydreams. Among the most famous are the benzene ring (Friedrich Kekule), the periodic table of elements (Dmitry Mendeleyev), and the theory of relativity (Albert Einstein) (Box 2.9).

BOX 2.9

What are your dreams telling you?

Select a dream (or daydream) that you had recently, or a recurring dream that comes back regularly. Can you recall a specific event that triggered the dream? What feeling(s) did you have in the dream? What are your associations concerning the dream?

Although these questions seem to be simple, the answers aren't the least bit easy. Let your mind float. Do some associative thinking. If you're remembering a night dream, think about whether some event that occurred the previous day could have been the trigger. Then work to understand the meaning of the presenting imagery. This may take some time. Interpreting dreams is a lot like doing a jigsaw puzzle; it's a painstaking process. But gradually, as the pieces fall into place, you'll discover yourself in new territory and the dream will take on new meaning. As you discover the stories behind your dream, you'll discover something new about yourself.

Escaping your psychic prison

Many executives don't pay much attention to their inner world. In fact, they keep themselves busy (with the help of the "manic defense") just to make sure they don't have time to reflect. It's rarely a conscious avoidance, but it's an avoidance nonetheless. They run faster and faster, giving very little thought to what they're running for or where they're running to.

many executives don't pay much attention to their inner world

Many of the executives I talk to are stuck in what amounts to a psychic prison. And yet they rarely try to escape from their self-imposed house of detention. They're mired in their old ways of interacting, engaged in what psychoanalysts describe as repetition compulsion, an (unconscious) urge to reenact troubling scenarios in the hope that repetition will eventually lead to liberation from this need. Many otherwise very bright people engage in a form of magical thinking: they believe that by doing the same thing over and over again, they will produce a different outcome. They fail to realize the common sense behind the old Sioux saying, "When you discover that you're riding a dead horse, the best strategy is to dismount!"

The challenge for people who are stuck is to find a way out of that prison – to find other, better ways of doing things. Although at age 30, two-thirds to three-fifths of one's personality is formed (according to the estimates of some developmental psychologists), there's always ample room for change. Mental health is all about having a choice. And we *do* have a choice, always. It's true that our inner theater stays largely the same – a certain amount of "hardwiring" is inescapable – but we can choose to react differently to our core wishes.

We all need to be the architects of our own fate, the authors of our own script. If we turn that scripting over to others, we're not really living, we're just playing a part. How much better it would be to *own our own lives*. And we can – if we're willing to open ourselves to the possibilities of change. To change, however, you have to stop at times to reflect on your life.

NOTE TO CHAPTER 2

1. A word of caution: I'd like to emphasize that questionnaires are of limited usefulness in the context of measuring emotional intelligence, because so many of the factors pertaining to emotional intelligence are sensory based (relating to touch, sound, and smell) and are therefore hard to capture in a questionnaire. In addition, the "social desirability factor" affects the results: people respond to such questionnaires not with the truth but with the way they'd *like* to be perceived.

3 The mussel syndrome

Those who know do not tell; those who tell do not know.

LAO-TZU

You can't step into the same river twice. HERACLITUS

Oysters are more beautiful than any religion ... There is nothing in Christianity or Buddhism that quite matches the sympathetic unselfishness of an oyster. SAKI

The lowly mussel has a lot to teach us about change and stasis. This mollusk has to make only one major existential decision in life, and that's where it's going to settle down. After making that decision, the mussel cements its head against a rock and stays put for the rest of its life. I've discovered that many people are like that: they're so resistant to change that they might as well be cemented in place. If leaders share that trait – if they suffer from what we might call the "mussel syndrome" – the results can be devastating for their organizations (Box 3.1).

many people are so resistant to change that they may as well be cemented in place

BOX 3.1

Do you show symptoms of the mussel syndrome?

Respond TRUE, FALSE, or I DON'T KNOW to the following statements. Be as honest with yourself as you can be. (I realize this exercise is not going to be easy.)

TRUE   FALSE   I DON'T KNOW

- I like to keep most of the organizational decision-making power to myself
- I tend to be more reactive than proactive in my decision making
- I've been accused of subscribing to the "not-invented-here syndrome"
- I don't like people to contradict me
- I often get quite impatient when I listen to others
- I'm usually right in the things that I do
- I don't always manage to make my priorities clear
- I like to keep information about the company's operations and financial picture to myself
- I tend to be rather suspicious of people
- I've been known to blow up at bad news
- I have a tendency to split people into two camps – those who are with me and those who are against me
- I prefer people to be quite dependent on me
- There's a big discrepancy between my point of view concerning the future of the organization and that of others
- I have a tendency to blame others when things go wrong
- I'm quick to take offense
- I like to "blow my own trumpet;" I'm eager to tell others about my successes

If many of these statements are TRUE for you, you might want to reassess your way of making decisions in your organization. There's a danger that you're headed for the mussel syndrome. If you've gotten stuck in your leadership style and are resistant to change, you're setting up your organization for failure.

Corporate consequences of the mussel syndrome

The mussel syndrome is very common in organizational settings. Let me illustrate its dynamics. Once a year, in February, *Fortune* magazine comes out with a "hit parade" of the most admired companies in North America. The criteria for this list are such factors as quality of management, quality of products and services, creativity, innovation, long-term investment value, and financial soundness. *Fortune* polls something like 11,000 people before compiling the list, which first came out in 1983.

That initial year, IBM was in first place; by 1997 it had dropped to 102. Exactly where it is now is hard to say, since the rating system changed in 1998. (Companies are now ranked by industry, with the exception of the top ten.) Certainly IBM is handling itself better in the new millennium, although an enormous amount of capital destruction has taken place. Digital Equipment Corporation (DEC) had an even more dramatic drop: it went from number seven to number 386 during that same 14-year period; and in 1998 it was taken over by Compaq, a competitor, which then was taken over by Hewlett-Packard.

The crucial question is, Why did these companies fall so dramatically in ranking? What went wrong? Let's narrow our focus and ask more specifically, What happened to DEC? What was going on in this organization that led it to plummet so precipitously?

One of the problems at DEC was the person originally responsible for its success, its founder, Kenneth Olson, and the corporate culture he created. During his early years with Digital, Olson showed that effective, time-appropriate leadership does make a difference for the future of an organization. However, he went on to prove that effective leadership at one point in a person's life-cycle can turn disastrous at another. After he found himself on the cover of *Fortune,* the fame and success went to Olson's head. Although he was extremely innovative when creating DEC, he gradually became a mussel. No two ways about it: he got stuck. He held onto outdated ideas about product development while the marketplace around him changed. Increasingly narcissistic, he was sure that he had all the answers, so he stopped listening to his customers and to his own people. In 1977 he made the following "prophetic" statement: "There is no reason for an individual to have a computer in his home." He began to surround himself with yea-sayers, people who told him only what he wanted to hear. In the meantime, the changing market passed him by. Only when he was pushed out was it possible for the company to begin to readjust itself, to experiment with other cultural values – not sufficiently or timely enough, however, to prevent a takeover.

Was what happened to Olson and DEC a fluke? Not by a long shot. Olson's story is repeated day after day, in organization after organization, by leaders who have succumbed to the mussel syndrome. But are all organizations destined to move from success to failure? Is a decline inevitable? Again, not by a long shot. However, success can be maintained only if an organization is able to adapt to change (Box 3.2).

BOX 3.2

How do you see the future of your organization?

Try to make some predictions about how you think your company (and its market context) will look three years from now. What do you view as the most probable scenario?

	PRESENTLY	THREE YEARS FROM NOW
• Organizational form		
• Core competencies		
• Leadership style		
• Ways of working with each other		
• Customers		
• Market context		

Compare your predictions with those of other members of your organization to arrive at some kind of consensus. You might also want to talk to some of your outside constituencies to get an additional perspective on what kinds of changes are likely.

The changing organizational paradigm

The world around us is changing. So are organizational and leadership practices. Throughout much of the twentieth century, organizations modeled themselves after such institutions as the Catholic Church and the army. The "modern" organization had a pyramidal structure, a hierarchical organization, staff departments, top-down decision making, functional and divisional structures, and position power. Given the increasing irrelevance of this model, the question becomes, What kind of leadership and organization will be most appropriate in the twenty-first century? Although it's hard to predict discontinuity, a few trends are apparent on the horizon. Let's look at three, turning first to a shift in mindset.

From the three C's to the three I's

Organizations dominated by control, compliance, and compartmental-ization (the three C's) are being outpaced by organizations that focus on ideas, information, and interaction (the three I's). In today's business world, people and processes have become the central themes. With the survival of companies in the "cyber age" dependent on attracting people with the right kind of expertise, good people are now a scarcer resource than capital. Companies need people who know how to handle strategic innovation, who are entrepreneurial minded, who have the skills and know-how to lead in a global world.

We are experiencing nothing short of a paradigm shift in the workplace. The old mindset was focused on stability, had a national (rather than global) orientation, and was technology driven, hierarchical, and inclined toward autocratic leadership. The new mindset is predicated on both continuous and discontinuous change, has a global orientation, is customer driven, calls for a networking architecture, and subscribes to authoritative (or respect-based)

in today's business world, people and processes have become the central themes

leadership rather than authoritarian (or position-based) leadership.

This paradigm shift demands a radically different kind of organization. There are several prototypes of that new organization: the "virtual" organization (one made up of parts that are loosely connected), the "chemical soup" organization (one in which new combinations evolve continuously), and the "amoeba" organization (one that continually splits off parts). Companies such as Virgin, Southwest Airlines, Gore Associates, Oticon, Patagonia, and Goldman Sachs fit these new patterns. Hierarchy is much less prominent in all organizations modeled on these new prototypes. They tend to be flat and organic rather than hierarchical and fixed, and many (recognizing that organizational form can offer a competitive advantage) have innovative designs. In addition, they're extremely fluid and action oriented.

From the traditional psychological contract to the paradox of employability

With the new paradigm comes a change in what's often called the "psychological contract" – an unspoken understanding of the obligations implied for both employer and employee in an employment relationship. Under the old paradigm, the implication of this psychological contract was that loyalty to the employer would be exchanged for job security until retirement and good pension rights thereafter. Given the increased discontinuities in the world around us, it has been increasingly difficult for organizations to deliver on the obligations that this psychological contract implies. In fact, the contract has been broken so often that neither side makes any pretence of it any more, and the mutual obligations are being rewritten to fit today's circumstances.

Organizations today are far less protective of their people; the concept of "corporate caring" is much less prominent (employee assistance plans and the like notwithstanding). The hire-and-fire culture – otherwise known as management by letting go ("Either you make an input or you're an output!") – certainly isn't universal, but it's common, Enron's "rank and Yank" culture being an extreme example.

With the breakdown of the psychological contract, corporate loyalty has lost much of its meaning. The new companies in the information age subscribe to the "employability" concept instead. No longer can good corporate citizens expect steady promotion and a pension at the end. A new, more "adult" (but also less intimate) relationship between employer and employee is the result. That new relationship encourages employees to be proactive in taking advantage of the learning opportunities offered by the organization (and, as an unintentional byproduct of the loss of loyalty, encourages them to look for opportunities elsewhere).

There is a paradox in the employability issue: even as organizations set their people loose, they encourage them to remain. If the new psychological contract at a particular organization includes considerable training and development – and if employees take charge of their own employability by keeping their skills updated so that they can work for anyone – then employees are *de facto* building job security with their employer. (Of course, this assumes that the employer values highly skilled and motivated employees.) Similarly, an organization that offers a lot of training and development is more likely to retain its employees, because it creates a challenging environment peopled with highly motivated workers.

Sounds good. But unfortunately, this new psychological contract of turning employees into independent contractors (as it were) fails to address the dependency needs that are basic to human nature. Unless these are addressed in some way, people inevitably feel disconnected from their organization; they lose the belief that the organization is fair. In the absence of a genuine display of caring, organizational cynicism and alienation rise, as does turnover at all levels. With executives in information technology and investment banking being more in demand than ever before, and with the newfound wealth that stock options often bring, there's little incentive to stay with an organization that lacks heart. Organizational leadership, now more than ever, needs to find ways to bind people to the organization.

organizational leadership, now more than ever, needs to find ways to bind people to the organization

From autocratic paternalism to new forms of leadership

Leaders in organizations that have made the paradigm shift have assumed a different role than their predecessors. They are no longer leaders in the traditional paternalistic, autocratic sense. Instead, in addition to being CEOs, they are "chief knowledge officers," transmitting knowledge from one part of the organization to the other. One of the best examples of a leader who's taken on this role has been Jack Welch, former chairman of General Electric. Welch recognized that given the diversified portfolio of his firm, the transfer of technology and best practices was essential.

Effective CEOs also have to become "chief storytelling officers," inspiring people through their stories and rallying them behind their vision. As Richard Branson, one of the people the British most admire as a businessman, puts it, "All business is show business." Thus CEOs become "lead actors," setting an example (both in the daily grind and through occasional **no organization can function without a set of clearly outlined rules and procedures** symbolic acts) that emphasizes themes they see as critical for the future of their organization. Jack Welch made his focus clear to his followers when he said, "An organization without a future is an organization that has its face toward the CEO and its ass toward the customer."

With less hierarchy and flatter, more organic structures, today's leaders need to pay more attention than their predecessors to processes, implying improved relationship building and cross-functional teamwork. Furthermore, the complexity of global organizations necessitates finding ways to simplify and accelerate decision-making processes (so as to avoid bottlenecks, which sure enough can usually be traced to the "neck," meaning the top of the organization).

While innovative leadership is needed to facilitate all these processes, there's a dirty little secret that we have to keep in mind: in spite of the new focus on networking structures and the death of hierarchy, flat organizations still require a degree of authority and discipline. No organization can function without a set of clearly outlined rules and procedures. Moreover, hierarchy is an intricate part of the human condition; the human animal can't do without it. We need look no further than our close relatives, the primates, to see hierarchy in action (Box 3.3).

BOX 3.3

Where's your organization now?

Rate the mindset of the people in your company, placing an X where you believe they're positioned (from 1 to 10) on the following dimensions.

1 2 3 4 5 6 7 8 9 10

- People in our organization value: stability   continuous change
- People in our organization have a: national orientation   global orientation
- People in our organization are: technology driven   customer focused
- Our organization tends to be quite: hierarchical   networking oriented
- Our corporate culture is one of: dependency   interdependency
- The leadership in our organization is: autocratic   authoritative

The higher the rating is on the different dimensions, the more you believe that the people in your organization subscribe to the new paradigm of organizational processes (and, if your perception is accurate, the higher your organization's chances of survival).

Companies that endure

Earlier in this chapter we looked at factors that made DEC (and other organizations) plummet on *Fortune's* list of successful companies. We also saw how the mussel syndrome can prevent leaders from making the paradigm shift that today's world requires. Now let's approach the issue of success from the opposite side and investigate how certain companies have managed to stay at the top of the hit parade during all the years that *Fortune* has published its results. What makes these companies different? What is it about their organizational practices that's made them so successful?

The companies that manage to stay at the top of *Fortune*'s annual hit parade are rarely positioned in the latest high-tech industries. Since we're not talking about flash-in-the-pan circumstances, their high ranking can't be a temporary artifact due to "hot" market conditions. The founding dates make that very clear: for **the companies seem to know how to reinvent themselves** example, 3M was founded in 1902, Coca-Cola in 1886, and Procter & Gamble in 1837. Yet these companies seem to know how to reinvent themselves: they are able to recognize and deal with changes in the environment, and they are skilled at dealing with paradigm shifts (Box 3.4).

So what do successful, enduring companies look like? What makes them different? I don't have all the answers, but in studying high-performance organizations, I've noticed the following ten shared characteristics:

1 These companies usually are concentrated either on one business or have a very focused portfolio. *Leaders who do well do stay focused.*

2 These companies are extremely sensitive to the environment they operate in. They pay attention to even the most subtle shifts in customer demands, and they carefully monitor the effects of disruptive technologies. *Leaders need to keep closely in touch with their customer base.*

3 These companies tend to be cohesive, have a strong culture, share a common vision, and employ systems thinking. This cohesiveness complements the "glue" provided by effective information systems. *Their leaders view themselves as the "high priests" of the organization's culture and act accordingly.*

4 These companies firmly believe that leadership isn't an isolated quality for a select few. Proponents of "distributed" leadership, they foster leadership at all levels, not just leadership at the top.

Because leadership development can't happen in the dark, *these companies believe that information should be shared broadly.* Thus they keep secrecy to a minimum. *Leaders need to remind themselves of their coaching and mentoring role. They are in the leadership development business.*

5 These companies are characterized by constant innovation, which is the lifeblood of any organization. *Leaders should never forget that without innovation their companies will die. They need to play a key role as catalyst of innovation and entrepreneurship.*

6 These companies foster (and achieve) upbeat employee morale. Employees enjoy what they're doing. And that enjoyment is contagious: happy employees make for happy customers. *Leaders play a key role in creating the kind of climate where their employees enjoy themselves.*

7 These companies know the importance of superior customer satisfaction. All the processes in the company are aimed at satisfying their customers. *Leaders need to set the example in satisfying their customer base.*

8 These companies have a learning culture. They accept that making mistakes is part and parcel of the decision-making process and believe that people learn and grow from their mistakes. They appreciate diversity in thought and action. *Leaders are the key knowledge officers and they should act accordingly.*

9 These companies have a systems perspective. They realize the interdependence of the various units in the organization, and make a great effort to create synergy. *Leaders play an essential role as the bridge between the various units in the organization. They find ways to help these units learn from each other.*

10 Finally, these companies tend to be rather conservative in financing. They don't take unnecessary financial risks. *As chief resource allocators, leaders should monitor the key financial indicators in the organization very carefully.*

BOX 3.4

Has your organization made the paradigm shift?

For each of the elements listed, think about whether your organization is on target now, in today's market, and whether you think you'll be on target in the future, in the increasingly global market of tomorrow. Put a checkmark in the NOW column, the TOMORROW column, or both, as appropriate.

	NOW	TOMORROW

I believe that our organization has:

- the "right" vision
- the "right" strategy
- the "right" values
- the "right" core competencies
- the "right" skills, abilities, attitudes, and behaviors to execute its strategic intent
- the "right" executive team
- the "right" way of stimulating innovation
- the "right" cost structure
- the "right" way of looking at customers

If you have a lot of blank spaces in the TOMORROW column, it's time to rethink your basic organizational parameters. Your company may need to undergo a paradigm shift. Compare your results with those of others in your organization. Discuss the similarities and variances.

But even having all ten of these characteristics of success is no protection against failure. As we saw earlier with the plummeting corporate rankings in *Fortune,* success often has dire consequences. This is especially true if success breeds either arrogance or lethargy.

So how can leaders detect the danger signs of success turning sour? By learning to overcome the "boiled frog factor." *What's that?* you ask. Well, imagine that you're a frog. (This may not be easy, but try!) Now imagine that someone has put a large pot of water on the stove and brought it to a boil. As the bubbles steam and churn, he throws you in. What do you do? You try to jump out, of course. You're not going to sit there and philosophize about the meaning of life. Now is not the time for existential thinking.

Now, still in your frog mode, imagine that someone puts a pot of cold water on the stove and plops you in, turning the heat on very low. As the water slowly warms – ever so slowly – you don't even notice that you're gradually being boiled. By the time the bad news sinks in, it's too late to jump.

The latter scenario mirrors what happens to many people and many organizations. Unless organizations, and the individuals within them, are hypervigilant to the need for change, they'll be boiled alive. As a consequence of the "boiled frog factor," many **the way executives** of today's major companies won't even exist **operate in an** tomorrow; changing circumstances will have **organization** done them in. The "boiled frog factor" repre- **determines that** sents an insidious process whereby executives **organization's** recognize the danger signs of organizational **success or failure** decline far too late (Box 3.5).

And this brings us back to people: the way executives operate in an organization determines that organization's success or failure. In the next chapter, then, we'll take a closer look at leadership.

BOX 3.5

Will you be done in by the "boiled frog factor"?

Does your organization suffer from the following symptoms? Place a YES or NO beside each statement, depending on how closely it reflects your situation.

YES   NO

- The company suffers from a control mentality; rules and regulations reign supreme
- The company has a no-trust culture
- The company is characterized by tunnel vision, meaning that firefighting is the norm
- The company is torn by infighting
- The company has a "don't-rock-the-boat" mentality
- The company suffers from organizational arrogance; in other words, it has a know-it-all attitude
- The company is reluctant to adopt best practices from other organizations
- The company doesn't believe in people development
- The company's leadership is inaccessible

If you've answered YES to almost all of these statements, then your organization and its leadership are in serious trouble. If the situation doesn't change, there's a strong possibility that your company won't be among the survivors.

4   The failure factor in leadership

It is better to fall among crows than flatterers; for those devour only the dead – these the living. ANTISTHENES

Beware of what you want – for you will get it.

RALPH WALDO EMERSON

He was a self-made man who owed his lack of success to nobody. JOSEPH HELLER

Let's go back to the question of leadership and start with the basics. What does leadership imply? What does it consist of? What are leaders supposed to do? Perhaps I can present this issue in an even simpler, more personal way: What do *you* do when you arrive at your office? What do *you* find important? What do *you* spend your time on as an executive? What elusive leadership qualities manifest themselves in *your* daily work at the office (Box 4.1)?

BOX 4.1

What does your workday look like?

A   Describe a typical day at work (insofar as such a thing exists!).

B   What activities do you spend most of your time on?

C   If you were to group those activities into categories (such as industrial relations, customer service, market research, or leadership coaching), what would those categories be?

Executive behavior: myth and reality

Many executives find it difficult to answer basic questions about their work life. They have a hard time describing just what it is they do on the job and see no real pattern in their activities. They don't really know what it means to be chief executive officer or chairman of the board. Sure, they can paint a picture of their work in broad brushstrokes, perhaps echoing Henri Fayol (one of the founders of management theory), who said that executives *plan, coordinate, control,* and *organize.* But what does a description that broad really tell us?

One wit who wasn't convinced that senior executives do all that much came up with the following story. A woman went to a store to buy a parrot. Entering the store and seeing a particularly handsome specimen, she asked the proprietor, "How much is this one?" "Two thousand dollars," he replied. "That's a lot of money," said the woman reluctantly. The owner said, "Ah, but he speaks German, French, Italian, and Spanish, and knows everything about the regulations of the European Community." The woman shook her head. "Too expensive," she said.

She looked around a bit more and found another bird she liked. "How much is that one?" she asked. "Three thousand dollars," said the proprietor. "It speaks Japanese, Chinese, and Arabic, and is an information technology wizard." The woman looked up and saw another parrot sitting alone on a perch. "How much is *that* one?" she asked. "Five thousand dollars," the owner responded with a touch of pride. "My god, that's really expensive," the woman exclaimed. "What does he do?" The owner said, "He doesn't do a thing, but all the other parrots call him chairman!"

many executives find it difficult to answer basic questions about their work life

As the parrot example illustrates, it's not always easy to figure out what senior executives actually *do* (though fantasies about the executive role abound). An old friend and colleague of mine, Henry Mintzberg, who had long been curious about executive behavior, decided to see whether he could determine what it is that executives do. He took a stopwatch and a notebook and rushed off to the first company he could think of: the consulting firm Arthur D. Little in Cambridge, Massachusetts. He got his foot in the door and asked General Gavin – he was the company's president at the time – whether he could follow on his heels and observe him for a week. General Gavin must have had a sense of humor, because he agreed. After Mintzberg had observed General Gavin, he studied four other CEOs in a similar manner.

What did Mintzberg find out? He discovered that executives "run around." Executive work isn't nearly as ordered as Henri Fayol would have liked to believe. According to Mintzberg, executive work is a discontinuous, disjointed process that tends to break down into seven-minute bursts of activity. (Time-and-motion aficionados have said that executives spend on average 17 hours a week in meetings, 6 hours a week preparing for meetings, and an unknown number of hours recovering from meetings.)

Mintzberg didn't leave it at "running around," however. Being a great behavior classifier, he described the specific things that executives do while running around. According to his taxonomy, they take on interpersonal roles, informational roles, and decisional roles. To be more precise, they're figureheads, leaders, liaisons, monitors, disseminators, spokespersons, entrepreneurs, disturbance handlers, resource allocators, and negotiators – all this as need demands.

Mintzberg wrote up his findings, first as a dissertation, then as a book, and eventually as an article for the *Harvard Business Review*. The article won the McKinsey prize for the best article of the year and became one of the *Review*'s all-time classics. So why did people get so excited about his findings? Why did executives love the article? Perhaps one explanation is that the categories named in the article offered confirmation that the work executives were doing – however unimportant some of the tasks appeared to be – was important. Here we thought we were wasting our time at the copying machine; wrong, we were playing the role of disturbance handler. We thought we were merely gossiping on the phone; wrong, we were playing the role of negotiator. We thought we were just swapping funny e-mails; wrong, we were playing the role of liaison!

Mintzberg is a thoughtful management scientist. He's also quite a rational person. And that outlook is reflected in his findings. He studied *manifest* behavior and believed that what he saw was all there is to see. But is behavior really only that which the observer *sees* – the gestures, the comments, the words on the page?

Having spent many years studying executive behavior, I'm of the opinion that it's not. We all have a facade, a persona, a public self. What that persona does is what the world sees, but something very different may be happening deep inside, where our private self (or shadow side) hides. The public self that we choose to share generally bears little resemblance to the private self, a self so private that even we ourselves may know it only slightly. As I say at times, everybody is normal until you know them better!

> what that persona does is what the world sees, but something very different may be happening deep inside, where our private self (or shadow side) hides

That's why it's so hard to learn what executives do. They don't necessarily engage in rational behavior (or better, behavior *perceived* as rational), they don't necessarily know why they're doing what they're doing, and (even if they *do* know) they don't necessarily give the real reason if asked, preferring to offer a rationalization. Much of what they do is either out of conscious awareness or not for public consumption.

Rational and irrational behavior

Let me illustrate with a simple multiple-choice test that shows how irrational executives can be. I'll use as my examples two executives well known to everybody – people who, at first glance, seem relatively uncomplicated.

Let me start with Walt Disney. Here's the question: What did his breakfast typically consist of?

1 A bowl of *kumiss* (Mongolian fermented mare's milk).

2 Dunkin' Donuts drowned in whiskey.

3 Sushi (on the theory that it would be good for the circulation).

The correct answer is Dunkin' Donuts. Did you get it right? This particular choice is just a minor signifier, of course. But it's a giveaway for other things to follow. Here was a man who announced, "No liquor in my company" (but dosed himself daily on donuts and whiskey). Here was a man who said, "No facial hair in my organization" (but sported a mustache). Moreover, he was a special agent for the FBI. Clearly, Disney had a strange side to him; he wasn't exactly a paradigm of rationality at all times. But that doesn't detract from the fact that he was a creative, persistent, visionary man. When his brother Roy said, "Don't make a short animated movie with sound," he made *Steamboat Willy*. When his brother Roy said, "Don't make a feature-length animated movie," he made *Snow White*. When his brother Roy said, "Don't set up theme parks," he constructed Disneyland.

And how about Robert Maxwell, the late media mogul whom some British bankers facetiously called the "bouncing Czech." He met his demise at his own hand off the coast of the Canary Islands, committing suicide by jumping off his yacht after it came to light that he had been plundering a pension fund owned by one of his companies. Which of the following do you suppose describes Maxwell's idea of participatory management?

1　Bugging the telephone system at the office.

2　Keeping his employees informed about the financial performance of his empire.

3　Always being on time for appointments.

Did you get this one right? It was option number one. The second option wasn't even in the running: Maxwell certainly didn't keep his employees informed about the financial performance of his company; he believed in the mushroom treatment, keeping people in the dark and throwing "manure" on them. And he certainly wasn't a person to be on time for appointments. Not only was he notoriously late, he also had a tendency to schedule a number of people for the same timeslot. As a result, there were always large numbers of people waiting for him.

What I'm trying to illustrate through this rather simplistic quiz is that executives aren't the rational people we might expect. There's an irrational side to many of them – as the examples of Disney and Maxwell illustrate. If we look only for Fayol's categories of planning, organizing, coordinating, and controlling, we'll be disappointed. Even if we expanded our files to include Mintzberg's more detailed taxonomy, we'd be missing out on the irrational, shadow side of executive behavior – a shadow side that can negatively affect other people in the organization and even, in extreme cases, bring down the organization itself.

a shadow side can negatively affect other people in the organization and even, in extreme cases, bring down the organization itself

Where does this shadow side come from? Why do perfectly normal-looking executives turn into problem cases and wreak havoc around them? The rest of this chapter attempts to answer these questions. But be assured that leadership irrationality is *prevalent*. When I ask executives what their greatest source of stress is, a full 70 percent say dysfunctional leadership. When I ask their reason for leaving the organization, they mention the same percentage with reference to leadership problems. And a number of researchers on leadership have estimated that there's at least a 50 percent failure factor among leaders of organizations – an estimate with which I concur. That adds up to a lot of ineffective leaders (Box 4.2)!

BOX 4.2

What's your leadership style?

Respond to the following statements with a YES or NO, depending on how closely each reflects your situation.

                                                                              YES   NO

- Do you routinely try to avoid conflict?
- Do you sometimes engage in abrasive behavior?
- Do you tend to get bogged down in details?
- Does it seem as if you're always engaged in firefighting behavior?
- Are you difficult to get hold of in the organization?
- Do you find yourself preoccupied with the politics in your organization?
- Are you still without a successor?

If you answered YES to most of these statements, you may be steering your organization to failure. If so (and if your responses are confirmed by others who know you well), you'd be well advised to reflect on your leadership style and do something about it.

Dysfunctional patterns in leadership

It's tempting to assign responsibility for the failure factor in leadership to external forces, but we can find responsibility much closer to home, in our own shadow side. Let's look at some of the most common reasons leaders develop the failure factor.

Conflict avoidance

Although we tend to think of leaders as dominant and unafraid, many have a tendency toward conflict avoidance. There's a large group of executives who have a desperate need to be liked and approved of. The need to be loved is the key theme in their CCRT; it echoes in every line scripted for their inner theater. Afraid to do anything that might threaten acceptance, they're unable (or unwilling) to make difficult decisions or to exercise authority. They become mere empty suits, unwilling to accept the fact – and it *is* a fact – that boundary setting sometimes takes precedence over conciliation. Conflict avoidance is neither a successful nor, in the end, a popular leadership style: the leader who always appeases is like someone who feeds crocodiles hoping that they'll eat him last. There's nothing bad about being nice, but there comes a point when every leader has to say, "My way or the highway." I don't have an exact formula for success, but I know a sure formula for failure, and that's trying to please *everyone*.

The tyrannization of subordinates

Another pattern that leads to leadership incompetence is the tyrannization of subordinates. This pattern describes the Genghis Khans of the work world – those abrasive (and sometimes sadistically oriented) executives who obviously graduated with honors from the Joseph Stalin School of Management. These are the people who "like the smell of napalm in the morning." Robert Maxwell, with his tendency to engage in abusive behavior, was clearly at the head of his class. Former British Prime Minister Margaret Thatcher also possessed some tyrannical characteristics. She would make statements such as, "I don't mind how much my ministers talk as long as they do what I say," or "I'm extraordinarily patient provided I get my own way in the end." The "Iron Lady" could be a bit of a bulldozer.

The tyrannization of subordinates sometimes triggers a response that Anna Freud called the "identification-with-the-aggressor syndrome." Through unconscious impersonation of the "aggressor" (that is, the abusive boss), subordinates assume the leader's attributes and thus transform themselves from threatened to threatening, from helpless victims to powerful actors. This is a defensive maneuver, a way of controlling the severe anxiety caused by the aggressor. The people in the one-down position hope to acquire some of the power that the aggressor possesses. Unfortunately, all they accomplish is to become aggressors themselves, thus increasing the total organizational aggression.

Micromanagement

Another cause of leadership derailment is micromanagement. This is seen in executives who are so detail oriented that they can't let go of control. Anything less than perfection causes anxiety. Not trusting anyone else to do a job as well as they can do it themselves, micromanagers are unwilling to delegate. I once consulted for an entrepreneur who'd been quite successful at building up his company. He was a control freak, however. For example, he was in the habit of opening all the mail that came to the company, and he wanted all e-mail forwarded to him. This level of involvement was manageable as long as the company was in the startup phase, but once it had become a $20 million operation, the entrepreneur's lack of trust in the capabilities of others had a stifling effect on all organizational processes.

One of the most difficult transitions for many executives seems to be going from a functional to a more general management orientation. But, in fact, all micromanagement is good for is ruining morale and destroying organizations.

Manic behavior

Manic executives, possessed of apparently boundless energy, push themselves and others to the limit. But they're so hyperactive that they don't always notice what it is they're doing (even when what they're doing is dead wrong). There's a vast difference between working hard and working smart. Many executives hit the ground running but are going the wrong way.

A look at the history of Xerox reveals the effects of disconnected, manic behavior. In 1976, the market share in copying machines held by Xerox was around 88 percent. Six years later it was only 15 percent. Yet Xerox executives kept going their merry way. The firm became increasingly good at repairing machines and selling copying paper, but no one gave much thought to technological innovation. No one noticed that customers weren't as taken with broken-down machines as management was. On the contrary, customers liked problem-free machines. Canon, a Japanese competitor adept at reading customers, identified Xerox's weaknesses and determined to gain market supremacy. In just a short time it had succeeded.

Manic behavior forces companies to lose sight of their main mandate. Manic leaders become so inward looking that they forget their main constituency: their customers. Leaders shouldn't look in the mirror; they should look out the window! Only if they're externally directed can they remain close to their customer base.

leaders shouldn't look in the mirror; they should look out the window

Inaccessibility

Inaccessibility of leadership is another common problem. Some executives are so full of self-importance that they have no time for others. It wouldn't occur to them to lead by example or to walk around the workplace and marketplace listening to their primary constituencies. Lofty and unapproachable, they shield themselves behind a battery of secretaries and assistants and closed-door policies. One executive in a company I was visiting said, "Our president is like the yeti, occasionally seen in high places." Is it that such executives are looking for more grandiose people to interact with, or are they afraid that if people come too close they'll discover a fraud with very little to say?

Game playing

Every organization has its "operators" – political animals who are master power calculators. Like manic leaders and inaccessible leaders, these game players can talk and think only about themselves, and their attention falters when others talk (unless they themselves are the subject of discussion). Furthermore, their personal goals sway the organizational goals.

Game players follow their own golden rule: credit goes up while garbage goes down. They refuse to let their subordinates shine, using and abusing them rather than helping them grow and develop; and they do everything possible to steal the attention from their superiors. They try to hog the limelight, whether it's aimed below or above them. They're unwilling to plan for leadership succession, envying anybody who might take their place. Not surprisingly, game players experience high turnover among their people.

The two M's trap

All these behavior patterns contribute to the two M's of failed leadership: mistrust and malaise. The acid test of effective leadership is the extent to which people in the organization trust their leadership. If the trust level is low, some kind of malaise will occur; it's inevitable. Although the details will vary from firm to firm, some symptoms are universal: creative thinking will be suppressed, a cover-your-back mentality will prevail, and "bureau-pathology" (that is, an excess of paperwork and supportive documentation) will emerge. When these two M's sneak in, the consequences can be very detrimental for an organization, particularly when the executive who opened the door to them occupies a senior position.

So what comes over them that they allow the two M's to sneak in? In other words, as we asked earlier, how do perfectly nice executives turn into monsters? The preceding discussion of variations on the failure factor gives part of the answer, but for the rest we need to turn to the transference trap.

The transference trap

Although management seminars presenting "new" ways to lead are a dime a dozen, what they teach is often a recycled version of very old concepts. If, instead of pursuing current trends and techniques, we look back at those old concepts, we discover some very useful guidelines. Philosophers such as Plato, Aristotle, and Socrates, for example, had many interesting things to say about organizations and leadership, and their ideas are frequently helpful in explaining why leaders derail.

How the transference trap works

It is a very old concept indeed that lies at the heart of the mystery of executive failure – a concept that's governed human relations for all time, although it wasn't clearly articulated and labeled until the beginning of the twentieth century. The clinical term for this concept is *transference*. According to Freud and Jung, transference is the alpha and omega of doing work with patients. Most mental health practitioners would agree, I suspect, that it's the most important concept in psychotherapy. It's important out in the "real world" too. Anyone hoping to make sense of interpersonal encounters at anything but an intuitive level needs to understand transference.

What transference says is that no relationship we have is a *new* relationship; all relationships are colored by previous ones. And the relationships that have the most lasting potency, coloring almost every subsequent encounter, are those that we had with our earliest caregivers. Thus we often act toward people in the present as if they were people from the past: we behave toward them as children do toward their parents, for example, forgetting that we're now adults.

In other words, without even being aware of it, we're confused as to person, time, and place. As we relive those earlier, primary relationships again and again, stereotypical behavior patterns emerge. Thus the behavior of today has its roots in privileged relationships with early caretakers. There are few universals in life, but transference is one: an absolutely ubiquitous element of the human condition, it's the way each one of us processes information and organizes experience.

Maybe an example would help. Say you had a father who tended to be rather autocratic when you were growing up, and you were always arguing with him. Given that groundwork, there's a good probability that when you later meet someone who reminds you of your father, you'll fall back into that particular dysfunctional behavior pattern. Without understanding the reason (since transferential reactions happen at an unconscious level), you'll find yourself primed for a fight. And later you'll be unable to explain your behavior. "I don't know what came over me," you might say. "I lashed out at the new sales rep with no provocation at all!" The behavior of others can be equally inexplicable. Say you ask, in a pleasant and supportive tone, for a simple correction in a document and your assistant bursts into tears. Chances are that an unconscious transferential reaction lies behind the outburst.

So why do those early relationships have such staying power? Let's look at their dynamics. Send yourself back in time for a moment and imagine that you're riding your tricycle. You're gleefully cruising the neighborhood when suddenly a bully appears and threatens you. A big bully. What do you do? Realizing that with his long legs he'd easily outrun you if you fled, you might hold your ground and say, with all the force you could muster, something like, "I'm going to tell my father [or mother or older brother or sister]. He'll take you down a peg or two; he'll protect me." This is a normal reaction given your feelings of helplessness; you try to acquire power from those whom you perceive as being powerful. Obviously, the most prominent among these are your caregivers.

there are few universals in life, but transference is one: an absolutely ubiquitous element of the human condition

This type of reaction is an early step in the process of identifying, idealizing, and internalizing the important people in our lives. That process is a necessary part of each individual's narcissistic development – that is, the development of one's sense of self and self-esteem. Think about very small children and their tendency to imitate their caregivers. At times, parents can almost hear their own voices through their children's mouths. Eventually, these introjections or internalizations (technically known as "part objects") become "metabolized," we might say, and each child puts his or her unique imprint on them.

Along with that three-part process that culminates in the internalization of people who are important to us, "mirroring" is an important component of transference. Send yourself back in time again, this time to when you first managed to stay upright on a two-wheeler. "Look, look at me riding my bicycle!" you exclaim with excitement. And your father or mother most likely says, "Great, terrific – you're doing a fantastic job." They don't say (unless you're one of the unfortunate ones), "Don't do that; you may fall on your face." Instead, they try to encourage you by "mirroring" (reflecting back) your excitement, your feeling of mastery.

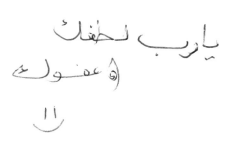

s generally the smiling eyes of
confirmation of the self.
sense of self-esteem – establish
ze ("introject") people who are
people to "mirror" what we're
knowledging our capabilities.
e many forms, these two – the
ions – are primary. They go a
e in the here and now.
w adults again; we're no longer
e of a department or an office or
quired power and authority. We
ul people for protection; others
tion. And yet, however small or
int or lofty our position in the
– our own signature patterns –
nave a tendency to recur. The dynamics of idealizing and mirroring don't disappear simply because we ascend the corporate ladder. Some people are (and always will be) more "mirror-hungry" personalities, while others are more "ideal hungry." Some people search for others to reflect them – to give feedback of the sort they want to hear. That feedback helps them reinforce their sense of self-esteem. Others search for people they can admire, can "idealize." They hope that identification with the admired person will cause some of that person's glory to rub off. What this example illustrates is that the most common, recurring transference patterns are of an idealizing and mirroring nature.

In analyzing the mirroring and idealizing patterns that we see in the workplace, we need to realize that the first "organization" we come to know is the family. How we deal with power and authority in the family dictates our later relationships with figures of power and authority. The predominant interaction patterns of childhood cast a long shadow over both our initial process of idealizing and mirroring and our later replications of that process. In other words, in adult life we can readily find replicas of our childhood behavior patterns vis-à-vis authority figures. In particular, idealizing and mirroring transferential configurations can have a devastating effect in an organizational setting when these go unchecked. People in a position of authority have an uncanny ability – without conscious awareness – to reawaken transferential processes in themselves and others.

For example, how do you react when an authority figure such as a police officer stops you for speeding? Do you anxiously try to please her, or do you get into a fight? When you're asked to go to the head office to make a presentation to the president of your organization, are you relaxed, or are you uptight? What kind of reactions will be acceptable to these authority figures? What kind of imagery occupies their inner world? What is happening to *your* inner world? Does mirroring and idealizing come into play? When we know the answer to these questions, we can extrapolate the nature of your relationship with childhood authority figures.

A world of liars

Let's look at another example of the after-effects of transferential processes. Say you're in charge of your organization, and you're running a project meeting. After the meeting, several members of the team come to you and compliment you on the great job you did conducting the meeting. That's nice feedback to receive, of course, but you might wonder what lies behind it. Did your employees react out of honesty, truly believing that you did an exceptional job, or were they just trying to please you? If the latter, they may have been deliberately "apple polishing" to gain political points. It's also quite likely, though, that they're responding unconsciously to a transferential reaction. They may be *ideal-hungry* personalities who have fallen into an idealizing pattern.

But there may be transference on your part as well. If you like to be mirrored by others, positive feedback of this sort feels so good that it can become addictive. Being *mirror hungry*, you want to be "fed." People who get to the point where they can no longer do without a daily "fix" of admiration may even fire individuals who don't praise them adequately. They need this type of daily oxygen. This end of the behavior spectrum suggests a narcissistic personality disorder – a narcissistic disposition (which, while still a mere tendency, is well within acceptable norms) that has been pushed to the extreme.

What does this example tell us? First, it implies that all leaders are surrounded by "liars." Senior executives need to recognize that many of the people who report to them are "lying," to one degree or another – whether consciously (for political reasons) or unconsciously (as a trans- ferential reaction). In hierarchical situations, people have a tendency to tell those above them what they think the superiors want to hear. People who don't acknowledge this are fooling themselves. Because *candor flees authority*, senior executives who aren't careful will find themselves eventually surrounded by sycophants. Guarding against this means creating an organizational culture where frank feedback is encouraged. Leaders need to continually ask themselves whether their own mirror hunger is encouraging dishonesty in the ranks.

Let me give an illustration. The well-known American movie tycoon Samuel Goldwyn wasn't exactly a soft touch. In fact, he was an extremely autocratic leader. His more famous statements include, "Don't say yes until I stop talking," and "When I want your opinion, I'll give it to you." Obviously, statements such as these discourage an open, participative atmosphere. Goldwyn apparently succumbed to the self-centeredness that threatens every position of power and authority.

He's not alone. I've spent a lot of time with CEOs and have seen how intimidated other people can become by the power and symbols of the office. I've also observed how power leads to dependency reactions and even physical illness in others. Any leader who says, "I don't *have* ulcers, I *give* ulcers," is probably right. Many top executives don't realize the extent to which people project their fantasies on them; how much subordinates are inclined to tell them what they want to hear as a way of dealing with their own feelings of insecurity and helplessness; how willing subordinates are to attribute special qualities to someone simply because of the office he or she holds. Even those who recognize these tendencies don't necessarily do anything to counter them. And that failure can lead a company astray. In fact, it's the lucky company that survives it.

As the author Jonathan Swift once said, "The only benefit of flattery is that by hearing what we are not we may be instructed what we ought to be." But somehow I doubt that leaders who encourage sycophancy see flattery in just that light. How much better it would be if those leaders would react to their subordinates' flattery by saying, "Don't tell me what *I* think. I know what I think. Tell me what *you* think!" Or they might try something along these lines: "You're such an easy bunch of people to get along with. Why don't you give me a really *tough* nut to crack, like 'What's your stock options package, sir?' or 'Are you planning to do any downsizing?' or 'When are we peons going to get a salary increase?'"

The role of attribution in leadership – the assumption that authority figures are worthy simply by virtue of their office – is well portrayed in the film *Being There*, based on the novel by the late Polish writer Jerzy Kozinsky and featuring actor Peter Sellers. The film looks at the life of an illiterate, reclusive, and rather slow gardener named Chance, who one day unexpectedly has to leave the protected world of his garden and finds himself in an alien environment. While crossing the street, he gets hit by a car. The occupant of the car (the actress Shirley Maclain), hoping to make amends, takes him home and introduces him to her husband, a financial wizard. When the host asks Chance what he thinks about the economy, the poor man hasn't a clue what he's talking about. Taking refuge in the only world he knows, he says something like, "You have to start at the roots." This simple statement is interpreted by the host as a great revelation. As an eventual result of his "wisdom," Chance is introduced to his nation's president, who asks him the same question. This time, after some thought, his answer is, "After the winter comes the spring." That does it. Everyone thinks of Chance as a deep thinker. He becomes front-page news, his autobiography is written for him (after all, he's illiterate), and his name is added to the spy lists of other nations. The parody continues with Chance becoming a candidate for the presidency. Wasn't it George Bernard Shaw who once said, "Kings are not born: they are made by universal hallucination"?

The symbolic trappings of power that come with high office add to the likelihood that a leader will become the vessel of subordinates' projected fantasies. Large, impressive office suites, chauffeur-driven cars, private jets, dynamic assistants, and secretaries who fawn and cater all contribute to the awe that surrounds many leaders. Awe on its own isn't so bad. It's when **awe on its own isn't so bad** leaders start believing their own press, and behaving accordingly, that the trouble starts. The early Romans had a relatively simple means for defusing this threat. When a conquering general entered Rome on his chariot, he would have behind him on the chariot a slave whose job it was to whisper, "You are human, Caesar, you are human." Some, however, did not listen very well to their slave.

The process by which executives are corrupted by power is so insidious that they don't sense their humanity slipping away. The principal actors in this dynamic – the senior executives who are the objects of the fantasies of the people around them, and the subordinates who idealize their leaders – simply don't realize what's happening to them, can't see how they've been co-opted in the process. Leaders at the extreme end of the narcissism continuum use their subordinates as extensions of themselves: they're like the mother who, when hungry herself, says to her child, "You're hungry, aren't you?" And the child, willing to be hungry if that's the mother's desire, says, "Yes, I am."

Avoiding the transference trap

Joseph Heller's *Catch-22* is a novel about a number of airmen who are on some kind of suicide mission. It describes the demented antics of an army air corps unit stationed on a Mediterranean island during the height of World War II. As time passes, the unit becomes progressively less concerned about the primary objective of the war: to end the conflict as soon as possible with minimal costs in personnel. In Heller's scenario, procedure takes precedence over substance. The policy of the officers in charge is to focus on the number of missions flown and on tight bombing patterns. The airmen whose lives are at stake get increasingly frustrated – and no wonder.

At one point a Lieutenant Scheisskopf – what a marvelous name, meaning *shithead* in German – beseeches the airmen to tell him the reason for their low morale and inadequate marching performance. One of the airmen, Clevinger, feels the urge to do so against the advice of his more canny friend Yossarian:

> "I *want* someone to tell me," Lieutenant Scheisskopf beseeched them all prayerfully. "If any of it is my fault, I *want* to be told."
>
> "He wants someone to tell him," Clevinger said.
>
> "He wants everyone to keep still, idiot," Yossarian answered.
>
> "Didn't you hear him?" Clevinger argued.
>
> "I heard him," Yossarian replied. "I heard him say very loudly and very distinctly that he wants every one of us to keep our mouth shut if we know what's good for us."
>
> "I won't punish you," Lieutenant Scheisskopf swore.
>
> "He says he won't punish me," said Clevinger.
>
> "He'll castrate you," said Yossarian.
>
> "I swear I won't punish you," said Lieutenant Scheisskopf. "I'll be grateful to the man who tells me the truth."
>
> "He'll hate you," said Yossarian. "To his dying day he'll hate you."

But Clevinger persists, falls into the trap, and tells Lieutenant Scheisskopf the truth. As a result of the lieutenant's wrath, he's brought before the action board on a charge of conspiring an overthrow by the airmen. His hope for a change of policies – ending the catch-22 – was futile.

It's clear, then, that when people in positions of leadership (whether in the military or business) say, "I'd like to get some constructive criticism," what they often mean is, "I want to hear some praise." It's also clear that when executives *do* get honest feedback, they often penalize the speaker. As the adage goes, "Tell the boss what you think, and the truth will set you free" – free from employment, that is. But the consequences of lying aren't any better. The irony is that whether employees lie or tell the truth, double-bind communication – communication that sends both a *tell* and a *don't tell* message – leads to suppression of conflict and false consensus, prevents mutual confidence and initiative, and leads to decision paralysis.

I recently conducted a leadership development workshop with a group of executives of a large pharmaceutical company undergoing serious merger pains. They weren't what I'd call happy campers, because they were under enormous pressure to deliver profit results in very difficult circumstances. At one point during the seminar I asked the executives to imagine that they were faced with a fun scale at work that ran from one to ten, with ten being the highest score and one the lowest. I then asked them where they'd fall on that scale. The first executive I questioned said three; the next one, four; the next one, three; and so on. Obviously morale was extremely bad, due largely to all the business reengineering that was going on. After the seminar I expressed my concern to the VP of human resources, who had been present at the seminar.

Less than a week later I taught the same seminar to another group of executives from the same company. As with the previous group, the population represented a random sample of the organization. There was one minor difference in this case: the chairman of the board of the newly merged company was present. He wanted to listen to what I had to say. This time, when I asked the fun scale question, the answers were remarkably different. The first executive said eight; the next, nine; and so on. When next I talked to the VP of human resources, I commented on the remarkable transformation the company had gone through. What a change in mindset in such a short time! As I said earlier, candor flees authority.

One of the most crucial tasks for any organization, then, is to create a climate where people feel comfortable dealing frankly with executives in senior positions. Effective organizational functioning demands that people have a healthy disrespect for their boss, feel free to express emotions and opinions openly, and are comfortable engaging in banter and give and take. It also demands that executives listen to what's being said.

The 360° feedback system in organizations is one of the more effective means I know for bringing a degree of openness into an organization. In such a system, organizational participants get feedback not only from their superiors (as in traditional performance-appraisal systems) but also from their colleagues and subordi-

candor flees authority

nates. The resulting communication redefines superior–subordinate relationships, reinforces a more open corporate culture, initiates constructive dialog, serves as an early-warning system for the need for change, and cautions people about their blind spots.

Clearly, if a fear of reprisals is prevalent, the 360° feedback system won't work, *can't* work. Executives who hope to implement such a system meaningfully in their organization need the courage to face any unpleasant truths that others reveal about them. Furthermore, they need to design and conduct an extensive educational program that allows participants to "practice" honesty in a safe environment; they need to guarantee that people won't be punished for telling the truth; and they need to be willing to stop making excuses for dysfunctional behavior and try to do something about it. It's not an easy transition, but it can be done. An increasing number of organizations are successfully implementing 360° feedback systems, making the injunction "Talk back to your boss" an important part of their corporate culture.

It's been estimated that only 10 percent of executives accurately assess themselves. Among those who get it wrong, twice as many people overrate themselves as underrate themselves. As a matter of fact, 70 percent of executives think that they're in the top 25 percent of their profession! Many executives suffer from blind spots, failings they're unaware of that impede effective organizational functioning. Executives can quickly learn how to be more perceptive in assessing themselves, however. While they may be far off the mark in the perception of their own capabilities the first time they go through the 360° feedback process, the next time they tend to be much more accurate.

The impact of narcissism

Having looked at the transference trap (and the only sure way to avoid it – honesty), let's take a closer look at the narcissism that underlies it. We've talked about narcissism in general terms on the preceding pages; now we'll get out the microscope and dissect it.

As my earlier reference to the tricycle indicates, the shaping of an individual's personality begins early in life. We learn from child psychologists that the first three years of life are particularly critical to development. These are the years during which the core patterns of personality are shaped, the years when we emerge as a person with a sense of our own body, gender identity, name, mind, and personal history. The foundations are laid in those early years for the kind of person we're going to be (and are likely to remain for the rest of our life). This doesn't mean that later life experiences are of no impor- tance, of course; it means simply that these tend **narcissism and leadership are intricately connected** not to have the same impact as our earlier experiences. There's a greater plasticity early in life that allows us to be shaped by what we see, do, and feel. The clinical term for the changes that take place during these early years is "narcissistic development." Although often fraught with negative connotations, narcissism is the engine that drives each one of us. And narcissism and leadership are intricately connected.

For our purposes here, we have to move beyond the limited everyday understanding of the word *narcissism*. What psychology labels narcissism is a stage of infantile development that each individual has to pass through, a stage during which the growing child derives pleasure from his or her own body and its functions. This early stage is a very delicate time in the child's life. The kind of treatment a youngster receives during this critical period of development colors his or her view of the world right through to adulthood.

As the tricycle and bicycle examples indicated, children cope with the inevitable frustration of growing up by trying to retain the perfection and bliss of their earliest days. They do so by creating both a grandiose, exhibitionistic image of themselves and an all-powerful, idealized image of their parents (the latter taking on the role of saviors and protectors).

The first configuration is referred to as the "grandiose self;" the second is the "idealized parent image." Over time, if children receive what can be called "good-enough" care, these two configurations that make up the "bipolar self" are tamed by the forces of reality. As indicated, however, remnants of these two configurations remain throughout a person's life, at times coming to the fore in interpersonal encounters.

The role of parents and other caretakers in the development of narcissism is obviously crucial. Parents, siblings, and other important figures in a child's life modify the child's exhibitionistic displays, channeling grandiose fantasies of power and glory in proper directions, thus laying the foundation for realistic ambitions, stable values, well-defined career interests, and a secure sense of self-esteem and identity. But that necessary process doesn't happen properly if a child receives an inadequate narcissistic supply due to inconsistent or harsh caretaking or to a series of significant deprivations.

Fortunately, *nobody* is perfect as a parent. After all, imperfection is a great teacher. Protecting our children from life's hardships is not really protecting them. Even with the best parenting available, the process of becoming a person is riddled with challenges; **fortunately, *nobody* is perfect as a parent** it's not at all like that comfortable pre-birth period of intrauterine existence when everything was automatically taken care of. Thus growing up inevitably implies frustration. If normal development is to occur, however, that frustration must occur only in tolerable doses. If the child experiences "good-enough" parenting, he or she will be able to deal with frustration and emerge into adulthood with a relatively balanced personality.

Sometimes, however, the caregiving that a child experiences *isn't* "good enough." Some parents overstimulate a child (that is, they overindulge the child and fail to set limits), resulting in prolonged disappointment; others understimulate (that is, are emotionally distant, overly critical, absent, or depressed); still others exhibit highly inconsistent, arbitrary behavior. All these parental shortcomings can lead to problems of a narcissistic nature in children (and the adults they grow into). If violence and abuse are added to the package, the stage is set for an inner theater rampant with malevolent imagery.

Children who have been exposed to these types of parenting may come to believe that they can't reliably depend on anyone's love or loyalty. As adults, they'll then act according to that conviction. While such people claim to be fully self-sufficient, they're troubled to the depths of their being by a sense of deprivation, anger, and emptiness. In order to cope with these feelings, and perhaps as a cover for their insecurity, they transform their narcissistic needs into obsessions. Such individuals become fixated on issues of power, beauty, status, prestige, and superiority. They try continually to maneuver others into strengthening their shaky sense of self-esteem, and they're preoccupied with thoughts of getting even for the hurts (real or imagined) that they experienced during childhood. They typically have an exaggerated sense of their own superiority, their uniqueness, and their talent; and they often have grandiose fantasies. They're extremely self-centered and self-referential: they don't care which direction they're going as long as they remain in the driver's seat (Box 4.3).

BOX 4.3

Is your narcissism held in check?

Answer the following questions with a YES or NO. Be as honest with yourself as possible.

YES   NO

- Do you feel superior in comparison with others?
- Do you have a tendency to exaggerate how good you are?
- Are there times that you engage in boastful behavior?
- Do you frequently have grandiose fantasies?
- Do you need a lot of attention?
- Do others see you as quite self-centered?
- Have others accused you of arrogant behavior?
- Do you use others to further your own interests without giving
  them credit?

The larger the number of YES responses, the more likely it is that you have strong narcissistic tendencies.

Reactive and constructive narcissism

As noted earlier, the narcissism we speak of in everyday conversation has only negative connotations. The mythological youth Narcissus (who looked at his image in a pond, fell in love with himself, and died of unrequited love) is held up as a reminder of what happens to those who look too kindly on themselves. But narcissism, in limited doses, is necessary for self-esteem and self-identity. And it's necessary in *moderate* doses in leaders, because dominance, self-confidence, and creativity can't exist without it. Thus having either too much or too little narcissism throws a person off balance. But how much narcissism is too much?

In determining what makes narcissism dysfunctional, I find the distinction between "constructive" and "reactive" narcissism helpful. Constructive narcissism develops in response to the "good-enough" caregiving described earlier. Parents who offer their children a lot of support, recognize the tolerance level of their children (and thus limit frustration to what's age appropriate), and provide a proper "holding environment" for their children's various emotional reactions, produce offspring who are well balanced and possess a solid sense of self-esteem. Reactive narcissism, contrariwise, develops in people who have been "wounded" in one way or another. With all the problems we saw earlier – parental overstimulation, for example, or parental understimulation – children don't get the attention needed for a smooth developmental process. Faulty interaction patterns between caregiver and child generally lead to problems later in life. As adults, reactive narcissists behave like the hungry, whimpering babies they used to be – babies who haven't been heard and want attention.

From my in-depth study of many leaders, I've concluded that a considerable percentage of them are driven by reactive narcissism. In other words, they've become what they are for negative reasons: they feel a strong need to make up for the wrongs done to them at earlier periods in their lives. Having been belittled, maltreated, or exposed to other hardships as children, they're determined as adults to show everyone that they've amounted to something. If that determination stops at wanting to be valued (and working to be valued) or extends to making reparation, reactive narcissism can bear healthy fruit. If it turns into envy, spite, and vindictiveness, the fruit is sour indeed.

The Monte Cristo complex

People who choose to deal with the hurts of childhood through vindictiveness and spite – and it *is* a choice, albeit an unconscious one – suffer from what can be called the "Monte Cristo complex," after the lead character in Alexander Dumas's book *The Count of Monte Cristo*. The book tells the engrossing story of a man who has been terribly wronged and manages to get even, repaying one bad turn after the other – with interest. The count's passionate desire to get even touches a responsive chord in many people. Certainly we all experience similar feelings, at least fleetingly. The universality of the desire for revenge may explain why the autobiography of former Chrysler CEO, Lee Iacocca (in which he described how he got even with the second Henry Ford), became so popular.

But for people who suffer from the Monte Cristo complex, revenge is more than just a fleeting temptation; it's *the* major motivational force in life. Getting even is all that really matters. It's more important, even, than such prizes as wealth and power. It's a stressful way of going through life, however, because it locks the body and mind in a perpetual state of high alert. Examples of the Monte Cristo complex in the political arena include Adolf Hitler, Slobodan Milosevic, and Saddam Hussein.

for people who suffer from the Monte Cristo complex, revenge is *the* major motivational force in life

Making reparation

Revenge is a negative way of dealing with childhood wounds. Although in some sense it "makes things right," it consumes the person pursuing it and leads to destructive behavior. A more constructive way of dealing with the hurts of childhood is what we might call *reparation*. The thought behind reparation goes something like this: "I had a bad deal growing up, so I'm going to make things better for my children. I'll create a better life for them." Although reparation usually starts with the personal environment, the same reasoning applies in the workplace. Thus people with a reparation orientation try to assuage their hurt by making improvements in their organizations.

Many successful leaders fall into the category of reparation seekers. Those who do often share some or all of the following traits relating to narcissistic development:

- ❖ They often have a background of an absent father – either remote or diseased – and a strong, supportive mother. (This is the constellation for male leaders. There's as yet no clear constellation for female leaders, since there are presently too few examples of female top leadership in business.)

- ❖ They were forced to take on the authority position in the family early on (especially those who lost their father at a young age) and were thus somewhat overstimulated. They were age inappropriately put in a responsible position.

- ❖ They tend to be competitive (a pattern that manifests itself throughout life), and they're often willing to speak their mind and confront authority.

- ❖ Because they've found people who believe in them and support them, they demonstrate great courage and resilience in dealing with failure; they're not easily intimidated, and they strongly believe in fair process.

Many of the leaders I've studied fit this bill. Richard Branson of Virgin, for example, had a powerhouse of a mother, while his father was less of a presence. Shortly after Branson was born, his mother walked around with him saying, "My son is going to become prime minister." As he got older, she set high standards and drove him to be independent. How could he lose?

Jack Welch, former chairman of General Electric, was born on the wrong side of the tracks. His father, a train conductor, was rather aloof and not much present. His mother was a sickly Irish American who kept on pushing her son to do better, be it in sports, at school, or at work. When an article appeared in *Fortune* magazine entitled "The mind of Jack Welch," the accompanying picture showed a picture of his mother behind him.

I could list many more. I've had quite a few leaders recount times when they were the only people prepared to speak up against a difficult boss, a risky act of courage that in a positive scenario is remembered as gutsy. They said that when interesting opportunities emerged later in their organization, their courageous actions were remembered and they were chosen for the job.

Narcissism and resilience

It has always intrigued me why certain people do well in life despite disadvantages while others don't. What is it that makes them *resilient?* This clinical label is given to people who have not just a one-shot victory over a single obstacle but an ongoing outlook that helps them over repeated obstacles. In general, resilient people deal with emotionally difficult problems proactively, reframe experiences in a positive way, have a great capacity to fantasize a more optimistic picture of the future, give themselves time for self-reflection, and work hard at maintaining a network of supportive relationships.

resilient people deal with emotionally difficult problems proactively

Studies of children who come from deprived situations suggest that what differentiates those who ultimately do well – who develop the quality of resilience – is having someone who takes a special interest in them, a supportive figure who believes in them as youngsters and pushes them to greater achievements. The best person, of course, is the mother; but fathers count, as do grandparents, other family members, teachers, scout leaders, and so on.

Children of failure-prone fathers can be more successful than children of highly successful fathers, so paternal modeling obviously isn't always a determining factor. As a matter of fact, sometimes the worst thing that can happen to an ordinary person is to have an extraordinary father. Such fathers can be overbearing, stifling the developing child. Fortunately, the mother can serve as a neutralizing force. As Napoleon once said (oversimplifying, perhaps), "The future destiny of the child is always the work of the mother." Although he was thinking of positive mothering, many children are driven toward success by controlling, domineering mothers. Furthermore, research has shown that a considerable number of successful people come from markedly troubled homes, or homes plagued by physical handicap or bereavement. All these kinds of difficulties focus the mind of the developing child to find ways to overcome his or her particular challenge (Box 4.4).

BOX 4.4

How resilient are you?

Put a checkmark beside any of the following statements that define your situation.

CHECK

- I deal with emotionally difficult problems proactively
- I reframe experiences in a positive way
- I have a great capacity to fantasize a more optimistic picture of the future
- I give myself time for self-reflection
- I work hard at maintaining a network of supportive relationships

If you've checked most of these statements, you are quite resilient. And that's good news: you're likely to be more capable than many of your colleagues at dealing with the stresses and strains of daily life.

5 The Dilbert phenomenon

As to diseases make a habit of two things – to help, or at least, to do no harm. HIPPOCRATES

It is not enough to be busy; so are the ants. The question is: What are we busy about? HENRY THOREAU

Each of us needs time for mental self-renewal. WHIT SCHULTZ

The Dilbert comic strip, drawn and written by Scott Adams, is enormously popular these days. An endless stream of e-mail communications from executives keeps Adams supplied with inspiration for his parody of office life. The popularity of Dilbert is an indication of the extent to which people in today's marketplace experience career alienation and cynicism. Because in so many companies people recognize a disconnection between organizational rhetoric and organizational reality, they hear slogans such as "People are our greatest asset," "We're from the head office, and we're here to help you," and "Training is a high priority" with considerable suspicion. Like Dilbert, people the world over confront bureaucratic absurdity and managerial idiocy in their daily struggle to survive life in a cubicle (whether real or metaphorical). Treated like cogs in a machine by organizations whose annual reports speak with pride of "respecting the individual" – organizations that take their "human capital" for granted, rhetoric notwithstanding – they lose interest in their work (Box 5.1).

BOX 5.1

How well do you know your people?

What do your employees do when they're not working for you? Can you give specifics for five or more employees, either off the top of your head or with a little conversational research?

Many executives are astounded to discover how loyal, creative, vigorous, and imaginative their employees are – *except* during the eight hours a day they're on the job.

The stresses and strains of organizational life take their toll. If executives aren't given (or they don't take) the opportunity to renew themselves, they often begin to suffer from terminal monotony and burnout. Everyone has talent at 25 (as the saying goes); the trick is to have talent at midlife. This applies far more often to men than to women. The latter tend to be more active in midlife, frequently having had a different career trajectory; and they're usually better at diversifying their interests (Box 5.2).

BOX 5.2

Are you suffering from burnout?

Respond to the following statements by checking TRUE or FALSE. Answer as honestly as you can.

	TRUE	FALSE
• I feel down or depressed most of the time		
• I feel tired most of the time		
• I have trouble sleeping		
• I rarely feel hungry		
• I complain constantly		
• I feel a lot of pressure at work		
• I feel frustrated or angry most of the time		

▶

BOX 5.2 continued

TRUE   FALSE

- I have a sense of helplessness about my present work situation
- I feel nobody really cares about me
- I feel swamped by all my obligations
- I feel close to a breakdown

If you have three or more TRUE statements, you may be suffering from symptoms of burnout. Reassess your present job and family situation and look for ways to renew yourself. Professional help may be advisable.

The deadness within

The psychiatric concepts of *alexithymia* and *anhedonia* are relevant to this discussion. The first term, coined from Greek derivatives by psychiatrist Peter Sifneos in the 1970s, means (literally) "no word for emotions"; the second, also of Greek derivation, means the inability to derive pleasure from experiences that are normally pleasurable.

Alexithymia

In psychiatry, the word *alexithymic* is used to describe people who have a dead-fish quality. Alexithymics struggle, with varied success, to understand their emotions and moods, and they're incapable of perceiving the subtleties of either. Because they're not sure what they feel, they also have difficulty *expressing* affect. Instead of showing an emotional reaction, they focus on physical problems.

Despite the fancy label, identification of alexithymics isn't difficult. The symptoms of alexithymia include an impoverished fantasy life, a paucity of inner emotional experience, an inability to experience fun, and a tendency to adopt a lifeless, detail-oriented way of speaking. Furthermore, alexithymics radiate a kind of mechanical quality that precludes spontaneous reaction. Alexithymics appear unperturbed by experiences that other people would find emotionally shattering. A death in the family, a partner's infidelity, being passed over for a promotion – nothing seems to ruffle them. All experiences slide down into a black hole of inexpressiveness and blankness.

Alexithymics are as incapable of empathy as they are of self-awareness. This, combined with their mechanical, robotic responses to conflict, amounts to emotional illiteracy. Alexithymics are preoccupied with the concrete and objective; metaphors, allusions, and hidden meanings are like a foreign language to them.

The work environment many executives operate in contributes to alexithymia. Everyday life in some insurance companies and banks, for example, simply isn't conducive to wonder, curiosity, or joy. The lifeless quality of a moribund organization encourages executives to suppress their emotions – a process that takes a lot of energy. Executives bearing the burden of suppression eventually face exhaustion (Box 5.3).

alexithymics appear unperturbed by experiences that other people would find emotionally shattering

---

BOX 5.3

How alive do you feel?

Think carefully about the following questions and then respond with YES or NO.

                                                                         YES   NO

- Do you have difficulty communicating with other people?
- Do you prefer to describe an event in detail rather than offer your feelings about it?
- Do you use action as a substitute for expressing feelings?
- When you talk about feeling, are you able to find the appropriate words?
- Are you sometimes confused about what emotion you're experiencing?
- Do you find it difficult to describe your feelings about others?

▶

BOX 5.3 continued

YES   NO

- Do you find it easier to talk about physical problems than about emotions?
- Do you feel that your fantasy and imagination leave something to be desired?
- Do dreams and daydreams play little role in your life?
- Do you prefer movies with action over psychological dramas?
- Are you more concerned about what's happening in your surroundings than in your inner life and emotion?
- Do you find life boring most of the time?
- Do you rarely feel or show excitement?
- Do you feel people try to avoid you?

If you answered the majority of these questions in the affirmative (and if people close to you confirm your responses), you may be somewhat "colorblind" as far as emotions are concerned.

These days there's an emotional division of labor in organizations: the higher one finds oneself in management, the more emotional restraint one is expected to exercise. Across the board – from management to shop floor – there are more rigid norms about the management of emotions, due perhaps to the expansion of white-collar managerial roles and the service sector. Many organizations emphasize emotional management of some sort. Disneyland, for example – sometimes called the "smile factory" – encourages its employees to "act" happy. Other organizations make it clear that the expression of deep and intense feelings is inappropriate. Few companies have yet discovered that suppression of emotions (or extreme management of emotions) leads to regressive behavior and infantilization and contributes to stress symptoms (Box 5.4).

BOX 5.4

Is your organization stressing you out?

Because it's often easier to detect stress symptoms than symptoms of alexithymia in oneself, your stress level in the workplace is an important signpost of unexpressed emotional distress.

Respond to the following statements by circling   1 (RARELY)   2 (OCCASIONALLY)
3 (OFTEN)   4 (ALWAYS).

• I have a clear understanding of what direction our oganization is going	1	2	3	4
• I feel secure in my position in the company	1	2	3	4
• I believe that I can influence the direction of my career	1	2	3	4
• I have ample opportunities to engage in new initiatives	1	2	3	4
• I am inspired and motivated by my boss(es)	1	2	3	4
• There is a strong sense of teamwork in the organization	1	2	3	4
• People have a lot of trust and mutual respect for each other in this organization	1	2	3	4
• People are very open to each other in this organization	1	2	3	4
• People in the organization value and recognize my contributions	1	2	3	4
• I believe I can make a difference in this organization	1	2	3	4
• Working in this organization is a lot of fun	1	2	3	4
• The organization's policies and procedures are applied fairly	1	2	3	4
• People have a strong sense of accountability in this organization	1	2	3	4
• This organization offers me many opportunities to learn new things	1	2	3	4
• The reward system is extremely fair in this organization	1	2	3	4
• I have a great deal of control over my workload	1	2	3	4
• People in this organization strongly believe in a balanced lifestyle	1	2	3	4

Add up the responses for each question.

Scoring
34 or less: Your work environment is very stressful
35 to 51:   You're working in a stressful place, but the stress is manageable
52 and above: You should be pleased to work in such a positive environment

Anhedonia

Anhedonia is the inability to experience pleasure. Anhedonics feel a pervasive sense of apathy and a loss of interest in (and withdrawal from) all regular and formerly pleasurable activities; they're all but dead inside. They're unwilling to seek out new sensations, they have diminished attentional function, and they lack a zest for life.

True anhedonia is a serious psychiatric syndrome. What we're interested in is quasi-anhedonia, a milder form of anhedonia that develops in people who are capable of experiencing pleasure (and used to do so). Even quasi-anhedonia in a top executive can devastate an organization, however, because leadership takes a great deal of energy. A dead fish lacks the oomph to lead troops to success.

Resuscitating "dead" leaders

What can we do to regain our sense of excitement? What can we do to rediscover or even reinvent ourselves? Given that the most meaningful asset in organizations is human imagination, how can we tap our own creative abilities and those of our colleagues and subordinates?

A sense of flow

We need to rediscover what the psychologist Mihaly Csikszentmihalyi calls a sense of "flow" – a feeling comprised of exhilaration, concentration, and such total involvement in what we're doing that we lose all sense of time. How do we do that?

❖ First, we need challenge. If we work on "stretch" tasks *that are manageable*, we can get that "Everest feeling" that a sense of flow conveys. Challenge is crucial because it forces us to learn. Human beings have an in-built exploratory hunger that only learning assuages (as we'll see in Chapter 13). Organizations that emphasize learning, thereby creating opportunities for creativity and innovation, help their employees feel alive.

❖ Second, we need intermediate milestones. Small "wins" are important. If we set and meet milestones for each major goal as we proceed, we get regular feedback, gain a perception of control over what we're doing, and can "celebrate" progress along the way.

What does "flow" look like on the job? When I ask people what kinds of work activities they remember as being most intense and exciting, they often say starting up something new or turning a business around. These "highs" are even better if a high-performance *team* is involved (Boxes 5.5 and 5.6).

BOX 5.5

How's your sense of flow?

1   Think back to when you were 5, 10, 16, and 21 years old. At those various ages, what did you envision yourself doing when you grew up? Reflect on the transformation of your dreams.

2   Now close your eyes and think back again to being a kid, maybe 5 to 10 years old. What activities made you really feel alive then? What activities were so absorbing and fun that you completely lost track of time?

3   Can you come up with comparable activities in your life now – activities that would absorb you in the same way?

4   List at least three pleasurable things you'd like to try. Be imaginative. Take the item that's the easiest and begin with it today.

It's important that each of us recognizes the kind of activities that make us feel really alive and energized. It's even more important that we seek out and do those activities regularly.

BOX 5.6

Can you identify your leadership "peak"?

Your responses to the exercise in Box 5.5 may be of some help as you engage in the following leadership exercise, which is aimed at helping you identify when you're at your best as a leader.

1 Describe a time when you feel you were at your best as a leader.
2 What were the circumstances to make it a challenge?
3 What did you do that made this a defining moment?
4 What characteristics of effective leadership did you demonstrate?
5 What have you learned from this experience?

As you select and coordinate activities in your organizational life, keep in mind your responses to this exercise and the one that came before. Bearing in mind the sort of activities that give you the greatest pleasure and help you to be productive and effective as a leader may help you choose more wisely in the future.

Flow in the age of business reengineering

Reengineering almost always involves layoffs. When management literature addresses the issue of downsizing, it tends to focus on two groups of "victims": the people who are downsized out of a job and the people who remain employed but suffer from survivor guilt. There's a third group of victims, however, that we rarely talk about. This is the "executioners" – the people who do the dirty work. While the occasional person with a sadistic disposition enjoys wielding the axe, it's far more likely that executioners will suffer from depression and show signs of alexithymia and anhedonia.

When top executives suffer from symptoms such as these, it's hard for them to steer a true course for their organization. It's harder still for them to maintain the excitement and energy that are necessary to a sense of flow. Too much of their energy is taken up by personal concerns. And yet, given the importance of emotional management and the extent to which leaders serve as a walking symbol to their people, emotional expressiveness is critical. Symptoms of alexithymia, anhedonia, or dissociation prevent an executive from being truly in touch with his or her constituency. Faking it is an option, sure; but it works for only a limited amount of time. Eventually other executives and then subordinates will realize that their leader isn't emotionally present and doesn't have what it takes to keep the momentum going. Thus leaders have a responsibility to either prevent such symptoms or seek outside help (whether from a colleague or a professional) in defusing them. Only if leaders face these problems head-on can they continue to help their people feel really alive.

Whole-life strategy versus deferred-life strategy

BOX 5.7

How balanced is your lifestyle?

Ask yourself the following questions. If possible, have your spouse or partner respond as well, and then discuss areas of agreement and disagreement.

1   How do you divide your time between home and work?
2   How much time do you spend with your spouse/partner and children?
3   What's the quality of your personal relationships with others? Are there people you can go to for emotional support?
4   How do you assess the balance between giving and getting emotional support?
5   Do you ever reflect on the goals in your life, and periodically reassess how realistic they are?
6   How well do you cope with stress and anxiety?
7   Do you have interests and activities outside work?

It may be difficult to answer some of these questions, but it's important to think about the issues they raise. If your responses (and the reactions of your spouse or partner) are troublesome to you, it may be worthwhile to explore these issues further, perhaps with the help of a leadership coach, psychotherapist, or other professional.

Achieving balance between work and personal life clearly belongs at the top of the list of things that are easier said than done (Box 5.7). Even coming *close* to that balance is a challenge. The following steps lay the groundwork for a commitment to balance:

❖ Take stock of your life goals. Spend time thinking about what you hope to accomplish in life, and then make sure that you set aside time for those things to which you've assigned high priority.

❖ Stop measuring your life in terms of *quantity* – years lived, awards won, promotions earned. Look instead at the *quality* of your life.

❖ Give up being a superperson. Don't set unachievable targets for yourself.

❖ Stop focusing on what's *ideal* and begin accepting what's *satisfactory*.

❖ Learn to say *no*. And don't feel guilty when you do so. It's everyone's prerogative to set boundaries.

❖ Spend more time alone with yourself. Frightening as this may be to some, it will give you the opportunity to reflect on what's important to you.

❖ Spend quality time with individual members of your family, participating in special activities with one person at a time. Try to really know each person in his or her uniqueness.

❖ Avoid irritating, overly competitive "Type A" people, especially during your off hours. Make friends with "Type B" people – those who have a more relaxed outlook on life.

❖ Make recreation – that's "re-creation" – a priority.

❖ Cultivate your esthetic side. Start to appreciate beautiful things: music, art, theater, literature, or nature.

Many people who take the career track seriously opt for what I call the *deferred-life strategy*: they plan to work like the dickens today so that they can enjoy the nice house and fine car and cushy retirement later. While this strategy sounds good (or even necessary) at the outset, it leads inevitably to disappointment.

Unfortunately, committing time to home life at the height of a busy career – itself a significant challenge – is only half the battle. Executives have to be able to shed their CEO persona and become just husband, or friend, or dad, or daughter. Many executives who can't make the switch gracefully give up trying; they put in time at home but don't bother interacting, or interact exactly in the same way they do in the office. During the first week of my four-part executive seminar on leadership, the participants spend a lot of time talking about their work. That changes, however, in the second, third and fourth weeks. Once they feel more comfortable with the format and with each other, what they want to discuss is how to juggle the pressures of work and family – how to keep their life in balance. When I ask them the difficult question, "If you had only six months to live, how would you spend your time?" few focus on work projects. Folk wisdom has it right: nobody on his or her deathbed says, "I should have spent more time at the office."

The tragedies of success and near-success

From the stories these senior executives have told over the years, I've discovered that there are two tragedies in life: one is to be unsuccessful; the other, paradoxically, is to be successful. We can all understand the unhappiness that grows out of being unsuccessful, in part because we've all been there at one time or another. But how could *success* breed unhappiness?

there are two tragedies in life: one is to be unsuccessful; the other, paradoxically, is to be successful

The Faust syndrome

Many successful executives suffer from what has been described as the "Faust syndrome" (named after Goethe's *Faust*) – a melancholia or regret that surfaces once career goals have been reached. These executives are successful; they've made it to the top; they've become

CEO or member of the board (or whatever they were shooting for); they've *arrived*. And yet they're depressed. Is that all there is to life? they ask. Is this what I mortgaged my life for? Is the prize worth the price?

Torschlusspanik

While some executives become depressed when they meet their goals, others despair when they *don't*, even if they've had a very successful career by other people's standards. Those in this latter group suffer from what the Germans call *Torschlusspanik* – literally, panic due to the closing of the gates. Recognizing that their early career dreams are still unfulfilled (and worse, are unlikely *ever* to be fulfilled), they fear that time is running out. Some give up right away; others engage in a frenzy of goal-directed activity, usually without reaching their desired aim. Both groups, however, tend to end up depressed. Although hard work wards off depressive feelings for a time, executives who don't reassess their priorities in the light of failed goals stand a good chance of becoming depressed.

In one of my leadership seminars I had an executive who had been a good "soldier" in his organization. He realized something during a workshop discussion that he had successfully suppressed for years: although he had steadily moved up through the organizational hierarchy during his tenure, his career trajectory was not going to take him to board level in the time remaining to him; there were other candidates before him who were more qualified. That realization sent him into a depression that threatened to undo him. After the seminar, however, he managed to work through his depression with the assistance of a leadership coach who helped him redirect his career, and he eventually took a more senior position in another organization.

Imposture, real and imagined

Still other successful executives in top management positions feel like impostors. They question their capabilities and fear that they're not as competent or intelligent as others think they are. Sometimes, regrettably, they're right. A small number of executives reach the top through posturing or because of family connections. Such people often become excellent clients of consulting firms, which help them shine.

Other self-doubters, however, are good at everything but self-assessment: although they feel like impostors, they're quite competent. They attribute their success to luck, compensatory hard work, or superficial factors such as physical attractiveness and likeability. They are unable to accept that they possess intellectual gifts and abilities, and are amazed that their perceived incompetence isn't transparent. They live in constant fear that their fraudulent existence will be exposed – that they won't live up to others' expectations and that catastrophe will follow. Because of their perfectionism, they're unusually sensitive to rejection and social failure. The doubt about their abilities sown by their early caregivers keeps on haunting them.

The Nobel Prize complex

Some executives become paralyzed when they reach the top. After striving for years for a particular position (such as CEO), they fall apart once they achieve it. Because they fear the envy of others – a state that's been described as the "Nobel Prize complex" – they tend to "snatch defeat out of the hands of victory." Because they're afraid to stand out and be noticed by others, they sometimes engage – without conscious awareness – in self-destructive behavior.

The late U.S. president Richard Nixon was a good example of the Nobel Prize complex at work. For Nixon, success was surrounded by ambivalence, and thus he developed an uncanny ability to shoot himself in the foot (the Watergate affair being only one example of this). Nixon's father was an impulsive, violent, unaffectionate man who was unsuccessful at everything he touched. His mother was a domineering matriarch with a strong ambition for her son and a manipulative way of dealing with her difficult husband. The helplessness and fear that Nixon felt toward his father meant that he identified with his mother. But the family dynamics left a legacy of anger, bitterness, repressed hostility, secretive manipulative behavior, and a need for control.

Sometimes an ambivalence about doing well has to do with leaving family behind, becoming more distant from them. Individuals who haven't satisfactorily resolved rivalrous, ambivalent feelings toward parents and siblings see worldly success as an "Oedipal triumph" that's both wanted and feared. If retaliation is feared from the Oedipal competitor, success is a Pyrrhic victory at best. Executives who reach the top under these circumstances may be haunted by feelings of guilt and retribution.

sometimes an ambivalence about doing well has to do with leaving family behind, becoming more distant from them

The loneliness of command

Not all executives deal well with the "loneliness of command." Corny as that term may sound, there's a great deal of truth to it. Executives in middle management have a lot of people to talk to, peers who share challenges and frustrations. When executives reach the top, however, they're alone. The complex network of mutual dependencies that exists at the lower rungs is disturbed when the top executive intrudes. Subordinates always have, at the back of their minds, the awareness that the top executive makes decisions about them – their promotions, salary increases, and so on. Consequently, they keep their distance. With no organizational outlet for their normal attachment needs, top executives begin to feel disconnected. If they're not careful, they may find themselves isolated from reality, with nothing to test their perceptions against.

In the face of the huge battles that many executives have fought and won on their way to the top, this may seem like an insignificant, unimportant detail. But it isn't. People at the top need someone to talk to; they have to take care of their dependency needs and address the anxieties associated with their job. So what can they do?

Some go to the famous leadership conference held annually in Davos, Switzerland, where hundreds of CEOs rub shoulders, delighted to find that they're not alone with their problems. Others take my leadership seminar. Many participants have commented that a seminar of this nature has been their first opportunity to deal with the loneliness of leadership, and they've been grateful for the chance to make deep friendships with people with whom they can share their concerns. Still others hire a consultant or a leadership coach. Many a consultant's main function (although his business cards wouldn't say so) is taking care of lonely-heart executives. We *all* have a need for confidants, people we can talk with, people who provide a "holding environment."

A summary prescription for revitalization

The surgeon Sir William Osler is supposed to have said, in the late 1900s, that the best thing that can happen to a person is a mild coronary at midlife. There's some truth to this outrageous statement. Lying in a hospital with tubes conducting fluids in and out of the body forces people to reflect on the priorities in their life, to determine what it is that they really enjoy.

Those of us who aren't "blessed" with a coronary need to sit ourselves down periodically and reevaluate what we hope for in life and what we're getting out of life. We need to take our metaphorical pulse to determine our emotional health and then seek remedies that will make us feel better about ourselves and our situation. We need to look for signs that we're doing the following:

❖ Continuing to strive for a sense of personal growth through self-exploration.

❖ Surprising ourselves and others.

❖ Balancing our private and professional lives.

- ❖ Cultivating caring and trusting ties with others.
- ❖ Remaining physically active.
- ❖ "Owning" our own life.

This bare-bones list can be fleshed out as follows. In our private life, we should strive to "rediscover" our spouse, wherever possible breaking the routines that creep into any partnership and discovering new activities to do together. Other ways to reload include spending quality time with the children and grandchildren, expanding the horizon of friends and acquaintances to include people different from those we usually encounter, and exploring aesthetic interests (for both stimulation and relaxation).

In public life, we should seek stimuli for growth by accepting new challenges in the short- and long-term projects that cross our desk; by mentoring younger people, a process that results in vicarious gratification when protégés do well; by pursuing long-held (and long-deferred) dreams, as Gauguin did when he left his work as a bank clerk and went off to a Polynesian island to paint; and by becoming involved in activities that benefit society.

If we stagnate at home or on the job, or fail to balance work and home, the stress will take its toll. Around 20 percent of executives suffer from psychiatric symptoms of one kind or another. That's one out of every five! Depression and substance abuse top the list, especially among male executives. (The figures for depression are higher for women, while alcohol abuse tends to be lower among women.)

if we stagnate at home or on the job, or fail to balance work and home, the stress will take its toll

Executive stagnation and imbalance harm companies as well. How can an executive who is depressed or alcoholic (or overaggressive, vindictive, arrogant, manipulative, selfish, or overly distant) shape a creative and nurturing corporate culture? In the next chapter, we'll look at that pathology – the damage that an impaired executive can wreak on his or her organization.

6 The rot at the top

Convincing yourself does not win an argument. ROBERT HALF

The world is full of cactus, but we don't have to sit on it.

WILL FOLEY

The greater the ignorance the greater the dogmatism.

SIR WILLIAM OSLER

All of us have specific ways of thinking and perceiving, styles of experiencing emotion, methods of subjective experience in general, and modes of activity that are associated with various forms of neurotic behavior. As indicated before, these unique ways of dealing with the environment are based on patterns that are deeply embedded, pervasive, and likely to endure. The "fantasies" or scripts that make up a person's interior world – the stereotyped, well-rehearsed, constantly repeated ways of behaving and acting that determine an individual's particular cognitive and affective map – are essential to understanding that person.

Just as individuals favor a particular "neurotic style," likewise in a *group* of individuals a specific style tends to dominate, consistently coming to the fore especially in stressful situations. Thus in studying top executives and their organizations, I find it helpful to draw parallels between individual pathology – the excessive use of one neurotic style – and organizational pathology, the latter resulting in particularly poor corporate performance.

A Spanish saying echoes this linkage between ineffective leadership and decay: "Fish start to smell at the head." In organizations where power is highly concentrated – where the decision-making authority is centralized in the hands of either a top executive or a small, homogeneous dominant coalition – the person–organization interface is so close that any rot at the head quickly spreads throughout. In organizations where power is broadly distributed, by the same token, culture and strategies are influenced by many executives, and thus the relationship between leadership style and organizational pathology is more tenuous.

Neurotic styles and organizations

Strategy and organizational structure can be influenced strongly by the personality of the leader. So can organizational culture. Management literature is filled with evidence to support these contentions. Much of the research, however, has examined simple aspects of personality and related them to one or two organizational variables. Such studies have led to the over-simplification of often very complex phenomena. In looking at the interface between leader and organization, I prefer to focus on *clusters* of behavior patterns, person- **strategy and** ality styles that remain relatively stable over the **organizational** years, as opposed to simple *dimensions* of **structure can be** behavior. The former may enable us to better **influenced strongly** link what happens in the inner world of the **by the personality of** executive with his or her actual behavior. **the leader**

My central thesis in this chapter is that the stable psychological orientations of key organization members are major determinants of the neurotic style of their organization. On the basis of their "core conflictual relationship theme" (or CCRT; see Chapter 2), top executives may create "shared fantasies" that permeate all levels of personnel, influence organizational culture, and underlie the dominant organizational style (which in turn greatly influences decisions about strategy and structure). The stronger the personality of the CEO, the more his or her way of behaving will be reflected in the culture, structure, and strategies of the firm. This is especially true, as noted earlier, in highly centralized organizations.

Although pathological organizational styles seem to mirror the dysfunctions common to certain individual neurotic styles, it's important to note that organizational pathology isn't *necessarily* the result of pathological leadership; it can be based on a number of factors, either singly or in combination. For example, depressive organizational pathology might be paired with "healthy" leadership in a firm that has dwindling markets because of a declining industry or too much foreign competition, in a firm that's been acquired and dominated by another organization, or in a firm that has too few resources to be able to initiate a significant turnaround. Mixed types are quite common. In fact, healthy firms tend to have a mixture of styles (see Table 6.1).

Table 6.1 Summary of the five dominant constellations

Organization	Executive	Culture	Strategy	Guiding theme
Dramatic				
Characterized by overcentralization that obstructs the development of effective information systems; structure is too primitive for its many products and broad market; lacking influence at the second-tier executive level	Attention seeking; craving excitement, activity, and stimulation; touched by a sense of entitlement; tending toward extremes	Well matched as to dependency needs of subordinates and protective tendencies of CEO; characterized by "idealizing" and "mirroring;" headed by a leader who is catalyst for subordinates' initiatives and morale	Hyperactive, impulsive, venturesome, and dangerously uninhibited; favoring executive initiation of bold ventures; inconsistent diversification and growth; encouraging action for action's sake; based on nonparticipative decision making	"I want to get attention from and impress the people who count in my life"

Organization	Executive	Culture	Strategy	Guiding theme
Suspicious				
Characterized by elaborate information processing, abundant analysis of external trends, and centralization of power	Vigilantly prepared to counter any attacks and personal threats; hypersensitive; suspicious and distrustful; overinvolved in rules and details to secure complete control; craving information; sometimes vindictive	Fostering a "fight-or-flight" mode, including dependency and fear of attack; emphasizing the power of information; nurturing intimidation, uniformity, and lack of trust	Reactive and conservative, overly analytical, diversified, and secretive	"Some menacing force is out to get me. I'd better be on my guard. I can't really trust anybody"
Detached				
Characterized by internal focus; insufficient scanning of external environment; self-imposed barriers to free flow of information	Withdrawn and uninvolved; lacking interest in present or future; sometimes indifferent to praise or criticism	Lacking warmth or emotions; conflict-ridden; plagued by insecurity and jockeying for power	Vacillating, indecisive, and inconsistent; growing out of narrow, parochial perspectives	"Reality doesn't offer any satisfaction. Interaction with others is destined to fail, so it's safer to remain distant"
Depressive				
Characterized by ritualism, bureaucracy, inflexibility, excessive hierarchy, poor internal communications, and resistance to change	Lacking self-confidence; plagued by self-esteem problems; ignorant of success (and therefore tolerant of mediocrity and failure); dependent on "messiahs"	Passive and lacking initiative; lacking motivation; ignorant of markets; characterized by leadership vacuum; avoidant behavior	Plagued by "decidophobia;" focusing inward; lacking vigilance over changing market conditions; drifting, with no sense of direction; confined to antiquated, mature markets	"It's hopeless to try to change the course of events. I'm just not good enough"

Organization	Executive	Culture	Strategy	Guiding theme
Compulsive				
Characterized by rigid formal codes, elaborate information systems, ritualized evaluation procedures, excessive thoroughness and exactness, and a hierarchy in which individual executive status derives directly from specific positions in the organization	Tending to dominate the organization from top to bottom; insistent that others conform to tightly prescribed rules; dogmatic or obstinate; obsessed with perfectionism, detail, routine, rituals, efficiency, and lockstep organization	Rigid, inward directed, and insular; populated with submissive, uncreative, insecure employees	Tightly calculated and focused; characterized by exhaustive evaluation procedures: slow and nonadaptive; reliant on a narrow, established theme; obsessed with a single aspect of strategy (e.g., cost cutting or quality) to the exclusion of other factors	"I don't want to be at the mercy of events. I have to master and control all the things affecting me"

The dramatic personality/organization

The need for grandiosity

Dramatic individuals experience a great need to impress and get attention from others. Thus they often exaggerate their achievements and talents and display excessive emotion. Because they're driven by an unusually strong need for excitement and stimulation, they frequently lack self-discipline, have a poor capacity for concentration, and tend to overreact.

Many dramatic individuals possess a sense of entitlement. Although they may be superficially warm and charming, they often lack sincerity, empathy, and consideration for others. They take others for granted and

dramatic individuals experience a great need to impress and get attention from others

exploit people for their own gain. Furthermore, they alternate between extremes of overidealization and devaluation. Relationships thus tend to be unstable. When their fantasies of unlimited power, success, and brilliance are cut short, dramatic leaders may experience marked feelings of rage and anger and act vindictively.

The dramatic-style leader often gives rise to a specific role constellation in the firm. Dramatic leaders attract subordinates with dependent personality structures who tend to idealize dramatic leaders – that is, to ignore their faults and accentuate their strengths. Because they're prone to feel flattered by a few words of praise, they're easy to control and manipulate. And that's how dramatic leaders like it. They thrive on being "nourished" by subordinates' confirming and admiring ("mirroring") responses.

The charisma of the dramatic executive ensures that there's only one leader. With no rivals for authority, an unquestioning, trustful climate of subordination grows up among group members. Zealous followers help create an atmosphere in which the leader is often perceived as well-nigh infallible. There's little reflection or analysis on the part of workers or middle management, since everyone relies on the inspired judgment of the boss. Independent-minded managers don't last very long in such a culture. They fall victim to the leader's power (both formal and informal), which is manifested in bold unilateral decisions.

Audacity, risk taking, and diversification are the corporate themes of the dramatic organization. Instead of reacting to the business environment, the dramatic decision maker attempts to create an idiosyncratic environment, entering some markets and leaving others, constantly switching to new products while abandoning older ones, and placing a sizable portion of the firm's capital at risk. The goal is unbridled growth, reflecting the top manager's considerable narcissistic needs and desire for attention and visibility. The result is hyperdiversification and overexpansion into (often utopian) mega-projects.

The structure of the dramatic organization is usually far too primitive for its broad markets. First, as we've seen, power is concentrated in the chief executive, who meddles even in routine operations in order to put a personal stamp on (and take credit for) everything. A second problem follows from this overcentralization – namely, the absence of an effective information system. External communication is poor because the top executive does little scanning of the business environment, preferring to act on intuition rather than on facts; internal communication is poor because, due to the leader's dominance, information flows mostly from the top down.

The dramatic style often includes people with histrionic, cyclothymic, and narcissistic personalities (although the latter are most common in the business world). John DeLorean of DeLorean Motors is a fine example of the latter. His narcissistic person-

the structure of the dramatic organization is usually far too primitive for its broad markets

ality led to the development of a new car, a new wife, a new face, cocaine – you name it. With his dramatic flair he could be very seductive, but the narcissism that provided the flash eventually led to his downfall. Sandy Weill, the former CEO of Citigroup, the world's largest financial empire, can be viewed as another example. Anyone who knew only a little about him realized that his assertions of the benefits of co-leadership (when the merger between Citibank and Travelers was announced) were mere propaganda. Weill wasn't known for sharing the limelight with anyone else. Given his giant ego, the bets were that he would end up running the merged financial powerhouse. Being in that sort of role would satisfy his need for grandiosity. As these examples signify, people with the narcissistic inclination that many dramatic personalities possess often forget to set boundaries for themselves.

Firms that are excessively dramatic should do the following to restore balance:

- ❖ sharpen their focus and divest their loss leaders
- ❖ set up a coherent structure
- ❖ establish solid coordinating and control systems
- ❖ revive the core business and scale down any mega-projects
- ❖ engage in leadership development/succession planning.

The suspicious personality/organization

The predominant concern associated with the suspicious style is the inner theater fantasy that nobody can be trusted, that a menacing, superior force is "out to get you." Being on guard, ready for any attack – real or imagined – is thus the major preoccupation.

The persecutory orientation

The suspicious leadership style is characterized by mistrust of others, hypersensitivity, extreme alertness, secretiveness, envy, and hostility. Suspicious executives are constantly prepared to counter perceived threats. They take offense easily and respond in anger. Preoccupied with hidden motives and special meanings, they easily misread and distort the actions of others, magnifying minor slights. Suspicious executives expect to find trickery and deception, and they're usually able to find "facts" to confirm their worst expectations. They have an intense, narrowly focused attention span and thus often come across as cold, rational, and unemotional.

In organizations that have a suspicious leader at the helm, inter-personal relationships between leader and subordinates at all levels are often characterized by a persecutory theme. Leaders who feel perse-cuted and mistrustful may react in a hostile manner toward subordi-nates – may even want to harm or attack them – as a defensive reaction. They justify their hostility by seeing subordinates as malingerers and incompetents, or as people who are deliberately provocative. Suspicious leaders act on their hostility in one of two extreme ways:

❖ **Exerting stringent control through intensive personal supervision, formal rules and restraints, and harsh punishment** This response removes all initiative from lower-tier managers, lowers their self-esteem, and increases the possibility that they'll engage in a contest of wills with the leader. The absence of opportunity for growth or development that this response ensures induces the most promising executives to leave.

❖ **Being quite aggressive, especially in dealing with subordinates who speak their mind** This response guarantees that subordinates get only the bare minimum in emotional and material rewards. Because aggressive leaders hold tight to power, they come out on the winning side of all "trades." The organization turns into a "police state," with people feeling that they're under continuous observation. Morale suffers a good deal under these conditions, as does productivity, because subordinates hold back their contributions. They fear to stick their necks out and concentrate on protecting themselves from exploitation.

Suspicious top executives generate organizational cultures that reflect their own distrust and suspicion. In these "fight/flight" cultures, the members come to fear the same things as the top executive. The atmosphere is clouded with fear of attack, and the preponderance of organizational energy is expended on identifying an enemy (or enemies) on whom all problems can be blamed.

Once enemies are targeted, they're vigorously analyzed and explicitly countered with a competitive strategy. The mobilization of corporate energy against these enemies cements a strong sense of conviction among organizational members about the correctness of their actions. But if there are enemies "out there," so too are there enemies within. Thus the paranoid culture tends to be contagious. Suspicious leaders are careful to hire, reward, and promote only those who share their views. People who dissent from the leader's opinions are mistrusted, regardless of their record with the firm. In consequence, they're ignored or refused promotion.

suspicious top executives generate organizational cultures that reflect their own distrust and suspicion

The suspicious atmosphere generally taints both interpersonal and interdepartmental functioning as well. Company wide, information is a power resource; therefore, those who are in the know about any project or problem hoard their knowledge or barter with it as a commodity. An adversarial relationship can develop from desk to desk, department to department, division to division, and subsidiary to subsidiary, making coordination difficult. Secrets abound and proliferate, and a "protect yourself" ethic prevails.

In the suspicious company, managerial distrust translates into a primary emphasis on organizational intelligence and controls. Managers develop sophisticated information systems to identify threats from the government, competitors, and customers. They develop budgets, cost centers, profit centers, cost-accounting procedures, and similar methods to control internal activities. This vigilance frequently calls for product diversification as well, to reduce the risk of reliance on any one item. But because diversification requires even *more* elaborate control and information-processing mechanisms, it actually reinforces the firm's paranoia.

This paranoia also influences decision making. The perpetual enemy identification that the "institutionalization of suspicion" results in leads to stereotyping; and because leaders who see people and issues in stereotypical terms are unable to perceive nuance, their decision making is rigid. Furthermore, key executives frequently decide that it's safer to direct their distrust externally rather than withhold information from one another. They share information and make concerted efforts to discover organizational problems and to select alternative solutions for dealing with them. This approach is positive in moderation, but the excesses that it runs to in the suspicious organization *cause* rather than *solve* problems. Multiple people are asked for similar information, for example – since any one source might be tainted – meaning that a necessary job gets done, say, five times rather than one.

Corporate paranoia can have a specific, identifiable trigger. It may take root during a period of traumatic challenge: a strong market dries up, a powerful new competitor enters the market, or damaging legislation is passed. The harm done by these forces causes executives to become distrustful and fearful, to lose their nerve, or to recognize the need for better intelligence.

Because of his uncanny information-gathering abilities, J. Edgar Hoover, illustrious former leader of the FBI, became all but untouchable. After all, who has no skeletons in the closet? Although Hoover may have been **who has no skeletons** quite capable at the beginning of his career, his **in the closet?** leadership (and his organization) eventually became an abomination. That decline reflected aspects of his personality. For example, according to the biography *No Left Turns*, Hoover was so intolerant of going "left" (with that word's Communist connotations) that vehicles in which he was a passenger had to reach their destination without ever turning left; multiple right turns had to be made to achieve a leftward orientation.

Harold Geneen, once in charge of ITT, brought a Hoover-like style to the world of business. Although Geneen created an impressive company, his peculiarities came to haunt ITT later in its life-cycle. Typifying the paranoid atmosphere in the organization, the controllers of the operating companies in the many countries where ITT was established – there were roughly 400 of these people – had to report directly to Geneen. He was continually in search of "unshakable facts" on which to base decisions. And he wasn't satisfied until he had *masses* of facts. People used to say that ITT was populated by seagulls – that is, people who flew in, ate, made loud noises, shat on everybody, and flew off again.

Once a month, leaders of all of ITT's businesses had to go to New York or Brussels for a review meeting. There they were met individually by a strange British accountant (Geneen) who had a habit of living in hotels and who read numbers while the visiting executives slept. He would say, in the James Bond-like war room where these meetings were held, "Mr. X, I don't understand; the number on page 27 doesn't match the number on page 223. Can you explain?" If the concerned executive, desperately trying to sort out the figures, hesitated at all, that was the beginning of the end. Geneen's cadre smelled blood and zeroed in for the kill.

In addition to people who were booted out, many left by choice. In fact, the organization was often called Geneen University because of the high turnover. Among those who stayed, some were lured by the money; Geneen "had them by their Cadillacs," as people said.

There were serious succession problems after Geneen's exit – he tried, with mixed success, to eliminate some of his successors – but the company went through a major demerger process. It's now only a shell of the company it previously was.

Firms that are excessively suspicious should do the following to restore balance:

- ❖ simplify decision-making and reporting mechanisms
- ❖ facilitate information sharing and minimize secrecy
- ❖ encourage trust-building activities
- ❖ adopt a more proactive attitude toward strategy making.

The detached personality/organization

Some individuals are guided by a detached style and fantasize that the outside world offers them no satisfaction. Because they believe that interactions with others will eventually fail and cause harm, they see distance as the better option.

A pattern of noninvolvement and withdrawal characterizes the detached style. Detached individuals are determinedly unwilling to enter into emotional relationships for fear of social derogation; they prefer to be alone and feel no need to communicate (or want to communicate but just don't know how). Although on the surface they may seem to be indifferent to praise, criticism, or the feelings of others, this mask is often a defense against being hurt. Whatever the reasons, the result is aloofness, emotional blandness, an inability to express enthusiasm or pleasure, and a spurning of the give and take of reciprocal relationships.

detached behavior can show up in otherwise healthy executives who have become bored with the daily work routine

Detached behavior can also show up in otherwise healthy executives who have become bored with the daily work routine. As activities not directly work related (social or political involvements, for example) come to seem more attractive, the executive is less available than before at the office.

Politicized cultures, schizoid organizations

Politicized corporate cultures are generally a product of executives who abdicate their responsibilities as leaders. Leaders whose detached style causes them to avoid contact with others delegate (by default) the management of their firms to second-tier managers, who tend to be unclear about authority and responsibilities. The members of the second tier turn into "game players" who spend their time jockeying for position and power against "rivals" in other departments. They fill the leadership vacuum by lobbying for their own parochial interests with the detached leader. In this, they see opportunities for enhancing their own sphere and resource base. Problems of coordination, cooperation, interdepartmental rivalry, and vacillating strategy often result. Little attention is paid to the internalization and maintenance of organizational values.

Strategy making in the schizoid organization resides in this shifting coalition of careerist second-tier managers, all trying to influence the indecisive leader and simultaneously advance their own pet projects and minor empires. The firm muddles through and drifts about, making incremental changes in one area and then reversing direction when a new group of managers gains favor. The initiatives of one group of managers are often either neutralized or severely blunted by those of an opposing group.

The divided nature of the organization prevents effective coordination and communication. Information is used more as a power resource than as a vehicle for effective adaptation; in fact, managers erect barriers to prevent the free flow of information. But this isn't the only shortcoming of the information system. Another is the absence of information about the outside business environment. The company's focus is internal, on personal ambitions; everyone caters to the top manager's desires (insofar as those desires can be intuited) and to their own. Second-tier managers simply ignore real-world events that might either reflect poorly on their own behavior or conflict with the wishes of the detached leader.

The elusive Howard Hughes is a clear example of the detached executive. He ran his various ventures – among them, his tool company, TWA, and casinos – with as little personal involvement as possible. In his combination office/living quarters in the Beverly Hills Hotel, he established a "germ-free zone," an area in the middle of the room consisting of a soft white-leather chair and matching ottoman, a small end table, and a telephone, all of which he painstakingly cleaned regularly to keep them free of contamination.

In the latter part of his life, he refused to go outside even for important meetings and forbade even close friends to visit him. He became so withdrawn that he made himself a virtual prisoner in his own corporate headquarters. He would often let urgent calls from Culver City (the headquarters of Hughes Aircraft) go unanswered, to the great frustration of his senior executives. Their desire for clarification of strategic issues and issues of authority went unheeded, leading to severe intracompany squabbles and jeopardizing deliveries to the U.S. Air Force. After 1965, Hughes was not just distant, he was truly mentally impaired.

Firms that are excessively detached should do the following to restore balance:

❖ revitalize and strengthen the leadership

❖ create strategic focus

❖ improve information flow within the organization

❖ emphasize organizational culture-building activities

❖ become more responsive to the outside business environment.

The depressive personality/organization

Depressive managers lack self-confidence and initiative, have a low sense of self-esteem, tend to be dependent, and (because of that dependence) have a strong need for affection and nurture.

In the depressive style, feelings of guilt, worthlessness, and inadequacy are pervasive. Individuals who are depressive downgrade themselves; they're self-deprecating and feel inferior to others, claiming a lack of ability and talent. Because of that sense of unworthiness, they abdicate responsibility, allowing others to assume charge over major areas of their life and work. In fact, they actively seek messiahs, people to protect them. Toward that end, they idealize others – consultants, important people such as bankers or directors, or other figures with whom they're in regular contact. Depressives tend to be ingratiating, adapting their behavior and submerging their individuality to please those they depend on.

Depressive-style leaders (if *leader* is the appropriate terminology here) are subject to feelings of powerlessness as a result of unpleasant past relationships. Anger about that powerlessness may give rise to feelings of guilt and wariness toward others. Depressives often turn their hostility inward in a phenomenon known as "moral masochism," whereby they seek psychic pain as a redemptive act. It becomes a form of restitution for prevailing guilt feelings. If they feel and want things that they perceive as unacceptable, defeat looks to them like a just reward.

Depressives display incompetence and fail to show any imagination. They wait for others to take the initiative, often fearing success because they think it will make people envious and hostile. Except for occasionally snatching mediocrity from the jaws of victory, they adopt a passive orientation, shying away from action and becoming reclusive.

Avoidant cultures, depressive organizations

The culture of a firm with a depressive leader is best characterized as avoidant. In some cases the leader's personality alone causes the depressive atmosphere; in others, an external force, such as the loss of the founder or a takeover, causes healthy executives to lose their sense of control, their authority, their self-esteem, and consequently their initiative. In either event, an avoidant culture is permeated by unmotivated, absentee executives who contribute only the minimum required of them. Buck passing and delays are the norm, as is an absence of meaningful interaction and communication among managers.

Most depressive firms are well established and serve a mature market, one that's had the same technology and competitive patterns for many years, with trade agreements, restrictive trade practices, and substantial tariffs. The low level of change, the absence of serious competition, and the homogeneity of the customers make administrative tasks fairly simple.

Although formal authority is centralized and based on position rather than expertise, the issue of power isn't very important in most depressive firms. Control is exercised by formalized programs and policies rather than by managerial initiative. Suggestions for change are resisted and action is inhibited, because top executives share a sense of impotence and incapacity; they don't feel that they can control events or have what it takes to revitalize the firm.

There aren't many examples of companies in a depressed phase, because in this new deregulated world, companies that express depressive characteristics don't last long. They go bankrupt, are taken over, or miraculously find ways to renew themselves.

At the Disney Corporation, for example, Walt Disney's death in 1966 prompted a virtual codification of the founder's viewpoints, tastes, and ideas. This idealization produced deepseated indecisiveness and a crisis in managerial spirit that took a long time for Disney's executives to shake off. Their founder's boundless inventiveness had seemed so invulnerable that they believed the appeal of Mickey, Donald, and Goofy would last for ever. The company kept on drifting until its rescue by Disney's nephew, who in 1984 brought in a new team of executives that reinvented the organization.

Firms that are excessively depressive should do the following to restore balance:

❖ revitalize and empower the leadership

❖ redefine the strategic orientation

❖ introduce and keep tabs on high performance-oriented organizational values

❖ simplify structures and processes

❖ become more responsive to customer needs

❖ update product service lines

❖ improve product service quality

❖ benchmark with high-performance organizations.

The compulsive personality/organization

Compulsive-style executives fear being at the mercy of people or events. Thus their overwhelming preoccupation is to master and control anyone or anything that might affect their life. They see relationships in terms of dominance and submission, and insist – where they have that authority – that others submit to their way of doing things. They can be deferential and ingratiating to superiors (although resentfully so) one minute, and markedly autocratic with subordinates the next.

Compulsives have a sense of perfectionism that interferes with their ability to see the whole picture. They're preoccupied with trivial details, rules, and regulations. Attracted by routines, they find it difficult to deviate from planned activity, lack spontaneity, and are unable to relax. Because they fear making mistakes and violating their precious efficiency, they're indecisive and prone to procrastination about substantive issues. Although they may come across as industrious because they're always doing *something*, working hard is not necessarily working smart. Compulsives are excessively devoted to work, to the exclusion of pleasure and productive personal relationships.

Bureaucratic cultures, compulsive organizations

In the compulsive firm, there's a high degree of mistrust between leader and subordinates. The leader's preoccupation with losing control robs subordinates of their sense of discretion, initiative, involvement, personal responsibility, and enthusiasm.

Above all, the bureaucratic group culture is depersonalized and rigid, permeated by top management's preoccupation with control over people, operations, and the external environment. Leaders manage by rules rather than through personal guidance or directives (even if many of the rules are legacies of the past, codifying the original founder's notions about how to run a successful company).

Compulsive organizations are set up to avoid surprises and to monitor what's happening throughout the firm. The only executives who can survive happily in this setting are bureaucrats who love to follow rules and who fear taking the initiative. Independent executives soon discover that they're not granted enough latitude to act on their own, and thus they leave. Even with a good support team, the controlling top executive isn't willing to relinquish sufficient control over operations to allow for a participative mode of decision making.

The mode of operating in the compulsive organization is highly ritualistic and inwardly focused. Every operative detail is planned carefully in advance and carried out in routine fashion. Thoroughness, completeness, and conformity to established procedures are emphasized.

Like the suspicious firm, the compulsive firm emphasizes formal controls and information systems, but there's a crucial difference. In the compulsive firm, controls are designed to monitor *internal* operations (production efficiency, costs, and the scheduling and performance of projects, for example), while in the suspicious firm controls are more *externally* oriented. Controls in the compulsive firm standardize operations and formalize policies and procedures. These policies cover not only production and marketing moves, but also dress codes, meetings (which are frequent and detail filled), and employee attitudes.

the mode of operating in the compulsive organization is highly ritualistic and inwardly focused

The internal focus of the compulsive firm is reflected in its strategy. A compulsive organization that takes pride in being the leader in the marketplace, for example, might continue to put out new products even if innovation is inappropriate in the light of market conditions. Because the firm's strong inward focus prevents decision makers from seeing the bigger picture, change is difficult. Thus compulsive organizations go from incremental innovation to stale product lines, from cost leadership to destructive parsimony, and from quality leadership to quality irrelevance.

The first Henry Ford's slogan, "Any color as long as it's black," was initially downright visionary: it created the assembly line and made for cheap, mass-produced cars. But times changed; consumer tastes became more sophisticated. As they did, Ford's focus on one model and on the utilization of mass-production concepts, initially brilliant, became his Achilles' heel. While Ford, unwilling to adapt to changing circumstances, stuck with a single formula, he lost two-thirds of his market share to General Motors. He couldn't accept the fact that customers were going elsewhere any more than he could accept the need for change.

Only after Ford's death, with his grandson's entry into the organization, was it possible for the company to change direction. And it was a close call indeed: the company was hovering near bankruptcy. So though Ford was an organizational and technological genius, he almost brought down the company he'd created. His tragedy was getting stuck.

Firms that are excessively compulsive should do the following to restore balance:

❖ "explode" existing bureaucratic structures

❖ engage in a diversification program in related industries

❖ invest in R&D

❖ encourage entrepreneurship and strategic innovation

❖ become more responsive to marketing and customer needs

❖ benchmark with firms that are leaders in specific operations.

BOX 6.1

Which leadership style do you favor?

Which organizational type best describes your organization?

AN INVENTORY OF ORGANIZATIONAL TYPE
Now that you've gotten a sense of the interface between leadership style and organizational culture, structure, and strategy, it's time to assess your preferred style. Although this questionnaire is elaborate, take the time to respond to each question thoughtfully. The results will help you to clarify aspects of your leadership style and will give you a better understanding of your organization's corporate culture.

For each of the numbered items in patterns A to E that follow, check YES or NO; then (referring to the following three-point scale) circle the number that indicates *your reaction* to that condition (or the lack thereof).

1 = favorable   2 = neutral   3 = unfavorable

▶

BOX 6.1 continued

	YES	NO	REACTION

Pattern A

- Is power within your organization highly centralized in the hands of the chief executive? 1 2 3
- Is the organizational culture so strong that everyone at the managerial level sees things in essentially the same way? 1 2 3
- Is the chief executive put on a figurative pedestal by many employees? 1 2 3
- Are dissent and contrary opinions handled by getting rid of or ignoring "rebels"? 1 2 3
- Does the chief executive seem overburdened with work because he or she tries to do everything single-handedly? 1 2 3
- Have grandiose and risky ventures depleted organizational resources? 1 2 3
- Does the chief executive make decisions rapidly and without consulting other people? 1 2 3
- Is the organization rapidly diversifying, introducing many new products or services, or expanding geographically in a way that depletes organizational resources? 1 2 3
- Does the chief executive appear to be vain or egotistical? 1 2 3
- Are sycophants promoted over those who speak their minds? 1 2 3
- Does most information flow down rather than up the hierarchy? 1 2 3
- Does the strategy of the organization reside mainly inside the chief executive's mind? 1 2 3
- Are growth and expansion pursued seemingly for their own sake? 1 2 3

Pattern B

- Is there an atmosphere of suspicion and distrust in the organization? 1 2 3
- Do executives blame external "enemies" (regulators, government agencies, competitors) for the organization's problems? 1 2 3

▶

BOX 6.1 continued

	YES	NO	REACTION
• Is there a strong leadership emphasis on use of information systems to identify inadequacies and assign blame?			1 2 3
• Are there organizational "spies" who inform top executives about what's happening at lower levels?			1 2 3
• Is organizational loyalty a big factor in assessing personnel performance?			1 2 3
• Does the chief executive have a "siege mentality," constantly defending against perceived external attacks?			1 2 3
• Is the organization's strategy focused more on copying other organizations than on trying new, unique approaches?			1 2 3
• Is there much secrecy regarding performance information, salaries, decisions, etc.?			1 2 3
• Does the organization's strategy vacillate widely according to external conditions?			1 2 3
• Is there excessive risk avoidance in the organization?			1 2 3
• Is the organization noticeably unfocused?			1 2 3

Pattern C

• Is the organization badly split, with much disagreement among the various functional areas or divisions?			1 2 3
• Does political infighting occur very often?			1 2 3
• Is the chief executive somewhat reclusive, refraining from personal contact and preferring to communicate by memo or e-mail?			1 2 3
• Is there a "leadership vacuum" in the organization?			1 2 3
• Do decisions get delayed for long periods of time because of squabbling?			1 2 3
• Do the personal ambitions of executives take dramatic precedence over broader organizational goals?			1 2 3
• Are strategies badly fragmented, vacillating from one extreme to another according to which senior executive the chief executive favors?			1 2 3

▶

BOX 6.1 continued

	YES	NO	REACTION

- Is the chief executive too busy with outside matters to pay much attention to the organization and its business?   1 2 3
- Do very few decisions emanate from the top of the organization, resulting in considerable drift?   1 2 3
- Is it difficult to perceive what the chief executive really wants?   1 2 3

Pattern D

- Is there a feeling of helplessness regarding the influencing of events on the part of the chief executive or other key executives?   1 2 3
- Has the organization stagnated while other, similar organizations have advanced?   1 2 3
- Are the organization's products or services antiquated?   1 2 3
- Is there very little "scanning" of the organization's environment?   1 2 3
- Are work facilities poor and inefficient?   1 2 3
- Are the organization's strategies very narrow and resistant to change?   1 2 3
- Is there a lack of action, an atmosphere of "decision paralysis"?   1 2 3
- Do many young, dynamic executives leave the organization because of the stifling climate and the lack of opportunity for advancement?   1 2 3
- Is there extreme conservatism when it comes to making capital expenditures?   1 2 3
- Do bureaucratic rules set long ago substitute for communication and deliberation in decision making?   1 2 3

Pattern E

- Does the organization favor bureaucratic red tape, regulations, formal policies, and procedures?   1 2 3
- Is there a tendency for precedent rather than analysis or discussion to decide issues?   1 2 3

▶

BOX 6.1 continued

	YES	NO	REACTION
• Has strategy remained essentially unchanged for many years?			1 2 3
• Is the organization slow to adapt to trends in the marketplace?			1 2 3
• Does the chief executive hoard power?			1 2 3
• Is the chief executive overly concerned with one or two elements of strategy (e.g., efficiency, productivity, quality, costs) to the exclusion of most others?			1 2 3
• Did a former chief executive leave a strategic legacy that's held to be sacrosanct by current executives?			1 2 3
• Are strategies precisely articulated, down to the last detail?			1 2 3
• Do information systems provide too much "hard" and too little "soft" data on customer reactions, trends, etc.?			1 2 3
• Does the chief executive prefer subordinates who follow directives very precisely and refrain from arguing?			1 2 3
• Is there considerable emphasis on position and status?			1 2 3

ORGANIZATIONAL-TYPE INVENTORY SCORING SHEET

1   Count the number of YES responses for each pattern and enter each total below.

2   Count the number of NO responses for each pattern and enter each total below.

3   Add the numbers circled under REACTION for each pattern and enter each total below.

Number of: YES responses   NO responses   REACTION responses

Name of pattern

Pattern A: The dramatic organization

Pattern B: The suspicious organization

Pattern C: The detached organization

Pattern D: The depressive organization

Pattern E: The compulsive organization

▶

BOX 6.1 continued

ORGANIZATIONAL-TYPE INVENTORY INTERPRETATION SHEET

Step 1
Determine which pattern collected the most YES responses. If you responded in the affirmative only once or twice within a pattern, you're probably *not* working in that type of organization. If you responded in the affirmative more than half the time within a pattern, you probably *are* working in that type of organization.

Step 2
By totaling your reaction scores for each pattern, you can determine the kind of organization that's most comfortable for you. The higher your reaction score is for a given pattern, the more unfavorable that pattern appears to you.

What do your scores suggest? Are you and your organization a good fit? Reflect on your answers.

Reflections on the five constellations

For purposes of simplification, I've focused on the characteristics of "pure" constellations. In reality, however, the clinical picture, for both executives and organizations, is usually much more complicated, with combinations of types blending in various proportions.

Further complicating matters, movement across types is often seen in organizations – movement that depends on who's in power and where in its life-cycle the organization finds itself. Moreover, a certain style may be very effective at one point in the company's history but later become destructive, or vice versa. It is *excess* in style that leads to pathology, and simply holding on to a particular style when the circumstances change can mean excess and corporate disaster.

It must be stressed that although the personality of the top manager can vitally influence an organization, a reverse relationship also exists. A failing organization, rife with disappointment, can cause a leader to become depressed. Likewise, a series of vicious threats from the competition can awaken dormant paranoia. Clearly, then, the influence between organizational orientation and leadership disposition is reciprocal. Mutual causation is the rule.

To executives or board members concerned about a failing organization, causation may seem less important than remedy. Yet some understanding of causation is necessary if the appropriate remedy is to be applied. The typology we have just examined, with its five constellations, helps organizational analysts both assess organizational health and trace organizational pathology in the following ways:

mutual causation is the rule

❖ It searches for common types (and the psychological and cultural factors that underlie them), avoiding the complexity of the "one-variable-at-a-time" approach.

❖ It treats personality in a global way, looking for major adaptive styles that motivate and characterize much of behavior, while eschewing narrow dimensions of affect and cognition.

❖ It gets at the roots of strategic, structural, and cultural problems in organizations.

The assignment of an organization to a particular type can alert organizational analysts to a range of unobserved but frequently related manifestations (thus helping in the selection of the appropriate intervention strategy). Instead of dwelling on specific symptoms related to, say, the distribution of authority or the design of information systems, analysts can search for the underlying cause of the conjunction of various symptoms.

With that causal information in hand, analysts can then move forward with prescriptions for change. But any prescriptions that seek to change the neurotic style of an organization must take into account the neurotic style of its top executive. Because, as we've seen, personal styles of behavior are deeply rooted, CEOs are very hard to change – especially when they hold all the power. Generally speaking, then, managerial prescriptions that run counter to the personality of the CEO will be resisted, and those that *are* implemented won't fit into the overall configuration of the organization (and will therefore lack appropriateness and impact). For this reason, significant organizational turnaround often requires either dramatic erosion of the power base of the CEO (whether through organizational failure or board fiat) or the appointment of a new CEO.

An organizational vicious circle

Companies that are headed by (or have been headed by) dysfunctional leaders may get stuck in a vicious circle (see Figure 6.1). Though current dysfunction is more typically the culprit, the ghosts of past leadership practices sometimes haunt the corridors of an organization. Having been institutionalized, they continue to play an important role.

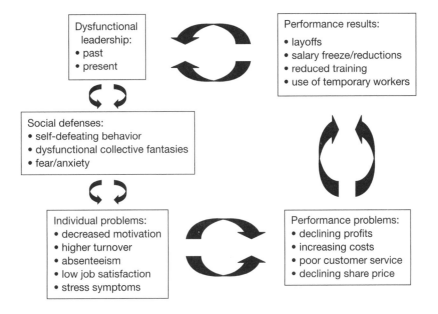

Figure 6.1 The organizational vicious circle: "neurotic" organizations

Dysfunctional leadership triggers a number of social defense patterns that detract from the real work of the organization. Free-floating anxiety and dysfunctional collective fantasies easily derail people from the company's principal task, resulting in a victory of procedure over substance. This in turn leads to morale problems among the organization's employees.

Indicators of a declining morale in the organization include such factors as decreased motivation, higher-than-usual turnover, increased absenteeism, and low job satisfaction. These individual problems contribute to organization-wide performance problems, such as declining profits, increasing costs, poor customer service, and eventually a declining share price (if the company is publicly quoted).

free-floating anxiety and dysfunctional collective fantasies easily derail people from the company's principal task

Organizational responses often include layoffs, salary freezes (or even salary reductions), reduced training, and the use of temporary workers – factors that *further* undermine the declining morale and start another round of the vicious circle.

Many CEOs, as they work through this vicious circle over time, begin to suffer from the four P's of dysfunctional leadership:

❖ They become addicted to *power.*

❖ They want increasingly expensive *perks.*

❖ They want to have more time front and center on the *podium.*

❖ They demand exorbitant *pay.*

Many leaders who at one point in their career had a stellar reputation have fallen victim to these four P's. The Enron, Tyco, and WorldCom scandals are good examples of leadership gone astray because of power, perks, pay, and podium. Many CEOs continue to award themselves fat salaries, stock options, and bonuses – and give plum jobs to family and friends – in spite of deteriorating corporate performance.

The ratio between the highest and the lowest paid workers in a company tells a lot about both the organization and its leadership. Although these ratios are changing rapidly, they reached in the United States more than 400. To put things in perspective, at one point in time the annual remuneration of Michael Eisner, the former CEO of Disney, equaled the gross national product of Grenada (or, closer to home, the

the ratio between the highest and the lowest paid workers in a company tells a lot about both the organization and its leadership

pay of all his 4,000 gardeners at Disney World in Florida).With figures like these, how is the average worker to feel valued or motivated?

Our task is to prevent the four P's from gaining a foothold so that organizational health doesn't become organizational pathology. We must create organizations that are prepared to deal with the challenges that success and innovation bring so that the corporate mindset, from corner suite to basement cubicle, reflects an openness to change.

7 Achieving personal and organizational change

A fanatic is one who can't change his mind and won't change the subject. WINSTON CHURCHILL

You have to stop in order to change direction. ERICH FROMM

Grant me the serenity to accept the things I cannot change, the courage to change the things I can and the wisdom to know the difference. REINHOLD NIEBUHR

An enormous pike was placed in a large aquarium divided into two parts by a glass partition. The pike had his half of the duplex to himself; in the other half were numerous minnows. A carnivore, the pike made many frantic efforts to get at the minnows. Every time it tried, however, it hit the glass. Eventually the pike gave up, realizing that getting at the minnows was impossible. Then the glass partition within the aquarium was removed, allowing all the fish to intermingle. As the minnows swam around the pike, it continued to ignore them! The pike had become caught up in a behavior pattern that it couldn't unlearn – at least, not without some help.

Change isn't a simple process, neither is it a comfortable one. The unlearning of habitual patterns can be decidedly anxiety provoking. People are often inclined to hold on to dysfunctional patterns, illogical as these may appear to others; and they can't seem to change their perspective on life without expending a great deal of effort. The reason that people cling so tenaciously to the status quo isn't easy to determine, since there are many conscious and unconscious obstacles on the path toward change. But cling we do, heedless of the proverb that warns, "All things change, and we change with them."

The process of change

The natural human resistance to change has a parallel in the domain of organizations. While the marketplace changes daily – advances in technology competing with improvements in communication – many organizations prefer to hunker down in the status quo. Yet in this age of discontinuity, the companies that last through the coming decades will be those that can respond effectively to the changing demands of their environment. How, then, can corporate leaders proactively drive the process of organizational change? How can they be most effective as change agents? How can they apply what's known about the dynamics of personal transformation to an organizational setting? These questions are critical now that change has become the rule rather than the exception for those seeking corporate survival and success.

change isn't a simple process, neither is it a comfortable one

Let me say it again: change is hard, whether we're talking people or organizations. Many change agents have discovered the wisdom that I noted in Chapter 1: it's often easier to change *people* than to *change* people. In other words, it's easier to start with a new crew (with a new mindset) than to transform the one you have. Even people who claim to believe in the value of change are typically half-hearted. They want *others* to change, but they don't want to change *themselves*.

Sometimes it's a matter not of resisting change but of being baffled by it. Many people have the *will* but not the *skill* to change. They need help to navigate the change process. Because old ideas die hard, it's essential that any change effort – whether it's personal or organization wide – be both cognitive and emotional; in other words, people have to be affected in both the head and the heart. Intellectually, they need to see the advantages that a change effort will bring, but cognition alone isn't enough. They need also to be touched emotionally.

The challenge, then, is to find ways to trigger the willingness (or even eagerness) to change. And this is true whether we're talking about personal change or organizational change. Both processes happen one individual at a time. Many organizational psychologists, basing their theories on the findings of developmental and clinical psychologists, view organizational change and transformation as embedded in the process of individual change. They argue that because organizations are made up of collections of people, the successful implementation of organizational change is dependent on an understanding of individual reactions to the change process.

The dynamics of individual change

So let's go back to square one: How is an individual's personality affected? What's the exact nature of personality change? What steps does a person need to take to make this process possible? These questions have intrigued developmental psychologists and psychotherapists for decades. After much research and reflection, different schools of thought have emerged as to the degree of change that's possible and how that change comes about.

During early childhood, the personality develops and changes as rapidly as the body. Adulthood rarely brings about that same kind of dramatic, revolutionary change, but most researchers of personality development agree that some change is possible at any point in life. Indeed, it's inevitable. Incremental change is ongoing in each one of us: during the various stages of our life, a gradual, unfolding developmental process occurs. And the principles underlying that developmental process seem to be relatively invariable from one person to the next.

It's because there's an invariability – and thus a predictability – to the change process that we can extrapolate from individual change to organizational change. By observing from a clinical perspective the different stages by which individual change takes place, we can reach parallel conclusions about the organizational change process. Then, by applying the insights derived from individual change to the domain of organizational transformation, we can induce, facilitate, and even speed up organizational change (Box 7.1).

by applying the insights derived from individual change to the domain of organizational transformation, we can induce, facilitate, and even speed up organizational change

---

BOX 7.1

How does your life look to you? A reassessment

In the "What's your CCRT?" exercise in Chapter 2 (Box 2.8), you took a preliminary step toward arriving at a better understanding of your personality structure. You also developed an action plan to deal with elements of your personality that cause you distress. Now that you've read further and have more information, take another look at your life. What are some of the critical issues that you're struggling with? What would you like to change about your life?

1   What were the worst times in your life? Who helped you get through those times?
2   What were the best times in your life? How about the times of which you're most proud? With whom did you share those times?
3   Describe an event/situation (be it personal, organizational, or both) that changed your life in a significant way.
4   Which person has had the greatest positive/negative influence on your life? Why? What made this person so special?
5   What has been your greatest regret?
6   What do you like best/least about your life?
7   If you could change three things in your life, what would these be?
8   Imagine that you're looking into a crystal ball and can see your situation five years from now. What do you see?

Take plenty of time to think about these questions. Listen to your inner dialog as you proceed, and ask yourself the meaning of your responses. Then review your responses with someone close to you and discuss with that person possible actions that you could take to improve your situation.

The five C's of change

Let's look now at the five C's of change – necessary components of any individual or organizational change process. They are *concern, confrontation, clarification, crystalization,* and *change.*

CONCERN: NEGATIVE EMOTION

If the human tendency is to resist change, how does the process of change ever get under way? Why does a person's resistance start to weaken? Given the relative stability of personality, getting the process of change into motion requires a strong inducement in the form of pain or distress – discomfort that outweighs the pleasure of "secondary gains" (psychological benefits such as sympathy and attention) that the situation may offer. People must experience a sense of *concern* about their present situation, whether the trigger be family tensions, health problems, negative social sanctions, an accident, feelings of isolation leading to a sense of helplessness and insecurity, problem behavior, distressing incidents happening to someone close, or basic daily hassles and frustrations.

Surveys of people who've undergone major internal change confirm that a high level of unpleasant emotion (anxiety, anger, sadness, or frustration, for example) exists in the period just prior to change, generally precipitated by a stressor such as one of those just listed. This negative emotion, which brings to awareness the serious negative consequences that can be expected if dysfunctional behavior patterns continue, makes the status quo increasingly difficult to maintain.

Even the insight that drastic measures are required doesn't automatically compel people to take action. However, it typically sets into motion a mental process whereby they consider alternatives to the adverse situation. Having made the transition from denying to beginning to realize that all is not well, they're able to undertake a reappraisal process. Initially every alternative to the troubling situation appears more frightening than the status quo.

CONFRONTATION: THE FOCAL EVENT

Beginning to accept the need for change is a necessary first step, but on its own it's no guarantee of action. People need a push, a *confrontation*, in the form of something that can be described as a "focal event." Although we typically think of a confrontation as something so acute that it's obvious, the focal event that triggers change is sometimes only retrospectively interpreted as a milestone.

The metaphor of the last straw is very appropriate here, because it indicates that if a person is prepared – if not actually ready – to take a decisive step, the triggering event can be minor: the final additional element (one among many) that puts matters into focus. Experience suggests that while major events certainly can be focal, the focal event is often a minor occurrence that's *seen* as focal (indeed, *is* focal) simply because it enables a discontented person to take that long-delayed first step. Thus it's the catalyst in the change process, whether it's perceived as major or minor to an outside observer.

A focal event often involves someone important to the distressed person. In the case of an executive I know, divorce from a husband of many years became the focal event. The divorce caused this woman's relatively comfortable life situation to fall apart and thus served as a wake-up call for her to reevaluate her lifestyle. She made some changes at home: she decided to spend more time with her children, for example, and to take up some activities that she really enjoyed. But the divorce triggered some work changes as well. She realized, as the divorce brought repressed feelings to the surface, that she'd been unhappy working for her present company for quite a while. She realized that she'd been using work as a crutch to forget a difficult home situation. What she really wanted – what she'd *always* wanted – was to work for herself. In her heart of hearts, she wanted to be independent, to be an entrepreneur. She'd postponed biting the bullet for years. Now the focal event of her divorce crystalized her discontent and provided the impetus for change.

A person's focal event can also be seen as a kind of "screen memory": while the incident, in some instances, may seem trivial at first glance, it's actually an indicator of a whole range of incidents that are symbolic of the experienced problem. Although it's *objectively perceived* as minor, it's *subjectively experienced* as significant, because it calls attention to a problem that's existed for a long time. It precipitates a moment of insight and leads to a reinterpretation of the person's life history. Of course, some focal events – such as the divorce in the earlier example, or one's own illness – are objectively as well as subjectively significant events of a very serious nature.

It's at this point in the process that people start to become prepared to take action. Their resistance is breaking down. They acquire new insights about their situation and see new possibilities, whereas before they knew only helplessness and hopelessness. Their emotional energy has been transferred from "concerns" of the past (such as dysfunctional behaviors) to aspects of the present and the future. They feel as if a heavy burden has been lifted, and they're mentally ready to tackle a more constructive future.

CLARIFICATION: THE PUBLIC DECLARATION OF INTENT

Change is so difficult that, even with the best of intentions, we can rarely manage it single-handedly. Thus the third step in the change process is a sharing of one's intent to change. People are now prepared to work on clarifying their intentions, to look in depth at the pros and cons of change.

Making a public commitment is crucial because it doubles momentum: it influences not only the person making the commitment but also the **change is so difficult that we can rarely manage it single-handedly** environment. Going public with one's intentions – to confront and clarify one's situation – enhances one's determination and enlists the support of others, thus working as a strong reinforcement for change. Furthermore, by taking a public stance, people give themselves an ultimatum: go through with it (whatever the change may be) or lose face.

CRYSTALIZATION: THE INNER JOURNEY

By this point the toughest challenges have been conquered. The personal resolutions of the clarification stage have laid the groundwork for a thoughtful, detailed reappraisal of goals and for experimentation with the new alternatives that have been envisioned. Ideas and plans become clear and definite in form. The destination of this sometimes-painful inner journey is increased self-knowledge and a new beginning.

CHANGE: THE INTERNALIZATION OF A NEW MINDSET

We all tend to talk big when it comes to change. But how many of the hundreds of "new leaves" we promise to turn over ever get so much as touched? The only true sign that change has been achieved is a new mindset. Inner transformation takes place only when a new way of looking at things has been internalized. (See Figure 7.1 for an overview of these individual steps to change.)

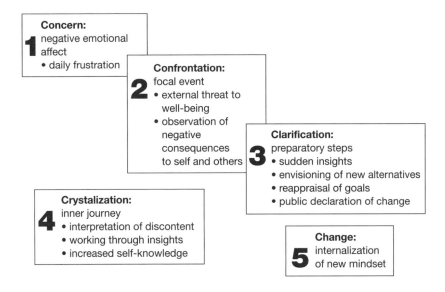

Figure 7.1 The five C's of the individual change process

Recalibrating inner forces essential to change

During each of these stages, three internal forces work with and against each other, interweaving a net of minuscule change experiences. In the end, once change has been accomplished, those three forces have been recalibrated, strengthening and deepening the person's new orientation to life.

The three forces involved are defensive structures, emotional reactions, and perceptions of self and others:

❖ What habitual defenses do we use to deal with stressful situations? Are there certain patterns that we can recognize? What can/should be changed about these defenses?

❖ What kind of emotions come predominantly to the fore? How might we express emotions more effectively?

❖ How do we perceive ourselves? Do we feel secure about who we are? How do we perceive others? Do we constantly see ourselves in a one-down position? Are we capable of honest self-appraisal?

Change requires that we relinquish defenses, express affect honestly, and perceive self and others in ways that accord with reality. (See Figure 7.2 for an overview of these forces.)

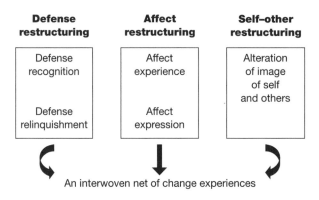

Figure 7.2 The interwoven forces of personal change

The dynamics of organizational transformation

Organizational "pain"

Organizational transformation can't occur without some "pain" in the system. Who wants change when things are going well? But if sales are down or layoffs are pending – well, who wants the status quo? And if the pain comes from both within and without – that is, when customers and the broader marketplace add their concerns to those that the ledger reveals – that's better still. When people in organizations experience a double-whammy call to change, they're much more likely to act.

Among some of the external factors that can cause pain in organizations are threats from competitors, declining profits, decreasing market share, scarcity of resources, deregulation, technological demands, and problems with suppliers and consumer groups. Examples of internal pressures are ineffective leadership, morale problems, high turnover of capable people, absenteeism, labor problems **who wants change when things are going well?** (such as strikes), increased political behavior in the company, and turf fights. All these factors negatively affect the mindset of the people in the organization. The resulting malaise corrodes the corporate culture and has an impact on patterns of decision making.

Although I'm no fan of pain, no leader (whether involved in a directed change process or not) should ever allow his or her people to become too comfortable. If any of the pressures just mentioned exist, they should be talked about company wide rather than hoarded in secret.

What we might call the "disorganizing function" of leadership – that jarring of comfort – can be taken too far, however. It's a delicate balance: too much organizational change can be as problematic as organizational stagnation. In fact, Machiavellians go so far as to argue that continuous reorganization is just a device by which top management hides poor decision making.

The process of organizational transformation is particularly difficult if we're dealing not with incremental change but with discontinuous change. Effective executives need to engage in a balancing act that allows them to deal effectively with both. They need to encourage the day-to-day changes that are part and parcel of organizational life; but at the same time they need to watch out for potential inflection points that could change the nature of the business altogether. When they spot such points, they need to act quickly and skilfully. Many studies have indicated that few top executives survive the major turnaround of a tottering company. Discontinuity comes at a high price in the form of human capital. It's a rare leader who can handle both forms of change well.

As with individual transformation, organizational change tends to be of a sequential nature, and that process begins with discomfort in the organizational system. Pain in the system can be seen as the main lever that sets the change process in motion. However, pushing that lever is easier said

pain in the system can be seen as the main lever that sets the change process in motion

than done, because (as in the case of individual change) there are a lot of resistance factors to deal with. Organizational participants may not see, at first glance, that the change process is in their self-interest. Even those who are aware that all is not well can find infinite ways of avoiding the issue of change. The fear that the proclaimed benefits of a particular change will not outweigh the costs involved sets many unconscious defenses in motion. Thus there's a significant challenge inherent in this dilemma (Box 7.2).

BOX 7.2

What's your attitude toward change?

Read and think about the following statements. If you can hear yourself making them, mark YES; if not – if they've never (or rarely) crossed your lips – mark NO. As with many of these exercises, try to check your responses with someone close to you.

                                                                    YES   NO

- We've been doing it this way for many years
- No one has ever tried this before
- Someone else has already tried it, and it bombed
- From a theoretical point it could work, but *practically* . . .
- From a purely practical point of view, it *could* work.
  We have to think of the wider implications, however
- It won't work in a small/large organization
- It needs further investigation
- We don't have the money/the resources/the equipment/
  the time
- It will affect our overheads adversely
- You'll get trouble from . . .

▶

BOX 7.2 continued

YES   NO

- (S)he is against it/won't like it
- You shouldn't try to teach an old dog new tricks
- Let's not rush things
- It needs sleeping on
- It's not how we do things here
- We're different, and we should stay that way

If the majority of your responses are in the affirmative, you may have an attitude problem toward change. If that seems to be the case, look into ways that you can develop your change readiness.

Organizational "mourning"

In spite of lavish claims made by many consulting firms, organizational change takes time. As in the case of loss in the personal sphere, people who have to leave behind old ways of doing and being in organizations have to go through a kind of "mourning" process, grieving over what has been lost.

Especially in the case of dramatic change in an organization, those who successfully make the transformation move through a number of stages in this mourning process: they move successively through *shock, disbelief, discarding,* and *realization/acceptance*:

❖ **Shock** People's first reaction when they learn that their company has been taken over, say, or that the financial figures are so deep in the red that layoffs are certain, is typically shock. This stage is characterized by numbness and disarray, and people tend to seek comfort in mindless, routine tasks.

❖ **Disbelief** Then people move into disbelief. Refusing to accept the changed situation, they dwell on the past and idealize the way things used to be. Their responses are reactive rather than proactive, and any tendencies toward dependency are exacerbated.

❖ **Discarding** This stage involves self-examination and a redefinition of self and situation that brings people to a recognition of the problem and a willingness to address it. Through that process, people gradually become willing to discard old ways and tentatively explore new ones.

❖ **Realization/acceptance** At this stage, people look forward rather than back. As action toward a better situation is taken, they begin to see and appreciate gains. Wanting to maintain and enhance those gains, they continue the new behaviors until they become natural. The result is a reshaping of people's outlook and the acceptance of a new reality. (See Figure 7.3 for an overview of the organizational "mourning" process.)

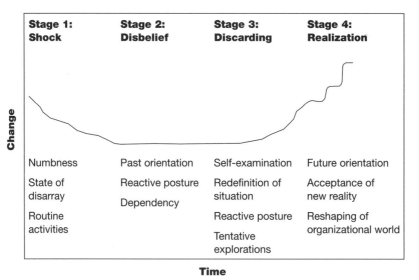

Figure 7.3 The organizational "mourning" process

Organizational resistance

For many people in an organization, change implies a loss of the security that goes with a specific job. They may fear the unknown and hang onto old patterns of behavior even when it's clear that those patterns are destructive. Other people – those who expect that change will require them to learn a new job or work harder – may fear that they lack the skills and stamina needed for change. Still others may be afraid that good working conditions or a sense of freedom will be taken away. Some individuals may fear that change implies a loss of responsibility and authority, with concomitant status implications. They may dread the perceived loss of status, rights, or privileges that they expect the change to bring. Other people may interpret change as an indictment of their previous performance. Furthermore, change sometimes threatens existing alliances, implying the loss of important friends and contacts. The fear of having to leave friends and familiar surroundings can arouse intense resistance. For those workers who deal with budgets, there's also the question of sunk costs: they may be reluctant to accept a change that entails scrapping costly investments. Finally, change may be resisted because of something serious such as the fear of losing one's job or facing a demotion.

the fear of having to leave friends and familiar surroundings can arouse intense resistance

One way to overcome the resistance that all these fear factors engender is to make it clear to all those involved that hanging onto the present state creates more problems than diving into the unknown.

Jump-starting the organizational change process

HIGHLIGHTING THE PAIN

As we saw earlier in this chapter, awareness of the need for change is achieved most effectively when people feel pressure from both within and without. Gradually, the majority comes to realize that something needs to be done or the future of the organization will be endangered. (This is the organizational equivalent of a personal crystalization of discontent.)

Because the awareness of organizational pain is crucial to any transformation effort, leaders who want to jump-start the change process must identify the challenges faced by the **benchmarking is a good way to illustrate performance gaps and their consequences** organization, point out the source of the distress, and clearly present the negative consequences of a failure to act. A popular tactic is to create some kind of "burning platform" – pointing out the undesirability of the present state. Benchmarking with other organizations is a good way to illustrate performance gaps and their consequences. By articulating the reality of the situation, organizational leaders define the existing state of discomfort.

They have to be careful, however, to keep the discomfort at a tolerable level; otherwise, through fear, people may tune out the problems or they may leave. To guard against excessive stress, leaders should present a viable alternative to the existing situation. What we might call a "collective ambition" – a picture of the future that everyone can stand behind – needs to be created. That picture must be realistic, however, not a pie-in-the-sky proposition, or communal support won't translate into communal action.

LINKING PAST AND PRESENT THROUGH A NEW VISION

When developing the outlines of a change process, the change leaders need to reframe the cultural guidelines that people in the organization have become used to, simultaneously reframing positive aspects of the change effort. They need to create pride in the organization's history and point out how this pride in tradition can anchor the organization as it moves into the future. By referring to the organization's past accomplishments while at the same time presenting a new way of doing things, leaders create a sense of hope – a dual approach that garners support for a new beginning.

Employees must perceive the entire change process as inspired by vision and driven by solid corporate values. They must see that it not only aims at building and maintaining a competitive advantage but also addresses the individual needs of the people who will be affected. Finally, they must know that there are boundaries to the change process, that the proposed change effort has clearly defined parameters.

BUILDING SUPPORT AND SYSTEMS THAT ALLOW FOR CHANGE

Leaders have to align crucial players behind their new vision of the future and then put the appropriate organizational architecture in place to implement the new vision. So who are the crucial players? Well, *everyone*. Key powerholders in the organization are important, of course, because they can help to spread commitment and cooperation throughout the firm. But rank-and-file employees are equally important; change can't be implemented without their enthusiastic support.

Organization-wide support grows more readily when leaders create and celebrate "small wins." Leaders who divide a huge change effort into bite-size portions make the overall task more palatable and help convince people of the feasibility of the effort. Executives need to pick battles big enough to matter but small enough to win. Furthermore, they need to set a good example, taking personal action in crucial change areas. Their subordinates may doubt what they say but they will believe what they do.

While striving for small wins, however, leaders should also set high performance expectations. By stretching followers' potential, by offering them an opportunity to spread their wings, leaders encourage people to rise to the challenge. Successful stretching benefits both the organization and the individual, since reaching one's goals engenders considerable personal satisfaction.

Although employee support and development are at the heart of any change effort, leaders also have to make sure that the organizational architecture is "remodeled" as needed. If employee innovation, for example, is to be highlighted in the new organization, the performance appraisal system needs to be revised to reflect that change. Likewise, if decision-making authority is to be spread throughout the organization, the management structure needs to be overhauled.

Steps in the organizational change process

The preceding discussion hints at a number of steps that the process of organizational transformation moves through. These steps are as follows:

- ❖ **Creating a shared mindset** In this first step, leaders set the stage for change by creating a sense of urgency, building a "collective ambition" for the future, encouraging contrarian thinking to foster real dialog, managing anxiety at all levels, and fostering commitment and motivation.

- ❖ **Changing behavior** In the second step, leaders work to empower followers (by granting authority and responsibility), create cross-functional cooperation, emphasize a customer focus, initiate internal and external benchmarking, and align the corporate architecture.

- ❖ **Building attitudes, competencies, and practices** In the third step, leaders work to give employees what they need to make the change effort successful, fostering their development in emotional intelligence as well as in job-specific competencies. At this point "small wins" become important.

- ❖ **Improving business performance** As leaders start to enjoy the fruit of their efforts, they work hard in the fourth step to maintain the changes that have led to such indicators as higher profitability, lower operating costs, a greater market share, broader geographic coverage, higher share price, and community involvement that makes a social contribution.

Figure 7.4 illustrates these steps of the organizational change process graphically (Box 7.3 provides a checklist.).

1 Creating a shared mindset characterized by:
- a sense of urgency
- genuine dialog
- collective ambition
- controlled anxiety
- commitment and motivation
- openness
- action orientation

3 Building competencies, practices, attitudes in the following areas:
- marketing
- technology
- manufacturing
- strategy
- transnational effectiveness
- external linkages
- emotional intelligence

2 Changing behavior to foster:
- empowered leadership
- customer focus
- mutual sharing of information
- cross-functional cooperation
- internal and external benchmarking
- alignment of organizational architecture

4 Improving business performance:
- profitability and operating costs
- market share
- geographic coverage
- share price

Figure 7.4 Steps in the organizational change process

BOX 7.3

How would you rate your company's preparedness to change?

On a scale of 1 to 10 (1 = lowest, 10 = highest), rate your company's preparedness to change. If possible, ask several colleagues and subordinates to complete the same questionnaire.

RATING

- Is the organization as a whole dissatisfied with the status quo?
- Are outside and inside forces pressuring the organization?
- Does the organization have shared values, goals, and expectations?
- Does the organization have in place organizational architecture that will effectively support change?
- Does the organization have the right mix of competencies?
- Does the organization have the right quality of leadership?
- Do performance appraisal and reward systems encourage the kinds of behavior that the planned changes hope to foster?

BOX 7.3 continued

RATING

- Does the organization have the ability and resources to handle the kind
  of change that's required?

The higher the score, the better prepared your organization is for change. Discuss
your score with the others who responded to see how their perceptions of
preparedness for change differ from yours.

Leadership strategies for implementing change

There's change, and then there's *change*. Some organizations need just
a little strategic tweaking, while others need major transformation. The
degree of change needed depends on the organization in question and
the business environment it's competing in.

There are three main approaches: restructuring (getting smaller),
reengineering (getting better), and reinventing the corporation (getting
smarter). On the change continuum, these approaches move from
improving operations, to redesigning the organization, to massive
layoffs, to reconceptualizing the business, to engaging in strategic reorientation through the identification of core competencies, to revitalizing
the leadership of the organization, to changing the entire corporate
mindset. Because most organizations manage minor changes
adequately, we'll focus here on more radical transformations.

Downsizing and reengineering

Whether we're talking simple downsizing (which generally involves
only layoffs) or reengineering (which also encompasses a rethinking
of all remaining roles), drastic change is increasingly common in
the workplace. Although many organizations need the surgery of

reengineering – from here on I'll use that label to cover downsizing, restructuring, and reengineering – others resort to it only because it's "the thing to do." Far too many companies (generally stimulated by an explosion in mergers and acquisitions) have jumped on the business reengineering bandwagon, often with disastrous results.

The stated objectives of reengineering are generally some combination of the following:

❖ reduce costs and development time

❖ improve quality, service, and productivity

❖ increase profits.

Because these objectives sound reasonable and desirable, downsizing usually results initially in a positive blip in share price. The long-term effects of business reengineering are much less likely to be positive, however, in part because downsizing tends to lead to more downsizing. Soon companies aren't just cutting out the fat; they're cutting into the muscle – getting rid of people who are essential for a healthy organizational future.

strategic downsizing begins with a detailed vision of the future organization

Moreover, downsizing almost inevitably creates morale problems and leads to a company-wide trust disorder. Since some of the best people may leave if trust is violated, any company that decides to downsize needs to do it right. That means doing it *strategically* – grounding the process in an exciting vision for a new future and exercising thoughtful selectivity. Downsizing on the basis of headcount alone is doomed to fail.

Strategic downsizing begins with a detailed vision of the future organization. That vision makes it clear which management strengths should be a priority and thus allows executives to pinpoint which employees are essential. Managing layoffs well the first time also avoids the need to rehire unnecessarily fired employees (for a price!) or employ outside consultants.

Strategic downsizing involves deciding not just what jobs will be left but what those jobs will entail. Survivors in downsized organizations frequently complain that the dismissal of employees has resulted in an increased workload, putting an additional burden on already anxious and disoriented individuals. In order to avoid this unnecessary strain, management must clarify each person's new role, responsibilities, and workload.

Downsizing that's part of a comprehensive change process in the organization is far more likely to succeed than stand-alone downsizing. In other words, reengineering is better than restructuring in a more simple way. Reengineering usually involves layoffs, yes; but it offsets the departure of employees lacking the necessary skills and flexibility with an influx of new people who have the creativity, enthusiasm, and energy to reinvent the organization. It also involves making investments in people in the form of training and education, and in new technology.

When layoffs are deemed unavoidable for a company's survival, they should be implemented quickly. Human beings generally have a low level of tolerance for uncertainty. They waste a lot of energy worrying whether there's something as troubling as potential layoffs to worry about. There's bound to be some worry, of course. Executives can minimize that, and work to maintain credibility and trust, by communicating the steps in the reengineering plan constantly and in detail. Leaders can provide reassurance to those in need of it by being readily accessible, clarifying the situation as they see the need (and when asked), and being honest and open about the consequences of intended changes.

Leadership's attitude and behavior toward the victims is especially crucial to the success of the change effort. Careful handling of those who are laid off benefits the organization as well as the victims. Because survivors react strongly to what they perceive as unfair treatment of axed colleagues, their behavior, morale, and productivity are directly affected by the way layoffs are managed. By providing victims with tangible caretaking services (such as outplacement consulting and psychological and career counseling), actively trying to help them find new jobs, and assisting them in bridging the transition, leadership can make the best of a precarious situation.

Strategic reorientation

While some businesses that see a need for major change opt for reengineering, others favor strategic reorientation, or a return to the core competencies of the company. Many companies flounder once they've branched out into many different directions, especially if they've entered fields in which they have no special expertise. If the result is a diverse portfolio of companies that enjoy very little synergy, the company needs to restore a clear focus.

The first step toward that goal is a comprehensive assessment of what the company is really good at. What are its core competencies? What are the people in the company really good at? The second step is a careful inspection of the business environment. What kinds of challenges is the company facing? What's the competition like? What do the customers want? What possible discontinuities might the marketplace present? How will the environment look three years from now?

In many instances, going back to the core competencies, with any revisions in strategy that the market demands, is the best way to revive a floundering organization and restore corporate viability.

Changing the corporate mindset

Very often, neither business reengineering nor strategic reorientation, on its own, is adequate to turn a company around. Sometimes the entire corporate mindset needs to be transformed.

CREATING A SHARED MINDSET: REALIGNING THE CORPORATE CULTURE

The challenge for the instigators of any change process is to ensure that everyone in the organization takes personal responsibility for a part of that process. Blaming others doesn't lead anywhere. One organization may argue that it can't change because of the resistance of middle management, while another may claim that top management doesn't see the light. Both need to realize, as the American cartoon character

Pogo did, "We have met the enemy, and it is us!" Everyone in the organization – *everyone* – needs to ask him- or herself the question, What are
the impediments that prevent me from doing the kind of job I'd like to
do? And what can I do to remove those impediments (Box 7.4)?

BOX 7.4

What's holding you back (and what can you do about it)?

We've investigated the different steps that individuals usually go through in the
process of change. Now let's try to personalize that process, since "the enemy is us."
Take a good look at your organization and ask yourself the questions that follow.
Think through your answers carefully. Have others in your organization do the same
thing, then compare your responses and observations. Starting from the individual
action plans that this exercise calls for, work out a *combined* action plan for the
organization.

1   List on the left side of a piece of paper all the things that make your organization a
    great place to work.
2   List on the right side of your paper all the things that inhibit fun and creativity in
    your workplace. What do you see as the major problems in your organization?
    What would you get rid of or change immediately?
3   In the light of your responses to the two previous questions, what action steps
    could you take – you personally – to prepare your company for the future? What
    could you do to improve your own job effectiveness and the effectiveness of the
    company as a whole? (If you have trouble thinking of concrete steps, think back on
    a successful organizational change activity that you participated in. That history
    may give you some insight into the kind of levers you need to use.)
4   If you view other employees or departments or outside forces as impediments,
    what steps could you take to initiate an improved relationship or more conducive
    circumstances?

Your responses to these questions make the process of corporate transformation
more personal and help to clarify your personal contribution to organizational
effectiveness.

As anyone in a position of leadership soon discovers, you can't get people to be responsive merely by *requesting* it. Another way to put this is to say that leaders have to create a "shared mindset." To do so, you have to ask your people personal questions like the ones listed in the "What's holding you back?" exercise. How people react to these questions drives the process of corporate transformation, determining how – and whether – the process will move.

The shared mindset necessary to successful change combines specific goals for the future with those aspects of the organizational culture that support the desired future. That's a difficult task, however, because organizational culture – **organizational culture provides rules for behavior** a mosaic of basic assumptions expressed as beliefs, values, and characteristic patterns of behavior that are adopted by the organization's members in an effort to cope with both internal and external pressures – is largely beyond people's awareness. It's a kind of "invisible hand" that structures activities.

Organizational culture, although largely taken for granted, provides rules for behavior. It helps employees understand the dos and don'ts of organizational life. Organizational culture is also *descriptive*, telling of the organization's uniqueness and identity, and containing many symbolic elements that become expressed through language, rituals, stories, metaphors, artifacts, behavior, and other constructs that become part and parcel of the experiences of everyday life. Because it is rooted in identity, organizational culture tends to endure over time; it's not easily modified.

Identifying the values that make up the culture in your own organization isn't easy. Participants in organizations are like fish in water. Fish realize that they need water only when they're out of it. Notwithstanding that difficulty, however, values identification is crucial to any change effort. Leaders have to know what values are shared to know whether those values are worth keeping.

Although it's possible to highlight a number of cultural values that stand out in world-class organizations, there's nothing generic about those values. It's not possible to clone success by stressing specific values in the annual report (even if leaders model those values effectively). Every successful organization has something "extra," something beyond these values, that distinguishes the organization and how its people act. The companies that go places are typically rule breakers in some sense; rule *takers* tend to stay in the minor leagues.

Having said that, however, it's worth looking more closely at the values that tend to be present in successful organizations (Box 7.5):

- ❖ **Team orientation** The willingness to subdue one's personal objectives to those of the team.

- ❖ **Candor** Frank and open communication that shares information and minimizes secrecy.

- ❖ **Empowerment** The broad delegation of authority and responsibility.

- ❖ **Respect for the individual** A tolerance for cultural, gender, and skill differences.

- ❖ **Customer focus** A recognition of the need to be market driven, to satisfy customers.

- ❖ **Competitiveness/desire to win** An achievement orientation that drives all employees.

- ❖ **Speed** The speed with which decisions are implemented.

- ❖ **Entrepreneurial attitude** An openness to risk and innovation.

- ❖ **Fun** A playfulness that encourages creativity.

- ❖ **Accountability** A recognition that a result orientation is critical for the success of a company.

- ❖ **Continuous learning** An ongoing renewal of skills and attitudes.

- ❖ **Openness to change** A willingness to hear new ideas and suggestions.

- ❖ **Trust** The belief that others care and have the company's best interests at heart.

- ❖ **Integrity** Sincerity and authenticity in executive behavior.

BOX 7.5

What does your organizational culture value?

On a scale of 1 to 10 (1 = lowest, 10 = highest), rate the extent to which you believe people in your company share the following values.

1 2 3 4 5 6 7 8 9 10

- Team orientation
- Candor
- Respect for the individual
- Empowerment
- Customer focus
- Competitiveness/desire to win
- Speed
- Entrepreneurial attitude
- Fun
- Accountability
- Continuous learning
- Openness to change
- Trust
- Integrity

As we've seen, many of these values characterize world-class organizations. The higher the points you've assigned your organization, the more likely it is to fall into the high-performance category. Since individual perceptions are inevitably biased, share your responses with those of other people in your organization and reflect on the differences. Ask yourself whether people really "walk the talk," modeling the values that they espouse. Discuss with others in your organization what can be done to internalize more of these values.

MODELING ESPOUSED VALUES

Let's look at one value – trust – in more detail. Trust is the basic currency of success: any company's success is directly linked to the degree that top executives in the company are trusted. But how do you build trust in an organization?

The first thing we need to do is to communicate, a process that consists of two things: listening and talking. Most of us are terrible listeners. We're so busy formulating our responses that we forget to listen. If we're lax in this area, we need to learn "active listening" (see Chapter 2), which means staying tuned into the speaker and paying attention to nonverbal as well as verbal communication. And when we talk, we need to be honest but respectful. Nothing kills trust faster than a lack of respect. Mutual respect implies honesty, openness, consistency, competence, fairness, and integrity. If we want to build trust in the organization, we can't shoot the messenger. With trust, people engage in constructive conflict resolution, leading to commitments, accountability, and a positive effect on the balance sheet.

Powerholders in the organization have the responsibility to model trust and all other espoused values faithfully. They also need to monitor the practice of values at all levels and send people packing who can't meet the baseline for acceptable behavior that the espoused values set. This process of culture–person "fit" needs to be carefully managed, because it's the key to safeguarding cultural values.

This discussion of cultivating organizational values brings us to the issue of effective leadership. What characterizes effective leaders? What roles, in addition to values modeling, do they assume? What traits, qualities, and competencies and roles underlie their effectiveness?

8 Characteristics of effective leadership

I have always admired the ability to bite off more than one can chew and then chew it. WILLIAM DEMILLE

The world is divided into people who do things and people who get the credit. Try, if you can, to belong to the first class. There's far less competition. DWIGHT MORROW

You will never be a leader unless you first learn to follow and be led. TIORIO

It's hard for anyone who's not change oriented to be an effective leader. Contemporary society doesn't give us the luxury of choice between stasis and change. Change is here to stay, with or without our approval, and the rate of change escalates almost daily. Think, for example, about the differences in lifestyle between you and your grandparents. In just two generations, we've gone from horse **change is here to stay, with or without our approval** and buggy to space shuttle. Or think about this: one issue of the *Herald Tribune* contains more information than a person in the Middle Ages would have been exposed to in a lifetime.

As I made clear in Chapter 3, during the 1980s and 1990s the corporate world witnessed a major paradigm shift that has affected the modus operandi of many organizations. That shift came in response to changes in many aspects of society – changes that are ongoing in the new millennium:

❖ Major demographic shifts are taking place, including ever-growing urbanization and growth in what the West likes to term "minority groups."

❖ Information and communication technologies are exploding, as just noted.

❖ The "new economy" (or actually, better, the "old economy" with new technology), as reflected in e-commerce, is changing how we look at traditional business models.

❖ The euro is having a major impact.

❖ Since the fall of the Iron Curtain, Eastern Europe and Russia are continuing to undergo dramatic changes.

❖ Africa, the Pacific Rim, and the Far East, given their exponential growth, are dealing with critical issues in health, finance, education, ecology and government.

❖ Management is becoming increasingly globalized. The extensive restructuring and downsizing efforts I spoke of in the previous chapter are part and parcel of this trend. In addition, there's an increasing consolidation of businesses through mergers, acquisitions, and strategic alliances on a global scale.

Those leaders wise enough to realize that they can't ignore these changes are looking desperately for answers. They want to know – they *need* to know – what the implications of all these changes are for their organizations. They want to know what kind of leadership competencies will be needed to address those implications, and what the marketplace changes have to say about how we select and develop the leaders of tomorrow.

Leadership models

One of the problems, as we attempt to understand the concept of leadership, is that it can be looked at as both a property and a process. As a *property*, leadership is a set of characteristics – behavior pattern and personality attributes – that makes certain people more effective at attaining a set of goals. As a *process*, leadership is an effort by a leader, drawing on various bases of power (an activity with its own skill set), to influence members of a group to direct their activities toward a common goal.

The interactionist approach

Broadly speaking, as alluded to in Chapter 1, two extreme positions can be identified in leadership research. On one side of the spectrum are the "personalists" – researchers who argue that specific personality variables determine leadership effectiveness. These folks see leadership as a property and/or process. On the other side of the spectrum are the "situationists" – those who deny the influence of individual differences and attribute all variations in leadership effectiveness to environmental constraints. While personalists view leaders as "heroic" navigators, those in the latter camp claim that it makes little difference who's in charge – societal forces determine what action needs to be taken.

Of course, leadership isn't really one extreme or the other. As is the case with so many things in life, the truth can probably be found somewhere in between. Furthermore, leadership never happens in isolation. There can be no leaders without followers, and all leadership activities take place in context. Thus to understand leadership behavior we have to **leadership never happens in isolation** consider not only the personal makeup of the leader but also the makeup of the followers and the specifics of the particular situation. Certain styles of leadership simply don't fit certain follower types or situations.

It's this interface between leader, follower, and situation that makes leadership so complex. To successfully incorporate all these elements, an "interactionist" model of leadership is probably the most realistic. As Figure 8.1 illustrates, the personality, position, and experience of the leader play a role in the leadership equation, but so do the personalities of the followers (along with their values, attitudes, and beliefs, and the strength of the group's cohesiveness), combined with the situation

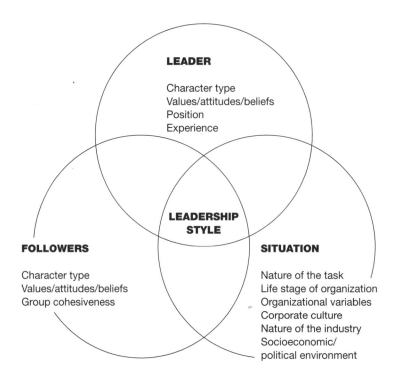

LEADER

Character type
Values/attitudes/beliefs
Position
Experience

LEADERSHIP STYLE

FOLLOWERS

Character type
Values/attitudes/beliefs
Group cohesiveness

SITUATION

Nature of the task
Life stage of organization
Organizational variables
Corporate culture
Nature of the industry
Socioeconomic/
political environment

Figure 8.1 The leadership domain

(the nature of the task, the type of organization, corporate culture, industry factors, and the socioeconomic/political situation).

The *situation* and *follower* branches of the leadership domain

If we want to dissect a particular episode of leadership, we need to look at the sort of task that has to be accomplished, the nature and health of the industry in question, the prevailing socioeconomic/political environment, the national culture the company is operating in, and the corporate culture that colors the microcosm of the organization. Even a particular leader's style of leadership – a very personal thing – is colored by the broader situation. It's an intricate outcome of personality, stage of life, national culture, and corporate culture.

After we've looked at the situation in an effort to understand some episode of leadership, we then have to assess the followers. What can be said about their mindset? What are their expectations of job and leader? What's their "power relationship" with their leader? Do they require strong guidance from above, for example, or do they work best in self-managed teams? (For an overview of superior–subordinate power relationships, see Figure 8.2.)

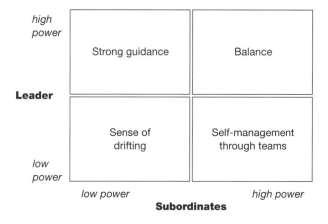

Figure 8.2 Superior–subordinate power relationships

The primary branch of the leadership domain: leadership competencies

We've seen that leaders don't operate in a vacuum; they're affected by the environment and their subordinates. Likewise, leadership doesn't *develop* in a vacuum. If we observe closely, we can read much about a person and his or her past in the leadership style we see exhibited. As we've noted, each leader adopts a particular leadership style and develops certain competencies (but not others) because of his or her "inner theater" – the scripting that results from the central needs of that individual. Let's oversimplify a bit for clarity. An individual's leadership style – as embodied in various roles that the person assumes while in a leadership position – is the consequence of a delicate interplay of the

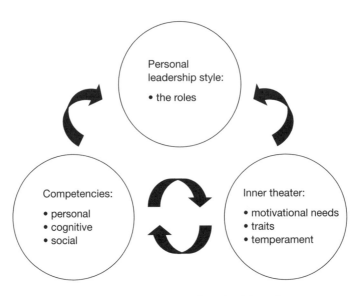

Figure 8.3 Dimensions of leadership style

forces in that person's inner theater (revolving around the individual's core needs) and the competencies he or she has acquired over time. (See Figure 8.3 for an overview.)

In Chapter 2, I pointed out ways of getting a handle on the various forces in a person's inner theater and highlighted the concept of a "core conflictual relationship theme" (or CCRT). I also discussed various defensive reactions and personality types, and tried to show that each personality type consists of specific constellations of character traits. These character traits are expressed in certain behavioral patterns that can be called *competencies*. In any given situation, a certain set of competencies contributes to effective leadership. The challenge for leaders (and potential leaders) is to develop a repertoire of competencies that covers most contingencies.

But what *are* those competencies? Or, stepping further back, what are the traits that trigger those competencies? What distinguishes good leaders from bad – what *specific, recognizable* characteristics can be identified? Over the centuries, many rather idiosyncratic selection methods have evolved. For example, consider

what distinguishes good leaders from bad?

Napoleon's (tongue-in-cheek) model of leadership assessment. It comprised a leadership competency matrix that consisted of two dimensions – intelligence and energy – which could be applied as follows:

❖ People who possess high intelligence and high energy would be made generals.

❖ People with high intelligence and low energy would be put in staff positions.

❖ People with low intelligence and low energy would be assigned to the infantry.

❖ People with low intelligence and high energy would be shot. They are the most dangerous.

Others have followed in Napoleon's footsteps. There was a good deal of scientific research at the beginning of the twentieth century designed to identify traits that would be universally beneficial in any setting of leadership. That research wasn't particularly successful, however. The results were conflicting, largely due to methodological problems in research design. Recently, however – after a long hiatus in trait research (and with the help of better measuring techniques) – trait theory is undergoing a revival. And the new research is promising, looking at behavioral outcomes of desirable traits *in context*. In other words, the traits themselves are less important than the fruit they bear.

Those studies that have gone beyond the simplistic approach of previous trait studies have identified a number of personality characteristics that consistently emerge, differentiating leaders from non-leaders – dimensions of character that can be mapped into the "Big Five" model of personality structure. (This Five Factor Theory, popular among many industrial psychologists such as Robert Hogan, names five categories of traits as most essential to human behavior: extroversion, agreeableness, conscientiousness, neuroticism, and openness to experience.) Thus, ironically, we've gone from a universal trait approach – via a long detour – to a competency model (Box 8.1).

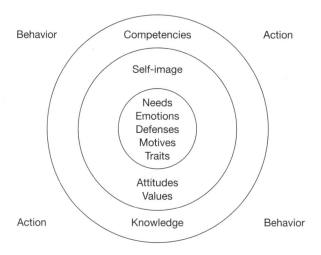

Figure 8.4 The circle of competencies

Most effective leaders possess clusters of competencies in three areas:

❖ **Personal competencies**, such as achievement motivation, self-confidence, energy, and personal effectiveness.

❖ **Social competencies**, such as influence, political awareness, and empathy.

❖ **Cognitive competencies**, such as conceptual thinking and a helicopter view.

In Figure 8.3 we looked at those competencies as one dimension of leadership. We can also see them as part of a layering process that has at its core needs, emotions, defenses, motives, and traits; these are followed by values, beliefs, attitudes, and self-image, which in turn are followed by competencies and knowledge. The effect of this set of interacting variables is expressed through behavior and action (Box 8.2). (See Figure 8.4 for an overview.)

most effective leaders possess clusters of competencies

BOX 8.2

What are your strongest competencies?

Rate yourself on the following characteristics, checking TRUE or FALSE for each statement.

	TRUE	FALSE
• I'm more of an extrovert than an introvert		
• I can be somewhat dominant		
• In interpersonal situations, I'm usually quite assertive		
• I tend to be very competitive in whatever I engage in		
• I'm extremely achievement oriented		
• Others perceive me as quite self-assured		
• When I promise to do something, I deliver		
• Other people see me as quite likable		
• I make a great effort to be helpful to others		
• I can be a real team player		
• I always make myself accountable for my commitments		
• I'm very willing to be flexible when the situation requires it		
• I'm very open to other people's ideas		
• I listen carefully to what others have to say (and how they say it)		
• I make a real effort to put myself in other people's shoes		
• I'm very effective in social situations		
• I get people to open up by talking freely about myself		
• I enjoy learning new things		
• I quickly grasp the essence of things		
• I have an amazing amount of energy		
• I relate very easily to other people		
• I can be quite playful		
• I have no difficulty controlling my temper		
• I have a rather optimistic outlook on life		
• Others consider me to have a realistic outlook on life		

▶

BOX 8.2 continued

If you labeled most of these statements TRUE, you're someone who easily wears the cloak of leadership. Whether your FALSE responses were few or many, give some thought to those areas before you continue along (or decide to take) the leadership path.

Let's end this chapter with a look at some of the competencies (closely tied to personality traits) that are most crucial to leadership effectiveness:

❖ **Surgency** This term applies to people who tend to have a more *assertive* character, who want (and know how) to get their own way. People characterized by surgency are very energetic and domineering. A strong *achievement orientation* distinguishes these individuals from lesser beings. True leaders have a fire in their belly; they are people who make things happen and are driven to beat the competition. They like to accomplish things. They are *action oriented*. Even when they don't feel confident, they're good enough at impression management to make others believe that they are. Because of their assertiveness, they get other people to do things they wouldn't have done otherwise.

❖ **Sociability** The most successful leaders have considerable social skills. (This competency is closely associated with the Big Five trait of *extroversion*, incidentally.) After all, leaders are in the people management business; they spend much of their time relating to people and need to enjoy that aspect of the job.

❖ **Receptivity** Successful leaders tend to be open to new ideas and experiences. They are somewhat adventurous. This quality is becoming increasingly important as the business world expands to global dimensions.

❖ **Agreeableness** Effective leadership is seen in people who are agreeable. Good leaders tend to be cooperative; they're flexible and likable. They possess a degree of trust in other people. They also know how to *reframe* difficult situations in a *positive* way. It is these characteristics that make them excellent *team players*.

❖ **Dependability** Effective leaders are conscientious (another factor of the Big Five). When they're asked to do something, they deliver; they're reliable, and they follow through.

❖ **Analytical intelligence** Most effective leaders possess more than average analytical intelligence. It helps them to think in a *strategic* manner. Too high an IQ can be detrimental, however, in that it encourages overintellectualization and the rationalizing of one's point of view (both of which impede right action).

❖ **Emotional intelligence** As noted in Chapter 2, successful leaders know how to manage their emotions and read the emotions of others. Having a solid dose of *empathy* is what differentiates these people. Possessed of a good sense of reality, they're aware of their strengths and weaknesses, know what they stand for, and know how to establish and maintain relationships. Furthermore, they're emotionally stable (a quality that we'll look at in greater detail in Chapter 13).

All these competencies (and the way they become expressed in actions) will stand leaders in good stead as they operate in today's global environment.

9   Leadership in a global context

Every nation ridicules other nations, and all are right.

ARTHUR SCHOPENHAUER

Nationalism: An infantile disease. It is the measles of mankind. ALBERT EINSTEIN

As the traveller who has once been from home is wiser than he who has never left his own doorstep, so a knowledge of one other culture should sharpen our ability to scrutinize more steadily, to appreciate more lovingly, our own.

MARGARET MEAD

With the increasing globalization of business, we can no longer ignore the fact that there's a strong cultural dimension to leadership – that is, that there are variations in what's acceptable as a leadership style depending on one's national culture.

Although what's a very effective leadership style for one country may be an extremely ineffective style for another, people aren't always aware that cultural differences exist at all. This is particularly true of people who inhabit the larger countries, who can easily live under the illusion of splendid isolation. People from smaller countries – for reasons of survival – don't have the luxury of this ethnocentrism. They need to reach out beyond their borders for various economic and political ends (e.g., to find an export market). Consequently, they're generally less culturally arrogant.

We all carry cultural stereotypes in our mind, and we need to be cognizant of those biases and counter them when necessary. We like to focus on differences – whether real or illusionary – between cultures. That desire is part of what's been described as the "narcissism of minor differences." Dividing people into in-groups and out-groups, while resulting in labels for others, is typically done to help us see who we ourselves are. In other words, we can better define who we are if we distinguish ourselves from others.

we can better define who we are if we distinguish ourselves from others

The wheel of culture

A nation's character (a concept here widely construed to include leadership style and choice of social and organizational practices) is rooted in its culture. *Character* implies deeply embedded, consistent, and relatively durable behavior patterns.

Whether in Western Europe, the United States, Africa, or Russia, cultural values can be seen as the building blocks for behavior and action. As such, they have an influence on leadership practices and institutional arrangements. Comprehending the building blocks of culture will help us better understand differences in leadership styles among cultures. Many aspects of leadership are affected by cultural differences:

❖ Varying attitudes toward authority from country to country affect how leadership is perceived (by both leaders and followers).

❖ Particularly in global corporations – which often attempt to "streamline" behavior patterns in the organization, wherever they're located – the interface between national and corporate culture is tightly interwoven.

❖ Styles of decision making vary culture by culture.

❖ Motivation and control can be understood only in the context of cross-cultural management.

❖ The management of multicultural teams requires a cooperative blending of elements from various cultures.

Culture is a highly complex topic; multiculturalism even more so. Because of that, many frameworks have been developed to simplify culture. Several of these introduce a number of dimensions to highlight specific cultural patterns. These dimensions, frequently presented in the form of polarities, can be summarized in a condensed form as follows:

- ❖ **Environment** One regularly applied dimension of polarity highlights the different ways individuals perceive both the world around them and their fellow human beings. Some of us enjoy a feeling of mastery over nature, while others feel controlled by our surroundings; some tolerate uncertainty well, while others avoid it; some view people as basically good, while others see them as basically evil.

- ❖ **Action orientation** Some people favor a *being* orientation, while others favor a *doing* orientation; some have an *internal* focus, possessing a sense of control over their lives, while others focus *externally*, feeling an absence of control.

- ❖ **Emotion** Some people are emotionally expressive, while others exhibit great emotional control and inhibition.

- ❖ **Language** In speaking and writing, some people favor language that is *high context* (in other words, that uses circumvention and is difficult to interpret), while others generally use language that is *low context* (i.e., that's comparatively easy to understand).

- ❖ **Space** Some people prefer to be in space that's private (and respect the privacy of those around them), while others prefer a public environment (and have little regard for the privacy of others).

- ❖ **Relationships** In the course of personal and business relationships, some people tout individualism and competition, while others rely on collectivism and cooperation; some believe in the application of *universalistic* rules that apply to everyone, while others argue for *particularistic* rules that depend on the specifics of the case.

- ❖ **Power** Some people believe that status is *achieved*, while others value only *ascribed* status; some favor equality and advocate position based on ability, while others stress the role of wealth, birthright, and other such factors.

❖ **Thinking** Some people have a deductive approach to issues, while others take a more inductive approach; some analyze phenomena into parts, while others have a more holistic orientation, seeing patterns and relationships in a wider context.

❖ **Time** Some people have a *monochronic* orientation (that is, they prefer doing one thing at a time), while others are *polychronic* (preferring to do many things at once); some are oriented toward the past, while others focus on the present or future.

All these dimensions have something to offer as we seek to better understand different cultural settings and leadership styles. (See Figure 9.1 for an overview of the various dimensions.)

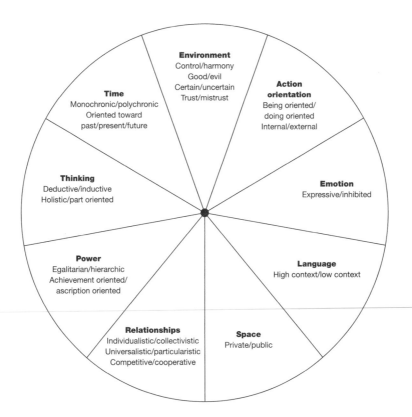

Figure 9.1 The wheel of culture

All of us feel more comfortable with certain cultures than others. That's in large part because of the ramifications of dimensions such as those just described. Take, for example, the low-context, high-context language distinction. In cultures that rely on high-context language (such as China, Korea, Japan, Vietnam, the Arab countries, Greece, Spain, Italy, and France), social trust needs to be established before effective communication can occur. Why is that? As an example, the Japanese have around 16 ways of saying no, not all of which *sound* like no. For example, the phrase *Eii doryoku shimasu* – literally, "We shall make efforts" – means no to Japanese. Given this complexity, personal relations stand central and negotiations are undertaken slowly and ritualistically. In contrast, low-context cultures (such as the UK, the Netherlands, North America, Scandinavia, Switzerland, and Germany) get down to business first. Personal relations play a much lesser role, meaning that agreements tend to be of a legalistic nature and negotiations are handled as efficiently as possible.

all of us feel more comfortable with certain cultures than others

Of course, low context and high context are in the eye of the beholder. Germans, for example, find it quite difficult to understand the Koreans but not so difficult to understand the Swiss. Koreans, by the same token, find it difficult to understand the Germans but not so difficult to understand the Chinese.

Let's stay with language for the moment, moving beyond the dimensions just listed. How about what we might call the language of locomotion? Swedish businesspeople, for example, tend to be rather serious and unexpressive. They don't gesture much with their hands, and their overall body posture tends to be stiff. Mexicans, however, are much more expressive with their hands and their bodies (although there's no kissing between men, as would be the case in Russia or Iran).

And how about touch? I once did a "time and motion" study to see how often people touched each other at a café. In Puerto Rico, in one hour, four people touched each other 70 times. In central Paris, in my own Café de Flore, four people touched each other 50 times. In London, the number was zero. Closely related to body language is the language of emotions. In Brazil, emotions drip all over the place, as they do in the Middle East. In the UK, on the other hand, the stiff upper lip prevails. People from other cultures are often surprised at how unemotionally British people can discuss highly emotional issues.

The French, particularly the Parisians, are often described as unfriendly, while Americans tend to walk around smiling at everyone, apparently friendly even to total strangers. When an American visiting Paris, for example, enters a shop and smiles, the shopkeeper doesn't smile back. He or she doesn't know the client and thus has nothing to smile about yet. (If the shopkeeper knew the client, he or she would certainly smile.) The upshot of this cross-cultural exchange is that the American concludes, "Those French – they're really unfriendly," while the Frenchman concludes, "Those Americans are odd people; they smile at everyone."

Even *silence* communicates. It's always interesting to listen to a conversation between a Finn and an American. There are many long silences in any Finnish conversation. Finns are comfortable with silences, because they're used to them. Theirs is a country of wide, open spaces. Americans, however, are made uneasy by silences, perceiving them as impolite. To break a silence in a Finnish–American conversation, the American (trying to be helpful) may finish a sentence that's been interrupted. The Finn will likely find this intrusive, unfortunately, seeing the American as "invading his space." Every culture has its

even *silence* communicates

conversational idiosyncrasies. When you talk with an African, for example, it's like talking on the phone. You have to make regular noises "at the other end" to indicate that you're actively listening; otherwise, the conversation will come to a halt.

Many global executives speak "bad English," a language in which one type of wording can bear several different interpretations, depending on the writer's/reader's cultural background. The language of time presents equally confusing translations, because different cultures relate to time in different ways. To illustrate, imagine that a Spaniard invites a Swede for dinner at eight o'clock. There's a strong probability that by ten to eight the Swede (who likely has a linear way of looking at time) is circling the neighborhood, planning to ring the bell at eight exactly. If she does so, there's an equally good probability that she'll find her Spanish hostess still in curlers and casual clothes.

Furthermore, some people deal with time in a polychronic way, while others deal with it in a synchronic way. The former do a lot of things simultaneously, while the latter do one thing at a time. Time is sometimes used as a power tool. In Ethiopia, the time required for decision making is proportionate to its importance. Thus low-level bureaucrats, trying to appear more important than they are, may take more time than they need. In Arab cultures, more important people get much faster service than less important people (and relatives have absolute priority). In America, too, time spent waiting for an executive is an indicator of the relative importance of host and client.

Each different time orientation can be quite irritating to the others. People in the one-down position have to adapt; those in the one-up position have the power to impose. I once had a Finn in my leadership seminar who was chairman of the board of a number of Irish firms that his company had acquired. He became so irritated by the lack of punctuality displayed by the other members of that board – Irish locals – that, after a few warnings, he fired the latecomers.

There's also the language of space. In America, proximity is familiarity. That's not the case in France. I've lived for more than 15 years in an apartment building in Paris, but I still don't know my neighbors. This would be unthinkable in America. What an office design communicates differs by country too. In America, having a corner office on the top floor is a sign of success. In France, the key office may be right in the center of the building, so that the CEO can keep an eye on everything. In Japan, too, the action is in the middle of the office area. If a person is put at the window in Japan, one assumes that he or she is a "window watcher" (*mado giwa zoku*). Moving the person out of the mainstream implies a desire, on the part of the company, to get rid of that person.

in America, proximity is familiarity

Space as it relates to physical closeness also differs by culture. What's a comfortable distance between speakers for Spaniards can be very uncomfortable for the British. Studies suggest that in the Northern European countries and the United States, the regular business distance is approximately 1.5 to 2.5 meters, while the distance for highly personal interactions is 0.5 to 1 meter. These distances are much smaller in Latin countries, which can lead to discomfort and awkward attempts at distance maintenance in cross-cultural dealings.

The language of friendship often requires careful translation. In certain cultures, making friends takes a long time, but friendships, once built, last for life. In other cultures, what are called friendships are really acquaintance relationships. What it comes down to is that in certain cultures, people show a lot of themselves – we might say that the public self takes up considerable space – while in other cultures, people are very private. This private–public dimension is also recognizable in noise levels. For example, Americans converse at a much louder level than do people from Sweden or Russia.

You want subtlety in communication? Let's look at the language of agreements. When it comes to a Finnish agreement, a promise is a promise. Finns are proud to see themselves as being very reliable. (After all, they paid reparations to the Russians to the last penny after World War II.) For Finns, promises are written in stone; one doesn't change them on a whim. So what if a Finn closes an agreement with a Greek, who typically has a very different attitude toward agreements? Greeks see every agreement as the beginning of a long-term relationship. They change the rules along the way – why not, since nothing is final? – which drives Finns up the wall. So Finns say, "Those Greeks – they're not reliable." The Greeks, for their part, say, "Those Finns – no flexibility; they're far too rigid."

Cross-cultural leadership styles

These different "languages" – these varying aspects of verbal and nonverbal communication that reflect a nation's culture – have serious implications for leadership practices. Organizational decision making, hierarchy, authority, and power are all affected by how a nation expresses itself through these "languages." Organizational design, for example, reflects a country's feelings about power. In certain countries, such as France, Venezuela, Pakistan, China, and Brazil, organizations tend to be quite "tall," with power concentrated at the top. In other countries, such as the Netherlands, Canada, and Finland, they tend to be quite "flat," with power more equally distributed.

In cultures that concentrate power at the top, hierarchy tends to be clearly defined and structures clearly delineated. People from such cultures often have trouble adjusting to global corporations, which typically have some form of matrix structure – that is, a structure where people have more than one person to report to. It isn't easy for people with a hierarchical mindset to deal with **we can distinguish between different leadership styles depending on the culture** networking organizations in which hierarchy is loosely defined, lateral communications dominate, people "bypass" (that is, forego hierarchical patterns of reporting), and many employees have more than one boss. Someone coming from a country such as Sweden, Holland, or America – a nonhierarchical country – would probably have an easier time of it than someone from a Latin country or (even more dramatically) the People's Republic of China, where there are more than 20 layers in the Communist party. In Chinese organizations, hierarchy and position play a critical role, mirroring the traditional family makeup there. No wonder matrix designs have problems in these cultures.

Broadly speaking, we can distinguish between different leadership styles depending on the culture. The *consensus model* is the norm in countries such as the Netherlands, Japan and those in Scandinavia. Japanese, Dutch, and Swedish followers expect a consensual leadership style, because group decision making is a core value. There's a tradition in these cultures of involving people – of allowing everyone to have a say.

The *charismatic model* is more typical in the Anglo-Saxon and Latin countries. North and Latin Americans expect their leaders to be assertive and decisive. They like their leaders to take charge, and to do so with flair. They want their leaders to be colorful, to be prominently visible. They're looking for people they can identify with, rule breakers who will guide them in new directions.

In the Germanic countries we find an *organizational processes* or *technocratic model*. This model can be seen as a reaction to the Nazi period. The German word for *leader* is *Führer*, a politically incorrect label that serves as a constant reminder of what abusive leadership can become. Since World War II, Germans have made a major effort to create a lot of checks and balances in their organizations (through worker councils and excessively large boards, for example) to prevent the abuse of power. It's interesting to note, however, that 50 years after the war charismatic leaders are again emerging.

The French favor a *political process model* of leadership. Charles de Gaulle stressed the importance of political processes when he said, "How can you govern a country which has 265 varieties of cheese?" The French are very skilled at coping with complex power networks. The *Grande École* concept of education plays a major role here. People who graduate from these schools – particularly *École Nationale d'Administration* (ENA) – are overrepresented among the political and economic elite. A small group of *énarques* (as graduates of ENA are called) have come to dominate the top positions in the country.

Many of the countries that used to be in the Soviet sphere of influence are characterized by a *democratic centralism model* sometimes described as "managed democracy". The Russians, after a long, painful history of troubled leadership ranging from czars to the KGB, retain a certain amount of paranoia about authority and strangers – a paranoia that shapes leadership in their business organizations. Under democratic centralism, a form of community decision making that links democracy and centralism, all members participate in discussions of issues and policies, and all members cast a vote for leadership. After leaders have been put in place, however, very little opposition to their ideas is permitted. In Russia, the notion of democratic centralism became particularly perverted under the Communist regime, resulting in extremely autocratic practices, a way of leading that is still very prevalent in the post-communist era.

Then there is the *patriarchical model* to be found in China, Malaysia, Singapore, Indonesia, India, many African countries, and some of the Middle Eastern countries. Leaders are expected to take care of their people. But again, what is meant well can easily become perverted. In some of the African and Middle Eastern countries it resulted in the "great man" concept, turning many leaders into tyrants. In other Arab countries such as Kuwait and Saudi Arabia, by way of contrast, the patriarchical model has a consultative side to it. Given the preference for a consultative pattern of leadership, open conflict is avoided and preference is given to subtle one-on-one negotiations.

Identifying global leadership abilities

As we look back at the various leadership models, and at cultural norms and distinctions, we can see that in our increasingly global world a number of patterns are converging (Box 9.1). The following characteristics and abilities are useful to leaders who have the opportunity to work cross-culturally:

- ❖ charismatic qualities
- ❖ teambuilding skills
- ❖ an openness to change
- ❖ an interest in the socioeconomic and political life of other countries
- ❖ an ability to relate well to people from other cultures
- ❖ good nonverbal communication skills
- ❖ an interest in and understanding of how cultural differences affect the way people function
- ❖ a willingness to hear and attempt to understand different views
- ❖ relative fluency in a second language (and an interest in languages generally)
- ❖ a desire to travel, learn new things, and try varied cuisines
- ❖ a sense of ease in culturally ambiguous situations
- ❖ the ability to work well in (and enjoy) multicultural teams
- ❖ a willingness to take risks when the potential for payoff is high

❖ a high tolerance for frustration and ambiguity

❖ adaptability to new situations

❖ an internal orientation (having a perception of control over one's life)

❖ a sense of humor.

BOX 9.1

Do you have what it takes to be a global leader?

Exceptional global leaders have specific competencies and character traits. Respond to the following statements by checking TRUE or FALSE. Answer as honestly as you can.

TRUE   FALSE

- I have a deep interest in the socioeconomic and political scene of the countries in which I work
- I'm very good at relating to people from other cultures
- I pay attention to nonverbal behavior when I communicate across cultures
- I spend time thinking about how cultural differences affect the way other people function
- I speak at least one language in addition to English
- I like learning new things
- Whatever country I live in, I make an effort to learn the language
- I'm comfortable in culturally ambiguous situations
- I enjoy working in multicultural teams
- I enjoy visiting other countries
- At times I like to do risky things
- I possess a high tolerance for frustration and ambiguity
- I enjoy trying a wide variety of cuisines
- If I were to discover a spaceship in my garden with the door open, I'd be adventurous enough to go inside
- I'm able to adapt to any situation
- I'm adventurous about eating different kinds of food
- I'm not considered dogmatic by other people
- I believe that I'm very much in control of my life
- Whatever predicament I find myself in, I keep my sense of humor

If you've answered TRUE to most of these statements, you're the kind of person who is likely to do well at assignments abroad.

Just as certain personal qualities enhance global leadership, certain organizational qualities increase a firm's chances of success in the global marketplace (Box 9.2).

How global is your organization?

As you think about your own organization and its global strengths and weaknesses, respond to the following statements by assigning the number 1 if a statement is FALSE, 2 if it's SOMEWHAT CORRECT, or 3 if it's TRUE.

- To create an overall corporate "glue," our organization devotes a large share of its resources to global executive development
- Global experience is considered essential to a successful career in our organization
- A considerable number of our employees live outside the home country
- A sizable percentage of our investments lie outside the home country
- The power of our subsidiaries is considerable
- Non-home-country executives are well represented on the board
- Our language of business is predominantly English
- The members of the executive board have extensive non-home-country experience
- Our organization is very experienced at handling expatriation/repatriation issues and offers executives considerable help with transitions
- We pay a lot of attention to preparing our executives for "foreign" assignments
- In considering people for assignments in countries other than their own, we look at many factors other than technical/functional expertise
- We lose very few of our executives due to unsuccessful foreign assignments
- Our organization doesn't favor home-country nationals for fast-track careers

The higher your score, the more your organization tends to be global. (If you're concerned about your score, keep in mind that these statements are diagnostic, not absolute.)

Those firms that are most successful across international boundaries are characterized by the following:

❖ a large number of employees who live outside the organization's home country

❖ sizable investment outside the home country

❖ extensive distribution of power to the subsidiaries

❖ strong representation by non-home-country executives on the board

❖ predominant use of English as the language of business

❖ extensive non-home-country experience among members of the executive board

❖ the belief that global experience is essential to one's career in the organization

❖ considerable experience with (and therefore help on) expatriation/repatriation issues

❖ careful preparation of executives for "foreign" assignments

❖ a weighting of factors beyond technical/functional expertise in making global assignments

❖ a good retention rate after foreign assignments

❖ an openness to consider non-home-country nationals for fast-track careers.

Global leadership development

When effective global leaders are asked what's been the strongest force in the development of their global skills, most respond with something from the five T's of global leadership: *tradition, travel, training, transfers,* and *team learning*. The most common response, however, is travel: living and working in a foreign country is typically the single most influential developmental experience. People who aspire to be global leaders tend to seek out and pass hurdles that enable them to successfully acquire these five T's.

The first hurdle: family influences

I'd go so far as to argue that if the right foundation is lacking in a given individual, global leadership training within the organization will be of limited use. Thus organizations would do well to look into the background of potential high-flyers, focusing on early childhood and educational experiences rather than limiting themselves to the career trajectory within the company.

The ease with which an infant or child relates to strangers is dictated by the security of the infant–mother attachment. The way that children react to initial encounters with strangers depends on the nature of their early attachment to primary caretakers. A strong sense of security encourages young children to explore their environment in a playful and creative way and establishes the foundation for healthy narcissistic development and realistic self-esteem. Parents who help children deal with their frustrations and disappointments – natural consequences of the child's growing curiosity and need to explore the world and push boundaries – in an age-appropriate manner provide a secure base for the youngsters' growing autonomy. Through supportive interaction with parents, children develop a cohesive sense of self and a set of core values that later allow them to function in a relatively problem-free way at work and in their private life. (At times, however, the need to explore can be of a counterphobic nature, it being a desperate effort at mastery of emerging insecurity.)

The culture of the community in which a child is raised is also a factor. For example, children who grow up in a trusting egalitarian or collectivist society – one in which interdependence and lack of paranoia are the norm – are more likely than others to become leaders who can generate trust and a sense of community in organizations of a global nature. Scandinavians, who tend to be more trusting than, say, Russians (with their historically induced fear of both authority and foreigners), are good at generating trust in a leadership role.

Likewise, children who grow up in a *doing* culture rather than a *being* culture (see the discussion of cultural dimensions earlier in the chapter) are more likely to do well at global leadership as adults. People in *doing* cultures have an internal locus of control – that is, they feel able to control (or at least influence) the direction of their lives – which empowers them as leaders.

Thus the foundation is laid at an early age for the ways in which a person reacts to new or unexpected situations. A positive sense of self-esteem developed in childhood helps adults to be more comfortable when interacting with people from different cultures. Furthermore, the more intercultural experiences children have early in life, the more likely they are to develop the kind of cultural empathy necessary for leadership effectiveness in a global setting. Xenophobia and ethnocentricity are culturally contingent for the most part; they're spawned by the kind of socialization a child experiences. To give a small example, European children of today are used to seeing text on their cereal box at breakfast printed in at least three languages. And they hear foreign languages often too, especially on television.

xenophobia and ethnocentricity are culturally contingent for the most part

Because of the impact of early socialization, exposure in childhood to different nationalities and languages can be a determining factor in how well an adult deals with cultural diversity later in life. Cultural exchange programs and summer camps open new vistas for young people. Dramatic examples include holiday camps for Israeli and Palestinian children, or Irish children from both Belfast and Dublin. These multicultural experiences can counteract home- or society-bred xenophobia. Children of mixed-culture marriages, bilingual parents, or diplomats or executives who move frequently also have an advantage – so long as the experience of cultural immersion is seen as positive by the parents. If the family doesn't provide a stable base from which the child can explore the world, cultural differences can turn into a frightening cacophony rather than a grand adventure. As children move through the developmental process, it's important that they retain a set of positive internal images that act as stabilizers in an often bewildering world. The strength of these stabilizers will be tested in later life – particularly in the case of global leaders.

The second hurdle: education and work experience

An international executive education has become almost a requirement for global leadership. An MBA program such as that offered at INSEAD, a business school in France and Singapore, which has no national identity, is a breeding ground for attitudes of cultural relativity. INSEAD students work in mixed-nationality study groups over their ten-month course: a typical group might include one American, one French person, one Russian, one Japanese person, one Swede, and one Brazilian. As these individuals work together on various projects, they develop the necessary cross-cultural mindset, minimizing ethnocentricity.

On-the-job training offers education of another sort, and it's no less vital. Exposure early in one's career to international leadership experiences – by *experiences* I mean concrete project responsibilities – is important. Such experiences hone a person's capacity to cope with difficult leadership challenges later in the career cycle, especially if they occur in conjunction with an internationally oriented human resource system and an organizational support system conducive to the management of global careers. (The hard truth is that the majority of expatriate assignments that fail do so because the family of the executive can't adapt.) This kind of early international experience is a good test of a young manager's global leadership potential.

Nokia, the world's number one producer of mobile phones, is now a household name. Founded in 1865, this Finnish company, once a manufacturer of everything from rubber boots and toilet paper to TVs, transformed itself under CEO Jorma Ollila into a producer of mobile phones at the cutting edge. A large part of Nokia's success rests on its ability to turn from a provincial organization which originally had the bulk of its business in Finland (and the Soviet Union) into a truly global organization with only a small percentage of its activity in Finland presently. The organization is flat and highly decentralized, with R&D centers in Japan, the UK, and Finland, factories in Texas and China, and the design center in California. Innovation on a global scale is a core value at Nokia. Not surprisingly, then, global leadership is a key preoccupation among the members of the board as their intense involvement in leadership development programs testifies.

Nokia stands out as exceptional because of its farsightedness in devoting time and money to developing truly global leaders. Organizations such as Nokia are ahead of the game: they already have in place a set of values, attitudes, and behavior patterns that center on cross-cultural empathy, and they've gone to great lengths to hire and build up a critical number of globally competent employees – the pool from which leaders of the future will come.

Contrast these leading global firms with companies that use their foreign subsidiaries as parking lots for redundant employees when times are lean at home. Or compare them to companies that send expatriates to take charge when an expensive and important new factory or project is due to come on line in a subsidiary, passing over the local employees who did the initial groundwork. Predictably, the local executives resent such decisions and act accordingly; the expatriates (and their families) are equally **companies that strategically develop people with global leadership qualities will have a competitive edge sooner rather than later** unhappy, stressed by a hasty move to an unfamiliar environment with little preparation (a cursory language program at best), often culturally isolated in an expatriate "ghetto," with no guarantee of a job in their home country when the foreign assignment is finished.

There's no easy solution to the development of leaders in a global age, but companies that carefully select and strategically develop people with global leadership qualities will have a competitive edge sooner rather than later.

The third hurdle: corporate culture

As noted earlier, however, one of the indicators that an organization is truly global is the number of nationalities represented on its board. Most U.S. organizations with global operations still have boards composed entirely of Americans. (The same point can be made of many

European and Asian corporations.) A mixed-nationality executive board shows the outside world that the organization is committed to globalization and integrates different perspectives, and it offers an antidote to signs of ethnocentricity within the organization. It also demonstrates that the top jobs aren't the exclusive bailiwick of certain nationalities. Most important, a truly global board can accomplish the function of effective decision making based on diverse perspectives.

Global leaders must create multicultural organizational communities by establishing a corporate culture that transcends these differences and establishes a number of "beacons" – values **global leaders must** and attitudes – that are comprehensible to **create multicultural** employees from diverse cultural groups. Thus **organizational** programs for developing global leaders must **communities** not focus exclusively on appreciation and accommodation of cultural diversity, but must also create awareness of the need for a shared organizational culture. (See Figure 9.2 for an overview of the developmental action steps involved in the making of a global leader.)

Global leadership competencies and attitudes are two legs of the global leadership triangle. How these competencies and attitudes are executed is the third leg. To understand that third leg, we turn now to the roles leaders play.

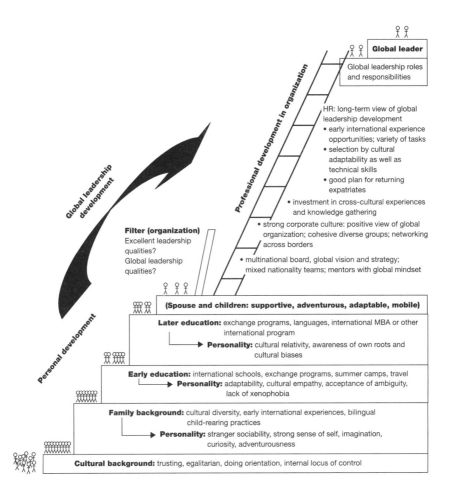

Figure 9.2 Global leadership development

10 Roles leaders play

Better to do a little well than a great deal badly. SOCRATES

A leader is a dealer in hope. NAPOLEON BONAPARTE

It is more important to know where you are going than to get there quickly. Do not mistake activity for achievement.

MABEL NEWCOMER

In the previous chapters we looked at some of the competencies that good leaders possess. In this chapter we'll look at what it is that effective leaders *do* – how they "act out" these competencies. We'll examine the various roles they play as they strive to bring out the best in their colleagues and followers.

Before we continue, take a moment to think about the following question: What are the major differences between a *leader* and a *manager*? How would you define each? Do you see the two as merely variations on a theme, or do you see them as taking on distinctly different roles?

The relationship between leadership and management has generated considerable interest in the leadership literature. It's also led to a great deal of confusion, both in classrooms and in the workplace. The political scientist James MacGregor Burns was one of the first to take up the challenge of delving deeper into this subject. He extended Max Weber's reflections on the sources of authority and charisma by making a distinction between *transactional leadership* and *transformational leadership*.

While transactional leadership can best be viewed as a mundane contractual exchange based on self-interest (often described in the organizational literature as the *manager's* role), transformational leadership seeks to satisfy the higher needs of followers – to engage in a process of mutual stimulation and elevation whereby followers transcend their own self-interests for the good of the group.

The word *manager* has its deepest root in the Latin word *manus*, meaning "hand." From that root, it branches etymologically into the Italian word *maneggiare* and the old French *manège* – meaning training and directing horses in the manège, or riding school. Perhaps not the most glorious activity now; but when the word was coined, centuries ago when horse power was crucial, the role must have been very important. In contrast to the etymological root of *manager*, the word *leader*, as we saw in the first chapter, comes from the Anglo-Saxon word *laed*, meaning "path" or "road." The verb *laeden* means "to travel." This etymological origin suggests a more distant, long-term orientation than does merely teaching a horse how to behave.

> **transactional leadership can best be viewed as a mundane contractual exchange based on self-interest**

Let's look at a few more differentiations typically made between leaders and managers:

- ❖ Leaders are interested in the future, while managers focus on the present.

- ❖ Leaders are interested in change, while managers prefer stability.

- ❖ Leaders tend to be long-term oriented, while managers focus on the short term.

- ❖ Leaders are caught up in vision, while managers (preoccupied with rules and regulations) focus on instruction.

- ❖ Leaders deal with the whys, while managers deal with the hows.

- ❖ Leaders know how to empower subordinates, while managers tend to control.

- ❖ Leaders know how to simplify, while managers enjoy complexity.

- ❖ Leaders use their intuition, while managers rely on logic.

❖ Leaders have a wide outlook that encompasses social concerns, while managers are more preoccupied by corporate concerns.

We need both leadership and management. Being an idea person is fine, but not at the expense of reality. Visionary leaders don't actually *lead* unless they take the steps needed to implement their vision. Vision without action is a hallucination. Likewise, managers can't take the steps they're so good at unless they know what direction to go. Thus instead of demonizing managers as bureaucrats who only shuffle papers, we should encourage all leaders to develop their managerial capabilities (Box 10.1). (See Figure 10.1 for an overview of various combinations of leadership and management.)

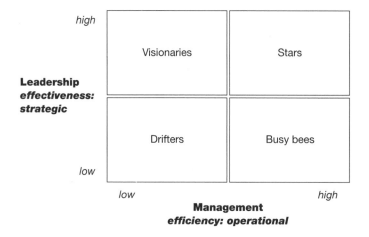

Figure 10.1 Leadership/management matrix

BOX 10.1

Are you primarily a leader or a manager?

Circle the word (or words) in either column A or B, depending on which option more closely reflects your outlook.

In running my organization (or organizational unit):

	A	B
• I focus on	the present	the future
• I'm more concerned about	stability	change
• I concentrate on	the short term	the long term
• To get my work done, I use	inspiration	instruction
• My goals are based on	immediate necessity	"inner theater"
• I always ask for	the how	the why
• My position is based on	authority	charisma
• When dealing with others, I tend to	control	empower
• My communication is characterized by	complexity	simplicity
• In decision making, I usually resort to	logic	intuition
• primary concerns are	corporate	social and corporate

If most of your responses fell in the B column, you tend to be leadership oriented. If they fell more often in the A column, you tend to be management oriented. If you were often unable to decide between the two responses, you share both orientations rather equally. Being in that position may lead to greater organizational effectiveness.

Leadership versus management

Private motives and the public stage

For truly great leaders, vision is deeply embedded. It's based on the inner theater, with its CCRT-based script. Let's take just one example.

Richard Branson was the first child and only son in his family. His father, the son and grandson of eminent lawyers, followed the family tradition and became a lawyer too, albeit a reluctant one. Branson's father wasn't terribly ambitious, although he was very supportive of his children. The driving force in the family, however, was Branson's mother, who had been (in her earlier years) a dancer and a flight attendant, traveling to South America when air travel still implied adventure and danger. Her stories about her travels must have had an effect on Branson as an impressionable young boy. And she aimed high for her son. As we saw in Chapter 4, when he was born she announced that one day he would be prime minister.

Branson's mother had very decided views on childrearing and pushed her children to be self-reliant, competitive, and responsible. No passive television watching in her household! In one of her lessons on self-reliance – an episode that understandably entered family lore – she put Branson out of the car at the age of four and told him to find his way home. He didn't arrive when she expected him to, and concern began to mount. The panicked parents later received a call from neighbors, who had taken in the young Richard.

Despite that hitch, Branson's mother was the person who convinced him that he could do whatever he set his mind to. She was also the family's role model for entrepreneurship, and she taught him the value of money (which was tight when he was growing up). Other role models during his impressionable years were his grandfather – a judge at the High Court – and Robert Falcon Scott, the Antarctic explorer. Overall, though, it was his mother who played the most decisive role in molding his personality. Branson once described her to me as having one mad idea after the other. She encouraged Branson's entrepreneurial ventures from the outset. His need to challenge the established way of doing things, his anti-authoritarian outlook, his need to play David against the Goliaths of enterprise – all these developed early and were encouraged at home. Thus Branson's upbringing set the stage for making him the successful person he is today. To really understand a leader, we have to heed his or her inner theater.

The enigma of charisma

Leaders are also supposed to have charisma – that mysterious "gift" that emanates directly from God, a quality thought originally only to be possessed by prophets. The charismatic element in leadership sweeps people off their feet; it's the basis for the influence of true leaders. (More on that later in this chapter.) Managers, in contrast, rely more on their hierarchical position for power and authority (Box 10.2).

If someone stood at the front of a room full of people and said, "Please raise your hand if you think you're charismatic," chances are not a single hand would go up. (Would yours, if you were in the group?) Even people who think that they possess charisma would be reluctant to say so publicly. Most likely, they'd worry that if they raised a hand people would think them **leaders are supposed to have charisma** arrogant or would laugh at them. But what if people were told to close their eyes and then were asked for a show of hands? Would that make a difference? Probably so. A "private" admission of charisma is much easier than a public one.

Yet I believe that *everyone* who has reached a leadership position has the potential to be somewhat charismatic as well. As we saw in an earlier chapter, when you're in a position of power and authority, others project their fantasies on you. You're the subject of their attributions. The question is, Do you have the kind of personality that will take advantage of these transferential processes? Will you in fact *encourage* them? And will you do what you can to ensure that the attributions are grounded in reality?

BOX 10.2

What's your take on charisma?

Give careful thought to the following questions and jot down your responses.

A   What does being charismatic mean to you?
B   Have you ever met a person whom you would describe as charismatic?
C   What qualities made this person so special?
D   Do you believe that you possess some of these qualities?
E   Are there ways you can acquire charismatic qualities?

Let's see if we can deconstruct charisma and isolate its component parts. First, charisma entails a determination to challenge the status quo. On a continuous basis, charismatic individuals articulate dissatisfaction with the present state. Truly charismatic people never take the present situation for granted; they keep on asking questions: *Is there no better way to build this mousetrap? Can't we do this a different way?* By asking these questions, they increase the level of discomfort in those around them, and they get people to think. But charismatic leaders don't stop there: they present viable alternatives. Complaining leads a group only so far; hope for a new beginning is required before complaints can lead to action. Charismatic individuals provide that hope, creating a new focus that speaks to the collective imagination.

In providing alternative solutions, truly charismatic leaders are masters of timing. They know that there's such a thing as the "historical moment," and they recognize it when it comes. Martin Luther, for example, knew when he nailed his demands on the door of the church in Wittenberg that the Catholic Church badly needed an overhaul. And because the time was right to lead such a protest, the Reformation took hold. The same canny sense of timing characterized Mahatma Gandhi's recognition that the time of the British Raj was up. His launching of a campaign against the tax on salt – a tax that affected the poorest section of the community – was a key event that transformed the psyche of the Indian people.

Charismatic leaders understand well the symbolic power of playing the David–Goliath theme. They see the wisdom of dramatizing the risk of their particular venture and know how to maximize the adrenaline that risk puts into the system. Richard Branson has been very good at orchestrating David and Goliath activities, as evidenced in his fights against British Airways, Coca-Cola, the National Lottery, and traditional banking. In many of his endeavors, he's played the underdog role, knowing that "righting wrongs" energizes employees.

Charismatic leaders are good at other forms of symbol manipulation as well. What we might call "the management of meaning" plays an important part in charismatic leadership. Like it or not, part of the leadership role is "theater." Leaders know how to create strong images to get people moving; they're good storytellers; they know how to make a point through ceremonies, symbols, **leaders know how to create strong images to get people moving** and settings. Furthermore, they're masters of language, adept at using similes, metaphors, and irony. Many politicians are especially good with words. Winston Churchill: "I have nothing to offer but blood, toil, tears, and sweat." Charles de Gaulle: "France has lost the battle, but she hasn't lost the war." Franklin Roosevelt: "The only thing we have to fear is fear itself." John F. Kennedy: "Ask not what your country can do for you; ask what you can do for your country."

In the business domain, Steven Jobs of Apple, an extremely articulate individual, is another good example of a leader who uses symbols and imagery to get his point across. He flew a pirate flag from the building where his people were developing the Macintosh computer, for example, and he introduced that computer on television with an extremely effective ad that aired during a Super Bowl match. The advertising message showed a large number of slave-like creatures sitting in rows in a dark auditorium, listening silently to the droning voice of an Orwellian "Big Brother" whose image was projected on an enormous screen. Then a young female athlete ran into the hall and threw a hammer into the air, splintering the screen (and dispatching the Orwellian image). As light flooded the room, all the slave-like creatures rose from their seats, revitalized. On the screen appeared the message that Apple was introducing the Macintosh computer. "Things will never be the same," it concluded. This advertisement wasn't the least bit subtle in portraying how Apple would beat Big Bad Blue – IBM. They'd be "blue busters!" Steven Jobs has continued to be a rule breaker in fields such as music and animation.

Charismatic leaders are also very good at building alliances. They know what to do to make people feel valued, singling out individuals and groups for special consideration. They display empathy through their actions. They also set a good example, walking the talk regarding all organizational expectations. Furthermore, they possess what I call "the teddy bear factor" – that is, they make people feel comfortable. Because they're an excellent "container" of other people's emotions, they put people at ease. Busy as they may be, they're masters at creating what may be an illusion that they have all the time in the world whenever someone wants to talk. And they really seem to *listen*; they pay attention.

The "teddy bear factor" is well portrayed in William Shakespeare's play *Henry V*. The play is based on the real Battle of Agincourt, where the British gained a decisive victory over the French in the Hundred Years' War. Before the battle, which took place on October 25, 1415 – St. Crispian Day – the odds were very much against the British. The French force, which totaled 20,000 to 30,000 men (many of them mounted knights in heavy armor), led by constable Charles I d'Albret, caught the exhausted British army (only 6,000 men strong) at Agincourt.

In Shakespeare's play, which contains some of the most famous lines on leadership in the English language, Henry V rallied his men for his cause by noting that on future St. Crispian days throughout history, a very few of them, the *happy* few, would be remembered. The play demonstrates the master-teambuilder qualities of Henry V, a man who knew how to create "mutual identification" (in other words, to create a group identity by establishing bonds between his soldiers and himself). He made his troops feel special and then went on to lead by example. In Act 4, Henry V says:

We few, we happy few, we band of brothers;
For he to-day that sheds his blood with me
Shall be my brother; be he ne'er so vile
This day shall gentle his condition:
And gentlemen in England, now abed
Shall think themselves accursed they were not here,
And hold their manhood cheap whiles any speaks
That fought with us upon Saint Crispin's day.

Henry V's speech, and his example, motivated his men. Energized by the king, who led from the front, the British turned the battle into a disaster for the French. After a three-hour struggle, the constable himself, 12 other members of the highest nobility, some 1,500 knights, and about 4,500 men-at-arms were killed on the French side, while the English lost fewer than 450 men.

Taken in combination, all the factors discussed in this section – the challenging of the status quo, the creation of hope, the dramatization of risk, the manipulation of symbols, the setting of a right example, and the teddy bear factor – create an organizational ambience that encourages exceptional effort, high commitment, intellectual stimulation, the belief in self-efficacy, and a willingness to take risks.

The dual roles of leadership

Effective leaders play two roles – a charismatic role and an architectural role. In the charismatic role, leaders envision a better future and empower and energize their subordinates. In the architectural role, leaders address issues related to organizational design and to control and reward systems.

Although the latter role has echoes of management, the two roles aren't just another way of stating the leadership/management distinction. *True leadership can't exist unless both roles are aligned.* And that appears to be a problem in far too many organizations. Neither role, in the absence of the other, is sufficient (although one role is often less dominant than the other, depending on the situation). The architectural role is far more than "mere" management; it's the imple-mentation by the leader of structures and policies that allow him or her to carry out the envisioning, empowering, and energizing duties of charismatic leadership. (See Figure 10.2 for a breakdown of these roles.)

effective leaders play two roles – a charismatic role and an architectural role

---

Charismatic role

• Envisioning
• Empowering
• Energizing

Architectural role

• Designing
• Controlling
• Rewarding

Figure 10.2 The dual roles of leadership

The charismatic role

Because of my training in psychoanalysis, my interest in the inner theater of executives, and my belief that aspects of charisma can be "learned" (if there exists a sufficient foundation within the individual), this book focuses on the charismatic role of leadership. Let's take a closer look now at the components of that role.

ARTICULATING AND COMMUNICATING THE VISION

An essential part of the charismatic leadership role revolves around visioning. Envisioning involves a number of things, including providing a road map for future direction, building excitement about that direction, creating order out of chaos, instilling confidence and trust in leadership, and offering criteria for success. Through the process of envisioning a better future, leaders provide meaning, forge a connection between themselves and other people in the organization, create a group identity, and trigger the collective imagination that connects people and helps them dream.

In the political domain we often hear visionary statements. John F. Kennedy, for example, set the goal of putting "a man on the moon by the end of the sixties." Mahatma Gandhi wanted to create harmony between Muslims and Hindus. There can be dark visions too, of course. Hitler wanted a Thousand Year Reich, and Slobodan Milosevic (although in prison) probably still dreams of his Greater Serbia.

In the business world, we also hear visionary statements (although they tend not to be quite so dramatic). Ingvar Kamprad, the founder of IKEA, wants to make "affordable furniture for the common man." Bill Gates wants to change the way people work through computer literacy. These visions become a general *leitmotiv* that gives direction to the organization.

Dark visions, like Hitler's Thousand Year Reich, can lead people astray. But so can visions that are far less flawed. It was the vision of Steven Jobs to have an Apple computer in every home. If he'd instead argued for the Apple *operating system* in every home, he could have been a Microsoft. John Akers, former CEO of IBM, thought that the future of computing belonged to the mainframe computer. His resistance to the more agile personal computer cost 70,000 people their jobs. It needed a man like Louis Gerstner to revive the dying giant.

The visioning that needs to take place in organizations isn't like Moses coming down from the mountain and making pronouncements. It's not a one-way street. All the different constituencies of the organization need to be offered the opportunity to give input. Visioning is only a small part of the equation. Speed of execution is the key. As has been said many times, behind every business that's successful is a leader who made a courageous decision.

Effective charismatic leaders not only *involve* large numbers of people in the company; they also *touch* many people. To illustrate this process: Three bricklayers were asked what they were doing. The first one said,

"I'm laying bricks." The second one responded, "I'm working to feed my family." The third one – the one who clearly had a visionary leader – said, "I'm building a cathedral!" If the leader's vision is inspirational, if it speaks to people's imagination, promising an exciting future, then it creates passion and a sense of pride among the people in the organization, pushing them to strive for further success.

Passion and pride is what drives leaders too: Richard Branson argues that whatever an organization undertakes, it should be the best at that enterprise. Jack Welch believes that any organization that isn't number one or number two in its particular business shouldn't be in that business. Larry Ellison of Oracle is after greatest market share. He is looking for people who are committed to that goal. Every senior executive at Goldman Sachs strongly believes that he or she is the best at whatever the individual responsibility is – a belief that's a major driving force at that organization. Being the best at something encourages people – leaders and followers alike – to stretch for even greater accomplishments.

Many senior executives make the mistake of stating the vision of their organization once and leaving it at that. Even if the initial statement is made articulately and with appropriate fanfare, the message needs to be repeated over and over again.

In this context of "being the best," business is rather like a combination of war and sport. Look, for example, at the competition between Pepsi and Coca-Cola, Hertz and Avis, Nike and Adidas, Nokia and Ericsson and Motorola, Goldman Sachs and Morgan Stanley. The competitive language that executives at Coca-Cola use about their rivals at Pepsi is downright intimidating; it's anything but subtle. The leaders in these organizations strive to keep the competitive spirit alive, making work feel like a race that the employees want to win. The battle cry of Canon's leadership was "Beat Xerox!" The president of Lufthansa used to say to his troops, "Fight British Airways!" The people at Honda went to battle saying, "Yamaha *wo tsubusu!*" ("We will crush, squash, and slaughter Yamaha!")

In addition to building a competitive spirit, the envisioning component of charismatic leadership involves shaping and preserving the organization's culture. Leaders are, in effect, the high priests of their organization's culture. As I noted earlier, they need to continually ask themselves the questions, *What does this organization stand for?* and *What* should *it stand for?* They also need to ask questions about the organization's "core ideology" – that is, the central belief that makes the organization different from others and is essential to its success. Because the core

leaders are, in effect, the high priests of their organization's culture

ideology encompasses both the core purpose of the organization and the core values, it touches on basic, implicitly held assumptions that people in the organization cherish. The core ideology is generally expressed explicitly in organizational artifacts, but it's also communicated through corporate practices that say much about quality of life and happiness (Box 10.3).

BOX 10.3

What's your organization's core ideology?

To get a sense of the core ideology that drives your organization, reflect on the following question. Your responses to the question may help you identify what is unique about your organization. Discuss your responses with those of others, looking for similarities and differences.

- Imagine that everyone in your organization is on the *Titanic* when it hits the proverbial iceberg. Your only option for survival is a lifeboat that can hold four people. Which four people would you put in the lifeboat to preserve the DNA of your organization? What qualities do these people represent that would enable them to reconstruct your organization?

The core ideology at Novo Nordisk, one of the world's major insulin producers, is to help diabetes sufferers live a relatively normal life. People who feel comfortable at Novo Nordisk typically have a great sense of social service; they're searching for meaning by helping other people. And that's true not just in the executive suite: people in the factories understand that problems in production can have serious consequences, so they strive for success.

If the core ideology is dear to all employees, not just to those who write the glowing corporate descriptions that grace public relations documents, the company develops an almost cult-like quality. The consensus among many students of organizations is that companies with that quality – that is, with a strong organizational culture (as I mentioned in Chapter 3) – outperform other companies by a huge margin. Strong cultures can be recognized by many different factors that reflect ideological unity, from organizational architecture, to language, to ceremonies, to interpersonal style. As an example, IBM in its glory days had a company song: "We are selling IBM, we are selling IBM. What a glorious feeling, *etc.*"

When the culture is *too* strong, however, a company can become destructively inward looking (as IBM, Philips, and General Motors discovered), forgetting the importance of one critical cultural value: openness toward change. (The discussion of the rise and fall of companies on *Fortune*'s hit parade in Chapter 3 addressed the importance of that value.) Although employees need to share organizational values to create a sense of continuity, at the same time they need to be able to deal with the discontinuities taking place in the environment.

Wal-Mart under Sam Walton pushed the organization's strong culture almost to excess, but, at the time, he managed to pull it off. (His successors are now facing different challenges.) In the mid-1980s Walton would speak to 100,000 of his "associates" (as the employees at Wal-Mart are called) via closed-circuit television: "Now I want you to raise your right hand and repeat after me that at Wal-Mart, a promise we make is a promise we keep – and I want you to repeat after me: From this day forward, I solemnly promise and declare that every time a customer comes within ten feet of me, I will smile, look him in the eye, and greet him. So help me Sam."

I ran a workshop at Sun City in South Africa a number of years ago for a financial services company named Investec. I really enjoyed interacting with the enthusiastic employees of this fairly young, successful company. At one point the executives in the organization made music together – literally, that is. To the outsider, this might have seemed silly. But the executives had fun. My experience with organizations suggests that people who play together – whether it's making music or just being playful on the job – stay together longer, have higher morale, and are more creative.

Herb Kelleher, now non-executive chairman of Southwest Airlines, strongly believes in "management by fooling around." And he's good at it: his antics in empowering and energizing his people and customers have contributed to the airline's success. By hiring people with "the right attitudes" and encouraging playfulness on the job, Kelleher has created a community of people eager to go that extra mile. A strong corporate culture based on shared values has allowed Southwest to substantially outperform many of its competitors. Branson too, in his various companies, looks for people with the right attitudes – people who are combative, fun loving, and entrepreneurial.

EMPOWERING COLLEAGUES AND FOLLOWERS

Another part of the leadership role concerns the execution of a well-articulated vision. The essence of this sub-role is empowerment: leaders must first involve large numbers of employees in the visioning process (as we've seen), thereby ensuring their stake in the vision; then they must transfer to employees the power and authority to make a difference in the organization. Empowerment means that people can do more than simply voice an opinion (although clearly that's important too); it gives a broad range of people the authority to make decisions that matter. Thus decision making needs to be pushed to the lowest level where an informed decision can be made. All people, wherever they are in the hierarchy, need to feel they can make a difference. Where's the fun in being passive recipients of someone else's vision – even if that vision is brilliant?

Empowerment shouldn't be confused with abdication of responsibility, however. Leaders should never attempt to empower people who don't have the necessary competencies or are afraid of decision making. If they do, what results isn't empowerment but anarchy. Empowerment works only when people are acquainted both with the general framework wherein decisions take place and with the details of each fic issue, while anarchy thrives on confusion and misinformation. ose who do best in an environment of empowerment are those who e both decisive – that is, willing to make a decision and stick to it unless circumstances change – and accountable.

As with so many of the challenges we've looked at in these chapters, empowerment is much easier said than done. Part of what makes it so hard is that it requires corporate transparency. In a fully empowered organization, secrecy is minimized so that sensitive information can reach everyone charged with decision making. Executives who see knowledge as power and believe that secrecy gives them an edge don't feel comfortable in that sort of organization.

Experimental studies on power have demonstrated that power is addictive: the more you have, the more you want. But it's also therapeutic. That's the conclusion of a large stress study I was involved in during the early 1970s. Participants who felt that they had control over their life (whether they did or not) had fewer stress symptoms than those who didn't. Thus a wise executive would do well to push power down, in the hope that when people are less stressed they'll work harder. Ironically, the power would eventually return to that executive, assuming that with the extra effort empowered employees contribute, the organization would grow in strength. Unfortunately, the short run usually wins out over the long run, resulting in the following repeated oscillation: a new executive comes in and decentralizes a company that's rather centralized; as empowerment kicks in, he or she gets scared of losing power and goes back to centralization; and then yet another new exec is brought in to fix the problems of overcentralization. Leaders seem to have a terribly hard time accepting the fact that the most powerful people in the world are those who know when to let go of power.

empowerment requires corporate transparency

As noted earlier, empowerment is an issue of ability as well as power. But which employees are equipped for decision making and which aren't? Two social psychologists at Harvard, Robert Rosenthal and Lenore Jacobson, conducted an interesting experiment in the late 1960s. In this landmark experiment, which became known as "Pygmalion in the classroom," researchers selected a group of children at random. Then they went to a number of teachers and reported that they'd selected a group of very special, gifted children. Would the teachers like to work with these children? The answer was yes, of course. And how do you think these children performed? They did extremely well. Performance is all about *stretching* people. The teachers had extremely high expectations of these children and treated them accordingly, demanding that they stretch. Napoleon understood the concept of stretch: he once said that every French soldier had a field marshal's baton in his backpack. People who are effective at empowerment follow the advice of Catherine the Great: "Praise loudly, blame softly."

ENERGIZING SUBORDINATES FOR POSITIVE ACTION

Being an effective leader or follower takes an enormous amount of energy. Energy comes in two primary "flavors": aggressive and affectionate.

Aggressive energy is ever-present. How it's manifested in the workplace depends on the kind of "fantasies" people have about each other. In general, though, it shows up in politicking of one sort or another – turf fights, rumors, back-stabbing, and other negative activities. Effective leaders try to direct that aggressive energy outward, beyond the organization's walls.

Affectionate energy is present only if leaders are successful at cultivating it. Good leaders are *de facto* psychiatric social workers. As I indicated earlier, they're the "containers" of their people's emotions. They provide an effective "holding environment" for all the anxieties that are part and parcel of organizational life. Sometimes people who ask to see their superior on a supposed business matter actually want to talk about something else. Effective leaders recognize the ruse and listen well anyway. Possessing what I earlier described as "the teddy bear factor," these leaders have considerable emotional intelligence; and they use that intelligence to choose employees wisely, build teams effectively, coach learners gently, and negotiate successfully.

Emotional management can also go too far, however, forcing natural emotional expression to assume a pseudo quality. The Disney organization has been called "the smile factory" because of the strict emotional guidelines found in its policy manual. Airlines also have a tendency to engage in excessive emotional management, which can sometimes feel quite artificial. The fact is that no one feels happy all the time. It's one thing to require that customers be treated with respect and professionalism even on a bad day; it's another to require that they receive a broad smile and a particular greeting. People should have the right to be themselves, even at work. Routinely presenting a "false self" comes at a high price – one assessed in depressive symptoms and increments of stress. If an organization strives to hire people with "the right attitudes" – people who fit well psychologically with what the company is trying to accomplish – the false self will have to make an appearance only occasionally.

effective leaders are dreamers, yes, but they're also doers

One of the best ways to energize an organization is through modeling. Effective leaders are dreamers, yes, but they're also doers. They *enact* their dreams. A wit once said that there are three kinds of people in this world: those who make things happen, those who see things happen, and those who wonder what's happened. Effective leaders have the persistence needed to put themselves into that first category. They don't give up until they've reached their goal.

As some of us know from hard experience, those who favor the middle of the road tend to get run over. The graveyards of business are full of people who kept their options open. Success requires hard decisions that lead to concrete action. It's better to light a few fires than complain about the darkness. Real leaders are often rather ordinary people with extraordinary determination.

The architectural role

As noted earlier, the charismatic role has to be combined with the architectural role if leaders are to be effective. One without the other doesn't cut it. All too many leaders have lofty ideas about where their organization should go but pay no attention to the details of the operation.

To bring their vision to life, leaders must adapt the organization's reward and control systems to encourage desired attitudes and behaviors, and they must amend the organizational design to embody the values behind their core ideology. Leaders have to think in these architectural terms (or find someone who can complement their own charismatic skills) as they seek to make their vision a reality. If they can carry out both roles well, there's a good possibility that their organization will be a high-performance winner.

11 The dynamics of succession

If you shoot at a king you must kill him. RALPH WALDO EMERSON

Young men think all old men are fools, but old men know young men are fools. GEORGE CHAPMAN

It's never too late to be what you might have been. GEORGE ELIOT

Some people turn into good wine as they age; others, becoming increasingly sour with each passing year, turn into vinegar. As I've heard it said, some people *immature* with age. Executives as a group have as much trouble (if not more) with the process of aging as does the larger population.

Many centuries ago the following lines were written:

> Midway in our life's journey, I went astray from the straight road and woke to find myself alone in a dark wood. How shall I say what wood that was! I never saw so drear, so rank, so arduous a wilderness! Its very memory gives shape to fear.

If you're familiar with Italian literature, you probably recognize these lines – perhaps the most famous lines in the Italian language – from Dante's *Inferno*. At its most personal level, this portion of the *Divina Commedia* draws on the poet's experience of exile from his native city of Florence. But the narrative is also an allegory that traces Dante's journey from darkness and error to the revelation of the divine light via hell, purgatory, and paradise – his midlife crisis, if you will. Thus the imagery of being alone in a dark wood is completely appropriate.

Dante, despairing, calls for divine help to get out of the wood. An apparition appears: Virgil, the Roman poet, who here represents the epitome of human knowledge. Virgil guides Dante on the first part of his journey, setting him on his way. The good news for Dante is that there *is* a way out of the dark forest. The bad news is that it's through hell! Like Dante, many senior executives find themselves lost and confused, and they see no easy way out.

As an aside, the wood Dante found himself in was populated with three animals. The first one was a lion, symbolizing power and ambition; the second was a panther, symbolizing lust; and the third was a she-wolf, symbolizing greed. Apparently not much has changed since Dante's time, because when I ask my MBA students what they want out of life, they say power, sex, and money, although not necessarily in that order (or in those exact words). Some include a balanced lifestyle in their list, but then most start working for hard-driving consulting firms or investment banks – say, McKinsey, the Boston Consulting Group, Bain, Goldman Sachs, or Morgan Stanley – so I don't give that vote much credence.

people don't usually join the ranks of senior executives until they're middle-aged

People don't usually join the ranks of senior executives until they're middle-aged. And with middle age comes a number of preoccupations apart from career. When we're under 35 we feel immortal; our perception of life is "time-since-birth." This perception starts to change after 35 to "time-left-to-live." We begin to feel that time is running out, and we experience a growing awareness of the inevitability of death. Because of this shift in perspective, we begin to feel an urgency about coming to terms with unresolved dreams and unfulfilled aspirations before it's too late.

Midlife dilemmas

Life at midlife is like a mirror that has three panels – a large central panel, with smaller panels folding out from each side. One side panel shows your children. The second side panel reflects your parents. Your role vis-à-vis your parents is changing now that you're in midlife and they're – well, they're *old*. While you used to be a "player" in the family, dependent on your parents for support and advice, you're now more of a "coach," taking the lead and offering *them* advice. As these parents who once seemed so powerful become increasingly dependent on you, your inner mental map becomes skewed. Looking at them (and feeling uncomfortable with the role reversal), you may wonder, "Will I really become like them in just a couple of decades, increasingly dependent and passive?" You see a caricature of what you fear you may become yourself.

The central panel of the mirror is the most frightening, however. It reflects you, as you are today. And what do you see? Someone who's losing hair or going gray; someone who's got wrinkles, a potbelly, and sagging breasts; someone who needs glasses and has dental problems. Given that decline, it's not surprising that midlife brings an increased preoccupation with body image. Men have concerns over no longer being a Don Giovanni, although they rarely voice such concerns out loud. The sexual prowess of most middle-aged men isn't what it used to be, and that realization causes great narcissistic injury. Women are not spared either: they have to deal with menopause and the realization that their childbearing years are over.

Both men and women often have concerns about the future of their marriage as they enter midlife, especially if they married young. They may feel that the relationship doesn't "click" like it used to, perhaps because the two partners have grown and developed at different speeds. What was good at 20 may no longer be good at 40. Because of a divergence of interests, they may share very few hobbies and activities. If there are still children at home, they may be all that holds a drifting couple together. Teenagers on the brink of moving on sometimes seem to sense their role as marital "glue": they "heroically" turn into "problem children," as if subliminally aware that if they left the house their parents' marriage would fall apart. If the children have already moved on to college or independence, the "empty-nest syndrome" plays an important role in marital equilibrium. With the children out of the house, what's left to talk about? The couple now has to face each other and attempt to communicate about *themselves.*

With middle age, the fear of physical illness grows, and people are more inclined to have hypochrondriacal concerns. As close friends suffer from serious illness or die, people become preoccupied with the question, Who's next? Even as they're plagued by occasional thoughts of a lost youth, their "phantom age" – the age they really feel – begins to catch up to their chronological and physiological age. It gets harder and harder to deny the reflection in the mirror.

Middle age also prompts a reappraisal of career identity, raising concerns about burnout and loss of effectiveness. The career clock and lifeline begin to get out of sync. We all have certain dreams when we start out on our career – organizational goals that we'd like to achieve over the years. Those dreams are delicate flowers that we nurture close to our heart; only to very intimate confidants are we willing to reveal them. As we carry those flowers up the career rungs, we see with increasing clarity that organizations are like upside-down funnels: there's a lot of space at the bottom but not much at the top. Eventually it dawns on us that not all our dreams are going to be reached – not without a miracle. There's no room at the top for them.

Some people who come to this realization – and it's the rare executive who achieves *all* his or her dreams – take out their frustration on other people in the organization. They suffer from generational envy, becoming resentful of the young "upstarts." They send promising subordinates to the organizational equivalent of Siberia or fire them for supposed incompetence – a "murder" if ever there was one – and then rationalize that fate so effectively that they think they're doing both organization and subordinates a favor. Still licking their lips, they speak with pride of being a "learning organization" and boast of creating leadership possibilities throughout the organization to develop young executives.

far too many executives are reluctant to engage in leadership development

Far too many executives are reluctant to engage in leadership development. Putting their interests far above the interests of others, they spurn good corporate citizenship and use young people only as extensions of themselves. As long as the young people are willing to accept that role, all is well. When they want to go their own way, however, envy strikes. This "desertion" is not taken lightly by executives who (having themselves had fantasies of overthrow – and more – when they were young) fear that the young people may try to depose them.

The life-cycle of a CEO

The word *life-cycle* is often used to describe the various developmental stages of an organism, whether plant, animal, or person. It can also be used to describe the tenure of a CEO. The life-cycle of a CEO generally has three stages: entry, consolidation, and decline. Although in the following discussion I focus on the CEO – because he or she is usually the most visible person in the organization – many of my observations are also relevant to senior executives put into a new position. For that reason, many executives who haven't yet reached a top-level position would do well to heed the cautionary notes made in this chapter. To be assigned to a senior leadership position comes with many traps attached.

Stage 1: Entry

The hiring organization's board of directors (or supervisory board) plays a critical role in the entry stage, orchestrating the hiring and acculturation of a new CEO. The board has to decide what kind of executive would be most effective at leading the organization into the future – a decision that rests on where the company is and where it hopes to go. The general rule in succession is that if you want *evolution*, you promote an insider; if you want *revolution*, you choose an outsider (preferably someone who's well acquainted with the industry in which the company operates).

One of the first things newly appointed leaders discover is that reaching the top of the organization changes a person's perspective on career. Once a person becomes head honcho, there are no obvious new positions to strive for (portfolio careers notwithstanding). It's success or failure; there are no other options. Several of the executives I've interviewed have said, in effect, "I've finally arrived, and now I'm in for the end game." This can create a powerful set of anxieties, particularly about being alone and (although few admit it) about whether they'll be able to handle the job. It also inspires fantasies about what kind of "monument" they want to create during their time in power to remind others of their tenure.

Although such doubts are frequently put to one side as the many pressures and diversions of the job take hold, other psychological forces are brought to bear. For example, incoming CEOs need to be aware that outgoing leaders are often overprotective of their legacy. For outgoing CEOs, relinquishing power may seem like a death sentence – one that only a favorable legacy can commute. Not surprisingly, then, retiring CEOs worry that their successor (especially if he or she is energetic) may disrespect their legacy and destroy their work. To avoid that result, they may (either unconsciously or not) work to ensure that their successor fails. The risk of such sabotage is heightened if, as is often the case, the retiring CEO stays on the board.

Another problem the newcomer may have to deal with is "romancing the past." All humans have a tendency to screen themselves from painful memories. Particularly in situations of stress, people struggle between the defensive process of denial and the force of memory. As in Daphne du Maurier's novel *Rebecca*, where the glorified memory of the previous wife hovers like a ghost around the new wife and everyone she deals with, new leaders may be haunted by idealized (and thus inaccurate) memories of their predecessor.

Newcomers also have to deal with unrealistic expectations. New leaders (especially those who come from outside the firm) are often seen as saviors who will quickly solve all the company's problems and make everything right. The more unhappy people have been with the previous regime, the higher the expectations of the newcomer are. But because such expectations are usually unrealistic, infatuation born of idealization soon turns into disillusionment born of disappointment. The temporary "messiah" quickly falls from the pedestal. In addition, "wounded princes" – leaders who were passed over in making the new appointment – may act out their revenge by orchestrating this change of mood, helping to ensure that the messiah becomes a scapegoat.

No two ways about it, the entry stage is fraught with anxiety. Not only are new CEOs fearful that they may not live up to the expectations just described, they're also bewildered, either a little or a lot, by the demands of the new role. CEOs who come from the outside have to learn quickly the formal and informal ways in which the company functions. They have to understand the principal forces that drive the organization. But there's no quiet hiatus for learning. From the very first day on the job, there's a lot of pressure to take action – *any* action. Furthermore, people want answers to their questions about the future. Even as new CEOs – again, especially those from outside – are attempting to grasp the "vision thing" in the organization, people are asking, What's your vision of the future? What are the kinds of performance criteria that need to be met under your leadership? What do you plan to change first?

what new CEOs coming from outside need to do first is listen, and then listen some more

Despite demands for action and clarification, what new CEOs coming from outside need to do first is listen, and then listen some more. An understanding of how the organization functions – and where they themselves can best add value – is critical. This understanding can be gained only by listening to *all* the stakeholders that make up the organization. Leaders who succumb to pressure to take action before the listening has been completed – that is, who fall into the "action trap" – all but guarantee that they'll have to reverse themselves later.

New CEOs have to identify the key players who will help them in the process of making their tenure a success. Although those who come as outsiders may bring some people with them into the organization, those colleagues shouldn't be the only ones put into key positions. Morale problems will be inevitable unless insiders are chosen for the second tier. Many CEOs assume that this means wooing the "wounded princes" – buying them off, as it were, with visible, responsible positions. But most CEOs who have gone that route say, in retrospect, that they should have "killed" the wounded princes much earlier. By bending over backward trying to get these people on their team – so says hindsight – they wasted precious time and energy that would better have been spent getting the company into shape.

The entry stage, with its many unknowns, is often characterized by experimentation. CEOs are usually chosen on the basis of a particular skill that the company needs at a given point in time – perhaps a skill in human resources, global strategy, finance, or turnaround. As new CEOs work to manage the "assignment" given to them by the board, they become very involved in the new challenge and feel fully alive, tackling and mastering a lot of new things. It's a time of intense work concentration, a period of great excitement.

In the process, new leaders search, either consciously or unconsciously, for business themes that match their inner theater. In other words, they look for a fit between their personal style and a strategy that suits the business environment in which they find themselves. They externalize their dreams and preoccupations in an organizational setting. Once they've found a congruent theme, the second stage can start.

Stage 2: Consolidation

As new CEOs start to produce results and corporate performance improves, they finally gain a strong sense of control. This is the hallmark of the consolidation stage. With a secure power base, the support of the board, the commitment of the management team, and a network of effective alliances, CEOs find themselves increasingly in a position to realize their dreams. Eventually – unless they're able to reinvent themselves – their performance peaks and they enter a plateau. This is a period that may last a good number of years.

But as elsewhere, success can carry within it the seeds of disaster. As time goes on, one dominant theme may emerge for the CEO – a theme that, because it reflects a deep-seated wish, may become a preoccupation. The danger (as we saw in the case of Kenneth Olson of DEC, cited in Chapter 3) is that when that central theme ceases to be in congruence with the organization's environment, rigidity sets in and the CEO becomes blind to the perspectives of others. As the saying goes, "When your mind is a hammer, you see only nails." If leaders don't reinvent themselves, they may lead the organization down the drain.

Stage 3: Decline

This brings us to the decline stage. Several characteristics mark the onset of decline in a CEO:

- ❖ executive myopia and arrogance
- ❖ an assumption that momentum equals leadership
- ❖ a refusal to listen to new ideas
- ❖ an internal focus at the expense of outside constituencies
- ❖ a lack of challenge to existing paradigms
- ❖ a growing, centralizing bureaucracy
- ❖ a lack of urgency to get things done, to change things
- ❖ repetitive reference to the overriding preoccupation
- ❖ waning excitement
- ❖ falling performance
- ❖ increasing cash reserves.

Earlier (Chapter 6) the first Henry Ford was cited as a good example of leadership in decline. For 19 years, from 1908 to 1927, Ford resisted any changes to the Model T. Indeed, when shown a slightly modified model by his engineers, he personally kicked it to bits in front of them. His preoccupying obsession was to produce a cheap car to help the farmer. (It's no surprise to learn that his father, with whom he had an ambivalent relationship, was a farmer.) Ford's view of the farmer's needs – "to get the farmer out of every hole" – became the oft-repeated theme in his internal theater. In spite of changes taking place in the business environment – such as new demands by consumers (who wanted greater choice and annual model changes) and an increase in competition – he refused to make any adaptations.

CEOs who get stuck and rely exclusively on a one-track, repeated formula block off new developments from within and "new blood" from outside. They stick with the same tired old group of senior executives, all of whom are committed (in word if not in concept) to the particular orientation of the leader. Having run out of ideas themselves (and being unwilling to hear the ideas of others), these declining CEOs hoard corporate cash rather than invest in innovation.

This third stage, if allowed to run unchecked, can have a devastating effect on the business, resulting in morbidity if not actual bankruptcy. As CEOs either pursue an outdated theme rigidly or seek their stimulation elsewhere – for example, in company perks (such as a corporate jet or exotic travel), in the thrill of chasing down mergers and acquisitions, or in charity, social, or public-sector work – only an ability to successfully engage in strategic innovation can save the organization. Whatever the particular **when the succession process is complete, the CEO life-cycle starts again** shape of an executive's decline, the board must step in and execute the review function properly. This isn't easy for people who have worked closely with the CEO, often over many years.

How traumatic the succession process is for the outgoing CEO and the organization depends on many things (including individual personalities and overall market conditions). Generally, however, a succession that's *planned for* can be carried out smoothly. An overlap between the old and the new leadership often smoothes the transition, although some CEOs find it too painful to work with their chosen successor during the handover period, given the deep loss the successor represents.

When the succession process is complete, the CEO life-cycle starts again.

Generational envy

When I ask CEOs how long top executives in general should stay in the job, the usual answer is seven years (give or take two). When it comes to their own individual careers, however, many CEOs would like to stay longer. As a matter of fact, a large percentage of senior executives don't want to retire at all. Some have to be symbolically carried out in a coffin, as was the case with the late Armand Hammer of Occidental Petroleum. In fact, it's estimated that 16 percent of CEOs *want* to go out that way. (Ironically, however, with the increasing pressure for shareholder value, the average lifespan of the CEO is rapidly diminishing and becoming too short to have any impact).

The process of handing over the baton isn't easy for most executives. The many conscious and unconscious forces that come into play conspire to make it extremely stressful. But because CEOs tend to be fairly close-lipped about their fears and feelings, top-management succession is shrouded in mystery. We have to read between the lines of the *Wall Street Journal*, *Fortune*, or the *Financial Times* to get an inkling of the difficulties inherent in the succession process.

Acknowledging the impending loss of power that stepping down will bring threatens the deep-seated wish we all have to believe in our own immortality. Let's face it: succession arouses basic fears of death. Many CEOs avoid thinking about succession for that reason, and loyal colleagues are wary of raising the subject lest it seem that they wish to hasten the CEO's demise. As a result of this two-pronged avoidance, many CEOs stay on far too long, fine-tuning the legacy they hope to leave. Other CEOs postpone leaving office because they fear the anger and disappointment of those colleagues who are passed over for promotion.

Sometimes CEOs, generally with the complicity of the board, postpone the inevitable through the ruse of a selection committee. They search and search for the perfect successor, only to conclude that no one inside or outside the company – with the exception of the present CEO, of course – possesses the required qualifications. Not surprisingly, the reigning leader's tenure is prolonged. Ironically, although 30 percent of senior executives don't plan for succession at all, those who plan most extensively, drafting convoluted, complicated plans for succession, are often the most reluctant to go.

Many senior executives have a hard time dealing with their successor, even if they themselves have named the "crown prince." A major reason is that CEOs are, almost by definition, masters at power calculation; power is an important property to them, and they know how to acquire and manipulate it. Appointing a successor changes the power equation. Power starts to flow away to the new candidate as soon as that person has been named, and CEOs experience subtle changes in power relationship patterns almost immediately. Loyalties quickly shift; relationships realign; new power structures begin to emerge. I've often said, tongue in cheek, that the major task a CEO faces is finding his likely successor and killing the bastard. Unfortunately, clinging to power through the derailment of that successor usually has disastrous effects on the organization.

It's not unknown for a CEO to change his or her mind and decide to stay on even after a successor has been chosen. As noted earlier, retiring CEOs are generally highly sensitized to shifts in power, and some simply can't face the reality of losing power. There are many examples of this in business history, especially in family business situations. Think about the first Henry Ford and his son Edsel. Almost every single recommendation Edsel put forward to change the way the company was run was vetoed by his father. Some people have suggested that Henry's inflexibility contributed to the cancerous stomach ulcer that did the younger man in. At Edsel's funeral, his widow ran up to old Henry and said, "You killed my husband."

The statistics regarding the survival of family firms are abominable. Many of the problems with which these firms struggle have to do with succession. One out of three family firms makes it to the second generation; only one out of ten makes it to the third. Rags to rags in three generations, I've heard it said.

Male entrepreneurs have an especially hard time dealing with their grown sons. (Daughters do much better – but that's a whole other story.) They have a tendency to "castrate" their oldest – that is, to put them down at every opportunity. The earlier mentioned Edsel Ford was a victim of this behavior pattern. Grown sons involved in a family business are always a symbolic (and sometimes a real) threat to an executive's power base. Thus CEOs fear (sometimes correctly) that their sons want to overthrow them. It's no accident that parricide has been a popular topic in literature.

But family-controlled enterprises aren't the only places where we encounter great succession dramas. Publicly owned companies, while not as susceptible, are nonetheless open to similar developments. For example, take the late William Paley of CBS, the man with "the roving eyes and roving hands," who (in spite of the fact that he was losing touch with the business because of his womanizing and other ventures) kept on firing his successors. The late Peter Grace of W.C. Grace is another notorious example. He "killed" his successor from his own deathbed, firing the younger man on the grounds of a trumped-up charge of sexual harassment.

The acid test of excellent leadership is what happens when the leader is no longer there. How seamless is the succession? Does the process occur without too much drama? Is the company still performing successfully after the old CEO is gone? Maybe you should ask yourself and the other execu-

it's no accident that parricide has been a popular topic in literature

tives in your company the following question: *Should you be hit by a bus while crossing the street, do you have a successor in place?* If not, give some thought to Charles de Gaulle's comment that the graveyards of the world are full of indispensable men. If, after reflection, you really believe that you're indispensable, put your finger into a glass of water, withdraw it, and note the hole that you've left.

Recognizing that no one is indispensable, CEOs should work to manage succession; but understanding that succession issues are heavily weighted with unconscious baggage, they should share all succession-related decision making. As noted earlier, board members need to be deeply involved in the succession process, looking regularly

---

BOX 11.1

How well is your organization dealing with succession?

As either a top executive or a member of the board of your company, respond with YES or NO to the following statements.

YES NO

1 The CEO and board members discuss at least twice a year who would take over in case of an unforeseen succession crisis
2 Members of the board are deeply involved in the succession process
3 Members of the board periodically review internal candidates against comparable outsiders
4 All potential candidates meet regularly with board members
5 Promising candidates get board assignments to give them exposure
6 CEO compensation is tied to development and succession planning
7 The CEO nurtures a succession culture whereby promising candidates are given jobs that stretch them

The more statements you've answered in the affirmative, the more prepared your company is for succession.

---

at potential internal and outside candidates and creating a reward system that encourages CEOs to both attend to the succession question and develop capable people internally (Box 11.1).

Companies that last – companies such as Nokia, BP, and General Electric – are far more likely to have succession plans in place than are their less successful counterparts. These organizations spend a substantial amount of their resources on executive development, and they do so in a consistent manner. They don't cut back on developmental activities the moment there are financial difficulties, for example. On the

companies that last are far more likely to have succession plans in place

contrary, they see such difficulties as reason for increasing the investment in development.

12 Leadership development

All who have meditated on the art of governing mankind have been convinced that the fate of empires depends on the education of youth. ARISTOTLE

Leadership and learning are indispensable to each other.
JOHN F. KENNEDY

The only real training for leadership is leadership. ANTONY JAY

A boy came home from school with a terrible grade report, so the story goes. For a couple of days he hid it from his father, but needing a parent's signature, he finally gathered all his courage and shared the report card. When his father saw the poor grades, he berated his son for his dismal record. When he was done ranting, his son asked him, "Father, do you think I did so poorly because of nature or nurture?" In another version of the story, the boy's father mentions a neighbor boy who lives a few houses away. "He doesn't get C's and D's, does he?" says the father. "No," the son admits. "But it's different with him. He has very bright parents."

I'm often asked whether leaders are made or born. When I turn the question back to those who asked, I get a wide range of responses. If the conversation takes place in a group setting, often a passionate discussion follows, with advocates of both camps making compelling arguments. The nature advocates point to prominent families who have produced a succession of leaders. For their part, the nurture advocates put forth examples such as the Dalai Lama. The basic developmental material in that example is a young boy who, because he recognizes clothing and other paraphernalia of his deceased predecessor, is whisked off to Potala Palace in Lhasa, where he's educated widely. Fifty years later he wins the Nobel Prize for Peace and is known as a leader of his people.

As with many traits, leadership is probably a combination of both factors. Although some twin studies suggest that the mixture is 60 percent nature, 40 percent nurture, the precise combination isn't especially important for people in the leadership selection business. What matters is the selection process itself. Most of the nurture that's going to happen in regard to leadership has already happened by the time people choose their career track; much of their personality development has already largely taken place. Thus an organization looking for "high potentials" (as future leaders are often called) would do well to start off *picking* the right person, not *developing someone into* the right person.

Selection problems

Ray Kroc, the founder of McDonald's, used to say, "You're only as good as the people you hire." Theodore Roosevelt once said, "The best executive is the one who has sense enough to pick good men to do what he wants done, and self-restraint enough to keep from meddling with them while they do it." It sounds as if the best way to prove that you're smarter than those you hire is to hire people who are smarter than you! As the saying goes: "First-class people hire first-class people. Second-class people hire third-class people."

But it's just plain hard to assess ability (whether leadership or otherwise) on the basis of scant information and brief acquaintance. When actor and dancer Fred Astaire did a Hollywood screen test early in his career, the report came back saying, "Can't act. Slightly bald. Can dance a little." When Jacques Chirac, the French president, met with Saddam Hussein in 1975, he said, "You are my personal friend . . . You are assured of my respect, my consideration and my affection." As both these examples show, we sometimes go wildly awry in assessing people. And if it's a CEO or other top executive we're selecting, we may be forced to live with a poor choice for a number of years and through a number of costly failures (Box 12.1).

BOX 12.1

Which criteria really matter?

Let's say it's time to elect a new world leader. Here are some facts about the three leading candidates

Candidate A associates with crooked politicians and consults with astrologers. He's had two mistresses. He chain-smokes and drinks eight to ten martinis a day.

Candidate B was kicked out of college twice, used opium as an undergraduate, now sleeps until noon, and drinks a quart of whiskey every evening.

Candidate C is a decorated war hero. He's a vegetarian, doesn't smoke, drinks only an occasional beer, and hasn't had any extramarital affairs.

Whom did you choose? If you opted for C, you may be surprised at what you get:

Candidate A is Franklin D. Roosevelt
Candidate B is Winston Churchill
Candidate C is Adolf Hitler

If we agree that the challenge is selecting the best people, the question becomes, What methods and criteria should we use? There are quite a few possibilities. First off, we can ask candidates about their leadership ability. That's an iffy approach, however. When I ask executives how they compare with others in the area of leadership, 75 percent rank themselves in the top 25 percent. So we have to question the reliability of self-reports. The judgment of family members and friends is equally unreliable. Especially in family firms, a formalized assessment of leadership potential is sometimes abandoned in favor of nepotism, often with very negative results.

Testing of one sort or another is another possibility. Psychological tests are helpful when it comes to revealing gross psychopathology, but they're not much good at assessing leadership ability. Directed testing may help tease out people for specialized professions, such as sales or marketing, but like psychological tests they don't read leadership well. The same can be said of the so-called tournament model, often used in France and Japan. Although the competitive judgment procedures which that model uses (the passing of professional exams, graduation from high-ranking programs or schools, and other assessments) can target high achievers, they're not predictive of leadership potential.

The best indicator of leadership ability (and predictor of leadership potential) is a person's track record. Unfortunately, an unedited record is hard to come by. Previous employers tend to modify the truth somewhat if the record is flawed, in part because of legal concerns and in part because they don't want to stab an ex-employee in the back. So somehow a candidate's true track record has to be ferreted out. Assessment centers have some value in this regard. They're helpful at separating the stars from the drones. They also help candidate assessors think about the kind of competencies that they're looking for in their organization.

these two factors together – track record and competencies needed – are as close to a magic formula as you'll get in the selection process

These two factors together – track record and competencies needed – are as close to a magic formula as you'll get in the selection process. If an organization looks to its vision of the future and determines which leadership competencies are needed to make that vision a reality, and then looks to its candidates and determines whose track record reveals those competencies, chances of a positive selection are high indeed.

What makes careful selection so important is that poor selection can be very costly. The figures vary, but estimates suggest that about 40 percent of new hires fail within the first 18 months. (One of the main reasons given for failure is the inability to build good relationships with peers and subordinates.)

The visible costs of selection are bad enough if an organization has to pay them repeatedly in a trial-and-error process of finding a good executive. (They run at about two to three times a person's annual salary.) But those visible costs are only the 10–15 percent tip of the iceberg. Add to them the additional hidden costs related to poor business decisions and opportunities lost due to ineffective leadership, and you've got a whopping price tag. The message of all this is that a new recruit's entry into an organization should be a great experience. It is a period in the development of the person that requires great attention. This also implies the presence of a sense of mutuality and alignment of vision and objectives.

Developmental tasks

After good candidates have been selected, what kind of developmental experiences are needed to make newly hired leaders successful? What key learning experiences are required? From my observation of and dealings with a great many companies, I've isolated several factors.

Broad exposure to different functions in the company early in the future leader's career

Not only does such exposure impart knowledge about the kinds of products and services the company has to offer, it also prevents manifestation of the us-versus-them syndrome, averts parochialism, and leads to a wider perspective on the company. All too often people at head office blame employees at the operating companies for stupidities, and vice versa. That blaming mentality sets the stage for fiefdoms and leads to the creation of organizational "silos."

Personal experiences that lead to greater sensitivity to customers and the competition

Although all the organizational functions are important, effective leadership requires special skills in the area of customer and competitor understanding. Standout leaders such as Richard Branson and Jack

Welch have always been very close to their customers, and they carefully monitor their competitors. These factors help to explain the success of their leadership styles. Thus organizations that want to "grow" effective leaders need to make sure that young candidates spend time working with good people in customer service and market analysis functions. Great companies continually invest in the development of their people.

Going to Timbuktu

When I ask people what made them a leader, many say something like, "When I was in my mid-twenties, my boss sent me to Timbuktu to set up a new sales office. Was I scared? Yes. Did I make mistakes? You bet! But let me tell you, I sure did learn!" Unfortunately, far too many companies fail to give their young employees early project responsibility and don't allow them to make mistakes. Instead, they waste these young people's time by putting them in irrelevant staff positions. They don't create meaningful jobs for them, or give them profit-and-loss responsibility and allow them to take risks. Giving young people autonomy and rewarding initiatives is essential.

It's simply not possible to learn leadership without making mistakes, and mistakes tend to be much cheaper when people make them young. There's a famous anecdote involving Thomas Watson Sr. of IBM, one of whose young executives once made a multi-million-dollar mistake. That was a lot of money in the 1950s. It's still a lot of money. After the mistake was discovered, the young man was called to Watson's office, where he nervously blurted out, "I guess . . . I guess you're going to fire me." To which Watson responded, "Fire you? *Fire* you? After all the money I spent on your education?" Mistakes that are handled well are a bridge between inexperience and wisdom. Failure teaches success. Success doesn't mean never making mistakes – it means never making the same mistake twice.

Positive mentoring from an effective leader

Another important factor in the development of leadership is mentoring. People learn the organizational "ropes" from mentors. Mentors help those under their wing understand the political systems in an organization, for example, and they often recognize serious mistakes in the offing and prevent them.

Even more important, mentors can teach through *constructive feedback*. An organization-wide culture of performance feedback is critical if a company is determined to develop its people well. Great companies coach and reward to maintain commitment. The leadership recognizes results. Unfortunately, many executives aren't terribly adept at giving constructive comments; they give feedback only by exception, perhaps not realizing the impact that constructive feedback can have. Offering suggestions for improvement and praise or thanks for a job well done can be extremely effective.

Most executives aren't very good at celebrating achievements, though celebrations are excellent development tools. As a wit once said, "Doing a good job here is like wetting your pants in a dark suit. It gives you a warm feeling but nobody notices!

Celebrations can be financial (in the form of stock options, bonuses, or profit sharing), but they need not be. They can be as simple as singling people out for a prize, putting people in the spotlight with the CEO, creating a "hall of fame," giving greater budgetary discretion, presenting tickets to sports or musical events, granting perks (club memberships, etc.), or offering coupons (which can be redeemed by exemplary "corporate citizens" for anything from an extra day off to additional financial rewards). Because a culture of constructive feedback starts from the top of the organization, constructive feedback needs to be strongly encouraged by its leadership. Executives need to ask themselves regularly how many smiles they've given that day.

Maintaining the balance between personal and public life

As I indicated in Chapter 5, if the balance between personal and public life becomes skewed, stress symptoms almost inevitably result. Furthermore, a diet of only work, with no diversions, stifles an enriched, creative life. Certain moments in private life won't come twice. Your children are young only once, for example. And real quality time with children and spouse won't be possible later in life if your loved ones have become alienated by your continued absence.

While it's clear that maintaining balance affects one's personal life, there are workplace ramifications as well. Personal time well spent has an important revitalizing function. People who allow themselves time for renewal and reflection outside the office make better decisions at work, deal more comfortably with their colleagues, and adapt better to office stress and fluctuation.

Because life shouldn't be what happens when we're busy doing other things, organizational leadership needs to encourage people to maintain the necessary balance. However, left to their own devices, too many top executives focus exclusively on their "magnificent obsession" – meaning their role in their organization – and thereby set up the expectation that subordinates should do the same. These executives may not even be aware of the imbalance. If they're asked about the amount of time they spend with their family, they may mention a far greater number of hours than would their spouse and children. In many cases, they're taking refuge in what psychotherapists call the "manic defense" (meaning running all the time to avoid true engagement).

A strong dose of emotional intelligence

Without the self-awareness that emotional intelligence brings, it's very difficult to manage other people. In the process of self-discovery, future leaders need to find out what creates a sense of "flow" for them. They have to ask themselves under what circumstances they're happiest, they feel at their best. They need to develop an awareness of others as well.

The "teddy bear factor" discussed in Chapter 10 – an *other*-awareness for which *self*-awareness is a prerequisite – is of great value in getting the best out of people.

As part of the crucial process of self-discovery, executives need to explore their strengths and weaknesses. They need to discover both where they add value and where their talents leave something to be desired. They can then either work on their weaknesses or search out others who can help them compensate for these weaknesses. Some executives have special competencies in technology, finance, or marketing, for example. Others are great vision-aries, having the ability to provide strategic insights. Still others fulfill a maintenance role, serving as the guardians of the company's culture. Some are good in execution, being particularly effective in an operations role. Those who are hired to come in and play a turnaround role often have exceptional transformational competencies. Some have specific human resource capabilities, motivating well and communicating clearly. Others have an innovative way of looking at the world. In leadership situations, it's important to create an "executive role constellation" that brings together all these competencies in a well-balanced group, enabling the executive team as an entity to tackle the challenges ahead. In general – and that can make executive role constellations so powerful – it is advisable to build on our strengths rather than find ways to deal with our weaknesses. Usually, the former comes with a greater payoff (Box 12.2).

executives need to explore their strengths and weaknesses

Good examples of effective role constellations are seen in the teams created by Richard Branson during different stages of his career. Branson's original claim to fame was the music business. However, as he willingly acknowledges, he's tone deaf. He compensated for this weakness by hiring a distant relative, Simon Draper, nicknamed "the man with the golden ears." It was Draper who picked Branson's winners in the record business. Reading balance sheets and looking at cash flows isn't one of Branson's strengths either. He found another formidable executive, Don Cruickshank, a Scottish accountant from McKinsey with an MBA. Cruickshank provided the systems that were

---

BOX 12.2

Where do you add value to your organization?

Check TRUE or FALSE as applicable. Compare notes with people who are familiar with your capabilities.

TRUE   FALSE

- My core competency is in a special functional area such as marketing/finance/operations management/information technology
- My core competency is as provider of strategic insights
- My core competency is in motivating people
- My core competency is as guardian of the corporate culture
- My core competency is as a change agent
- My core competency lies in the area of innovation
- My core competency is in execution and follow-up

Your responses to this quiz will indicate where you add value. Although each competency is important to the organization's well-being, the weighting of importance may differ depending on the organizational life-cycle. Your challenge is to find people whose core competencies are complementary, both to each other and to the situation your organization finds itself in.

needed in the company, which until he arrived had been run in a rather cavalier manner. This stellar executive role constellation was headed by Branson, who provided the vision, the inspiration, the energy, and the motivation.

Leadership in the "digital age"

Assuming that high potentials have taken on and succeeded at these developmental challenges, what will they – the leaders of the future – look like (Box 12.3)?

BOX 12.3

Are you ready for leadership in the "digital age"?

Answer the following questions YES or NO.

YES   NO

- Do you set your own goals when possible?
- Are you self-critical about your performance?
- Can you present complex issues to others in a clear and simplified way?
- Do you have a "helicopter view" – that is, can you see the forest and not just the trees?
- Are you comfortable with people from other cultures?
- Do you make an effort to understand the cultural specifics of people of other nationalities?
- Do you consider yourself to be action oriented?
- Can you put on a good "show" to create commitment to a plan of action?
- Do you enjoy mentoring younger people?
- Are you proud when you see executives whom you trained doing well?
- Are you at ease in team situations?
- Do you look for variety when creating a team?
- Do you enjoy working in multicultural teams?
- Do you feel that you bring out the best in each member of your team?
- Do you care about your employees when they have personal problems?
- Do you lead by example?
- Are you convincing when you make presentations?
- Do you share information freely?
- Do you inspire trust in people?
- Do you believe that people make an extra effort when working with you?
- Do people open up when they talk to you?
- Can you give frank, constructive feedback up front?

If you answered YES to most of these questions, then you're likely to be more effective in a global leadership position. As a check, compare your responses with those of other people who know you quite well.

Among the traits that characterize a charismatic, transformational leader at ease in the global context is *self-management*. Leaders need to be able to set their own standards and rewards, to engage in personal goal setting without prompting. Leaders with that ability are typically eager to learn and quick to adapt. They know how to reward themselves, but they're also their own worst judge. Organizations in search of leadership can single out such individuals by asking candidates about the things they did in their formative years. Because self-managers have "fire in their belly," those activities (whether scholastic, extracurricular, or professional) are sure to include great challenges.

Effective leaders in the digital age know how to *manage cognitive complexity*. This isn't a learned skill generally; it's a cognitive skill that people either possess by adulthood or don't ever have. Related to both forward thinking and reducing noise in the system, this skill is sometimes described as the "helicopter view" – that is, the ability to see the forest despite the trees. People with this skill quickly grasp the essence of a complex idea and can then simplify it for others. To test yourself on this skill, ask yourself whether you can take complex concepts and explain them to a child.

As noted earlier, *a sense of cultural relativity* is also necessary to effective leadership today. Ethnocentricity has no role anywhere in this world – but especially not in global organizations. Neither does navel gazing. Today's leaders need to be reflective, yes, but they also need an *action orientation*. Implementation and process abilities are thus critical. True leaders, wanting to get things done, put great emphasis on execution.

ethnocentricity has no role anywhere in this world

The criteria for leadership in the digital age include *generativity*. That's a concept introduced by the human development specialist Erik Erikson. It means to care, getting pleasure out of dealing with the next generation, mentoring well and with enjoyment. It's important that future leaders do not behave like the mythical Cronos, eating their own children. In the modern organization, leaders need to spend a lot of time on coaching their people. Any firm that wants to be a learning organization needs to have many mentors around to safeguard the transitional world of young executives – particularly those who find themselves with new responsibilities. Mentors provide the space and safety for personal exploration.

How can an organization test a candidate's potential for generativity? The answer is surprisingly simple. If there are children in the picture, the acid test often is whether the candidate is a good parent. Research suggests that good parents at home tend to become good "parents" outside the home. Conversely, executives who are extremely impatient with their employees are most likely impatient with their children as well. I've known some executives involved in the hiring process to invite a candidate with family in tow for a weekend away, to observe how the family members interact.

Team-building skills are also crucial. Many executives I know are excellent team *leaders* but very poor team *players*. Excellent team builders – individuals who are able to get the best out of others – are both players and leaders. They're also able to work well with diversity.

the effective global leader in the digital age is able to inspire *trust* in subordinates

The most creative forms of decision making take place in teams characterized by cultural, gender, and task diversity. Decision making may take longer in diverse groups than in homogeneous ones, but the quality of the outcome is much greater. (Remember that when everyone thinks alike, not many people are really thinking.)

Impression management is also an important skill. Good leaders have a little bit of the actor and storyteller in them, enabling them to convince many different constituencies of the wisdom of their vision and values. An essential part of this skill is the ability to positively reframe difficult situations. Believe it or not, lessons at acting school are often a good investment. Putting yourself on video and "reviewing" the "performance" with the help of others such as a coach can be very enlightening. Effective leaders use any means at their disposal to improve their communication skills.

Task-relevant knowledge is also essential. If you're in the automobile business, it's important that you like cars. If you work in the electronics industry, it helps if you know something about electronics. In this age of omnipotent financial executives, this point is sometimes forgotten.

And last but not least, the effective global leader in the digital age is able to inspire *trust* in subordinates and maintain that trust as vision becomes implementation. The need to inspire trust, and the desire to be worthy of trust, should be continually on executives' minds. Without trust, many of the other necessary qualities are useless. As mentioned before, the success of a leader is closely related to the degree that other people trust him or her (Box 12.4). (For a summary of leadership qualities in the digital age, with traits, roles, and practices interwoven, see Figure 12.1.)

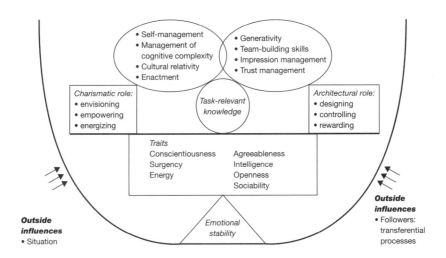

Figure 12.1 Leadership in the digital age

Any organization that promotes and nurtures the characteristics for effective leadership described in this chapter is well on its way toward success. The final challenge we face in this book is to identify what makes not just successful *leaders* but successful *organizations*. What can be said about the kinds of organizations that are emerging in this age of discontinuity? What are some of the characteristics that differentiate these organizations? And most important, what steps do leaders need to take to create such organizations?

BOX 12.4

Are you ready for action?

Based on what you've learned in this chapter (and in earlier chapters), you're now in a
position to identify the competencies and other qualities needed for effective
leadership in your organization, given your organization's specific strategic direction.
Make a list of the competencies your organization needs, those you possess, and
those you lack; then line out a development plan that fleshes out your competencies.

Leadership action plan

Required leadership competencies	Competencies I possess	Competencies I need to work on	Developmental plan
1			
2			
3			
4			
5			
6			

13 Best places to work
Authentizotic organizations

> *With regard to excellence, it is not enough to know, but we must try to have and use it.* ARISTOTLE

> *Keep your eyes on the stars and your feet on the ground.*
> THEODORE ROOSEVELT

> *Integrity begins with a person being willing to be honest with himself.* CORT FLINT

When we look at the first decade of this new millennium, we see many disquieting themes in the world of work. Prime among them is stress in the workplace. Statistics about illness, underperformance, and absenteeism tell a dramatic tale of on-the-job dysfunctionality, from the CEO to the mail clerk. In many organizations, the balance between work life and private life is tilted so far toward work that there *is* no private life. Horror stories abound about work overload, conflicting job demands, poor communication, lack of opportunities for career advancement, inequities in performance evaluation and pay, restrictions on behavior, and excessive travel – all of these leading to depressive reactions, physical symptoms, alcoholism, drug abuse, and sleep disorders.

Work doesn't *need* to be stressful, however. On the contrary, work can be an anchor of psychological well-being, a means of establishing identity and maintaining self-esteem. Sigmund Freud's dictum that mental health consists of *Liebe und Arbeit* (love and work) retains a ring of truth. But if *healthy* work is to happen, organizations need to be invested with psychological meaning. When they are, accomplishing something tangible on the job can give workers a dose of stability in a highly unstable, unpredictable world.

Given the importance of individual psychological well-being for organizational functioning, effective, responsible leadership is a major dimension in the workplace health equation. Leaders have the responsibility to create workplaces that are healthy – that allow people to "feel good in their skin" and that contribute to and reinforce adaptive functioning.

The best companies to work for

In addition to the list of strongest U.S. companies that *Fortune* puts out annually, the magazine has published a list of the "best companies to work for." In a recent *Fortune* article entitled "The 100 best companies to work for in America," the authors looked at the practices that make certain organizations special from the employees' perspective. Among those at the top (quite a delicate position to be in given the volatility of life in organizations) were Southwest Airlines, W. L. Gore, Patagonia, Starbucks, Container Store, Goldman Sachs, Genetech and Harley-Davidson. Working from a database of more than 1,000 companies, the authors narrowed down those high on corporate characteristics such as inspirational leadership, excellent facilities at the workplace, flexitime, generous perks, a considerable amount of training and development and a sense of meaning. Employees in the winning organizations trusted their management, took pride in their work and company, and enjoyed a sense of camaraderie with colleagues. In short, the companies high on this list went to great lengths to create a humane corporate culture that would affect mental health positively.

Architects of potentially exemplary organizations must try to deconstruct the humane philosophy that underlies the values, behaviors, and practices of these great-to-work-for organizations and then determine how those values can be dovetailed with the earlier described values of high-performing organizations. They must ask themselves, What steps do companies need to take to contribute to the well-being of their people? What are the psychological dimensions that make companies great places to work? How can we fully tap the human potential present in each organization?

Unfortunately, these questions, with their concern for the individual, run contrary to today's business climate, with its concern for the bottom line. Organizations are rarely the orientation points in a sea of change that they once were. In fact, life in organizations has never been more turbulent than in this day and age. The companies listed on the best-to-work-for hit parade are rare exceptions to the rule. As I mentioned in Chapter 3, in this era of business reengineering and excessive preoccupation with shareholder value, the psychological contract that existed in less hectic times cannot hold. Thus employees tend to become like independent agents, and organizational identification plays a diminishing role. As a result, organizational cynicism is on the increase, loyalty is on the decrease, and the organizational employee of yesteryear – that person with great emotional attachment to his or her company – has all but disappeared.

In the past, being associated with a company was an effective way to affirm one's role in the world. Making a commitment of loyalty helped integrate the self-experiences of the employee from a phenomenological point of view. Affiliation with an organization became one of the ways of coping with economic and social upheaval, and it thereby contributed a measure of stability. It's ironic, then, that in this age of discontinuity, one of the traditional pillars of stability – the psychological contract – has been taken away.

The implications of this loss for the psychological well-being of employees are significant. As noted earlier, by breaking the psychological contract, organizations have abdicated the "containment" role that they used to play (whether consciously or unconsciously). With senior management less willing to provide a "holding environment" in which to "contain" the anxiety of their people, workplaces have become more stressful, not less. And the mental health of employees is suffering in consequence.

The "healthy" individual

One way of getting answers to questions about what makes an organization an exciting, vibrant, and satisfying place to work is by looking at what makes for a well-functioning individual. Under what conditions does a person feel most alive, for example? Unfortunately, definitions of a "healthy" individual seem to vary widely, depending on the person making the observations (Box 13.1). My experience with a broad range of people in the workplace – experience that blends business concepts with a psychological perspective – suggests the following:

❖ Healthy people (or health*ier*, remembering that continuum) possess a stable sense of identity; they have a good sense of who they are.

❖ Healthy people have a great capacity for reality testing.

❖ Healthy people resort to mature defense mechanisms in dealing with the outside world. They take responsibility for their actions rather than blaming others for setbacks.

❖ Healthy people have a sense of self-efficacy and are resourceful. They strongly believe in their own ability to control (or at least affect) the events that impact their lives.

❖ Healthy people have a positive perception of their body image and body functioning. They don't engage in self-destructive activities due to cognitive distortions; neither do they suffer from eating disorders.

❖ Healthy people experience the full range of affect. They don't suffer from alexithymia, with its colorblindness to feelings. They live intensely; they're passionate about everything they do.

❖ Sexuality and sensuality are fulfilling experiences for these individuals. They are an important dimension of their lives.

❖ Healthy people know how to manage anxiety, and they don't easily lose control or resort to impulsive acts.

❖ Healthy people value intimacy and reciprocity. They have the capacity to establish and cultivate relationships, and they actively maintain a support network for help and advice.

❖ Healthy people view themselves as part of a larger group; they derive a great sense of satisfaction from the social context in which they live. They feel connected.

❖ Healthy individuals know how to deal positively with issues of dependency and separation. As youngsters, they went through the process of individuation in a constructive manner; thus they suffered no developmental arrest. They don't resort to clinging behavior; on the contrary, they're able to establish mature relationships.

❖ Healthy people, with their great sense of identity, have the strength to deal with the setbacks and disappointments that are an inevitable part of the trajectory of life. They know how to handle depression and have a great capacity for working through loss.

❖ Healthy people know how to handle ambivalence, and they're able to see others in a balanced manner.

❖ Healthy people are creative and possess a sense of playfulness; they have the capacity to nonconform.

❖ Healthy people have a positive outlook toward the world. They have the ability to reframe experiences in a positive way; they're always able to fantasize about a more positive picture of the future. Despite whatever setbacks come their way, they retain hope for what's to come.

❖ Healthy people have the capacity for self-observation and self-analysis. They're highly motivated to spend time on self-reflection.

BOX 13.1

How "healthy" are you?

Label the following statements TRUE or FALSE. Compare your responses with those of someone close to you.

TRUE FALSE

- I have a good sense of who I am
- I don't really want to be someone else
- I believe that I have a realistic way of looking at things
- I take personal responsibility for my actions
- I accept the fact that most people have both good and bad sides
- I'm at ease with my bodily appearance
- I have a satisfactory sex life
- I feel that I have a rich emotional life
- I often feel cheerful and downright happy
- I don't have trouble relaxing
- I feel that I'm less anxiety prone than most other people
- I rarely worry about getting a serious disease
- I have no difficulty controlling myself when that's appropriate
- It's relatively easy for me to establish close, intimate relationships with others
- I have people I can go to for advice and help
- I belong to one or more social groups
- I enjoy social interaction with other people
- I see myself as quite independent
- It's relatively easy for me to work myself through low moods
- I perceive myself as quite playful
- I tend to have an optimistic outlook on the world
- I don't feel compelled to follow certain rituals and routines
- I spend a lot of time reflecting on what I do
- I don't have a great need to control others
- I feel quite satisfied with my life

If the majority of the statements are true for you, you tend to be toward the stable end of the emotional spectrum. If a large number of the statements are false for you, you may want to look further into those negative areas and perhaps seek professional help in dealing with them.

A related question worthwhile exploring is: How happy are you? In the end, that's what really counts in life. The anchors for each of us are different, necessitating different life strategies. The following exercise may shed some light on this question.

▶

BOX 13.1 continued

HAPPINESS: LIFE ANCHOR EXERCISE

Read the following statements and rank on a scale of 1 to 10 the importance of each of them. The ones that describe you most strongly show the anchors to your happiness. Take the top five and make an effort to deal with these wishes.

WISH	STATEMENT	SELF-RATING
INDEPENDENCE	To be self-reliant is important to my happiness	
VINDICATION	It is important for me to prove my critics wrong	
ACCEPTANCE	I have a strong need to be loved, liked, and accepted	
SOCIAL CONTACT	I like to make contact, socialize, and be close to others/make friends	
POWER	It is important for me to be in a position of power, authority, and leadership	
ORDER	I like things to be organized/in order	
STATUS	People who have a high social position/own expensive things impress me and I wish to be like them	
HONOR	Integrity, fair play, and principled behavior are important to me	
FAMILY	My family is essential to my happiness	
FAME	I have a strong need for popular acclaim and public esteem	
AESTHETICS	Music, art, nature, and other beautiful experiences are essential for my well-being	
EXPLORATION	I love to learn and do new things	
ACHIEVEMENT	I like to achieve, to be competent, to be successful in what I am doing	
MONEY	Financial security is very important to me	
MEANING	I like to get involved in social causes/make a contribution to society	
SPIRITUALITY	My spiritual values contribute significantly to my happiness	
HEALTH	To be in good mental and physical shape is very important to me	
EATING	I love to eat, think, and talk about food	
SENSUALITY	Sensual and sexual gratification is a significant part of my life	
CARE	To care for others, to see them grow and develop is very important to me	

Motivational need systems

These characteristics tell us a lot about what makes for a "healthy" and "happy" individual. To make a "diagnosis" of health or ill-health, happiness or unhappiness, in any specific case, however, we need to take a closer look at what we've been calling the person's "inner theater."

The script of an individual's inner theater is drafted in response to the *motivational need systems* on which choice is grounded. These need systems become operational in infancy and continue throughout the life-cycle (although they're altered by the forces of age, learning, and maturation). Motivational need systems are the driving forces that make people behave the way they do.

There are five basic motivational need systems. Three of these impact the workplace only peripherally. The first encompasses a person's physiological requirements, such as food, drink, elimination of wastes, sleep, and breathing; the second encompasses a person's need for sensual enjoyment and (later) sexual excitement; the third encompasses a person's need to respond aversively to certain situations through antagonism and withdrawal.

motivational need systems are the driving forces that make people behave the way they do

In addition to these, there are two systems that impact the workplace directly and powerfully: the need for attachment/affiliation and the need for exploration/assertion.

Humankind's essential humanness is found in its need for attachment/affiliation – in the seeking of relationships with other people, in the striving to be part of something larger. The *need for attachment* drives the process of engagement with another human being; it's the universal experience of wanting to be close to another, to have the pleasures of sharing and affirmation. When this need for intimate engagement is extrapolated to groups, the desire to enjoy intimacy can be described as a *need for affiliation*. Both attachment and affiliation serve an emotional balancing role by confirming the individual's self-worth and contributing to his or her sense of self-esteem.

The other motivational need system that's crucial for the workplace – the need for exploration/assertion – involves the ability to play and think and learn and work. Like the need for attachment/affiliation, these needs begin early in life. Researchers observing infants have discovered that exploration – assessed in this case via a recognition of novelty and a linking of cause and effect – causes a prolonged state of attentive arousal. Similar reactions to opportunities for exploration continue into adulthood. Closely tied to the *need for exploration* is a *need for self-assertion* – that is, for the ability to choose what one wants to do. Playful exploration and manipulation of the environment in response to exploratory-assertive motivation produces a sense of effectiveness, competency, autonomy, initiative, and industry – whether the explorer/asserter is a developing child or a corporate CEO.

Because these last two need systems – the need for attachment/affiliation and the need for exploration/assertion – have a great impact on the workplace, organizational leaders need to build a corporate culture that addresses them directly. How? By crafting a set of meta-values that closely echo those need systems, building among their people a feeling of community that comes from being part of the organization (addressing attachment/affiliation needs) and a feeling of enjoyment and empowerment (addressing exploration/assertion needs).

The first meta-value, which we can call "love" or "community," seeks to help all employees develop a sense of collegiality with co-workers and a sense of belonging to the company. Attachment and affiliation are necessary not only to individuals but also to the organization. Only when attachment and affiliation have been achieved can trust and mutual respect grow; and as we've seen repeatedly in earlier chapters, trust is essential to organizational success.

A sense of community can be enhanced in various ways. Organizational architecture makes a big difference. For example, small units allow people to feel more connected. So does distributed leadership – that is, leadership that's spread throughout the organization rather than concentrated at the top. Mentoring builds community too: senior employees who help younger ones learn new skills and processes (and encourage them to feel good about their accomplishments) model a supportive attitude toward co-workers.

In addition to the meta-value of community, companies need to develop the meta-value of enjoyment. Employees who have fun at work feel free to exercise their need for exploration and assertion, and innovation and creativity result. Thus having fun improves the corporate bottom line along with the mental health of workers. Organizations that neglect a sense of enjoyment begin to feel like prison camps, their leaders nothing more than "guards" characterized by the alexithymia and anhedonia discussed in Chapter 5.

Humankind's search for meaning and congruence

The five motivational systems just described determine an individual's outlook on the world, creating a *subjective reality* that guides him or her through the *objective reality* of life. When these two realities are in conflict, stress and discomfort (or even, in extreme cases, mental illness) result.

Because people sense the need for congruence between their subjective reality and the world's objective reality, they seek out activities that reverberate with their basic motivational systems. Those activities that are congruent – whether at work or in the personal sphere – are perceived as personally meaningful.

people sense the need for congruence between their subjective reality and the world's objective reality

Work plays an important role in humankind's search for meaning. Work that offers congruence between subjective and objective realities gives people a sense of significance and orientation, and offers continuity in a world that's increasingly discontinuous. Furthermore, leaving a legacy through work (as discussed in Chapter 11) provides an affirmation of an individual's sense of self and identity, thereby offering an important form of narcissistic gratification.

Work can give meaning not only in the *personal* sense described, but also in the broader, *societal* sense of transcending one's personal needs to improve the quality of life, help people in need, or contribute value to society. Organizations whose goals benefit society encourage both leaders and followers to put their imagination and creativity to work.

Given the importance of meaning (whether personal or societal) to workers, organizational leadership needs to institute a *collective* system of meaning. By that I mean that work in any organization should be done – and if necessary reframed – in ways that make sense to the employees and should be directed toward goals that employees perceive as worthy. The resulting congruence between personal and collective objectives is essential to individual health, but it also furthers organizational health.

Let's look more specifically at what leaders should do to institute a collective system of meaning:

- ❖ They need to create a *sense of purpose* for their people. They can do this by articulating loudly and clearly the organization's vision for the future and its fundamental purpose and culture. By building support for that vision, they create a strong and cohesive group identity, purpose, and meaning.

- ❖ They need to create a *sense of self-determination* among their employees. For the sake of organizational mental health, it's essential that employees have a feeling of control over their lives. They need to see themselves not as mere peons in a larger scheme of things, but as actors who have choices to make.

- ❖ They need to build a *sense of impact* among employees. It's important that each organizational member be convinced that his or her actions can make a difference to the organization. This is what empowerment is all about. Leaders need to give their people "voice"!

- ❖ They need to foster a *sense of competence* among all employees, so that organizational participants have a feeling of personal growth and development. Continuous learning is essential: only when people's exploratory urges find an outlet can their creativity blossom.

- ❖ In addition, because *how* things are done says as much about meaning as *what* things are done, leaders need to develop a strong *sense of shared values.* Specifically, they need to espouse and embody those values of successful companies that we looked at in Chapter 7: team orientation, candor, respect for the individual, empowerment, customer focus, achievement orientation, entrepreneurial attitude, fun, accountability, continuous learning, openness to change, and trust.

To illustrate, Richard Branson works to build a collective system of meaning. He continually involves himself and his people in causes that seek to improve the world. He's worked hard to fight AIDS, for example, and has offered his planes for catastrophe relief.

Characteristics of the "authentizotic" organization

Organizations that meet the human needs discussed will set the standard in the twenty-first century. These organizations can best be described as *authentizotic*. The label *authentizotic* is derived from two Greek words: *authenteekos* and *zoteekos*. The first part of the label means "authentic". In its broadest sense, the word *authentic* describes something that conforms to fact and is therefore worthy of trust and reliance. Applied to an organization, it describes a place where the leadership walks the talk. Furthermore, it implies that the organization has a compelling connective quality for its employees, through its vision, mission, culture, and structure. In an authentizotic organization, the leadership communicates clearly and convincingly not only the *how* but also the *why* of the business, revealing meaning in each person's task. As a result, people find the sense of "flow" we discussed in Chapter 5; they feel complete and alive.

The second part of the label, *zoteekos*, means "vital to life." In the organizational context, it describes the way in which people are invigorated by their work. People in organizations to which the *zoteekos* label can be applied feel a sense of balance and completeness. In such organizations, the human need for exploration, closely associated with cognition and learning, is met. The *zoteekos* element of this type of organization allows for self-assertion in the workplace and produces a sense of effectiveness and competency, of autonomy, initiative, creativity, entrepreneurship, and industry. Although authentizotic organizations contribute only partially to the happiness equation, their importance should not be discounted.

As we move further into the twenty-first century, the prime challenge of organizational leadership is to create corporations that possess these authentizotic qualities. Organizations that are truly authentizotic offer an antidote to stress, provide a healthier existence, increase imagination and creativity, contribute to a more fulfilling life, and encourage a balance between personal and organizational life. These are the organizations we need to hope for. To quote an Arab proverb, "He who has health has hope, and he who has hope has everything!"

So what do these authentizotic organizations look like? They practice the values and meta-values mentioned earlier. They serve as a safe holding environment, offering a degree of safety and security for their employees despite the demise of the old psychological contract. They're very selective in taking on new employees, wanting to be sure that new hires are comfortable with and will "live" the values of the organization. They place a high priority on creating a sense of ownership among workers. To that end, they devote considerable resources to training and development and strive to revitalize their staff. (As Napoleon said, "The art of governing consists of not letting men grow old in their jobs.") They believe that attention to personal growth and development will encourage good organizational citizenship and prevent organizational parochialism.

the prime challenge of organizational leadership is to create corporations that possess authentizotic qualities

To foster a sense of belonging, authentizotic organizations favor an amoeba-type structure – that is, a structure in which units split off when they become too large. Alternatively, they create small companies within a large company structure, emphasizing the project team as the unit of responsibility. Grouped in small, flexible units, all employees can relate and interact with each other. Many exemplary leaders have been enthusiastic advocates of "small is beautiful" in one form or another.

Authentizotic companies are "flat," minimizing hierarchical differences (although it's in the nature of the human animal to differentiate itself) and spreading decision-making authority and responsibility throughout the organization. That doesn't minimize the role of leadership; it simply reshapes the traditional view. Leaders in the authentizotic organization don't render decisions from on high. They're accessible to their followers and responsive to their input. You might almost say that they manage by walking around.

Authentizotic companies spread accountability as well as responsibility. I remember once being on a podium with David Simon, who at the time was chairman of British Petroleum. He pointed out that, "What isn't targeted, what isn't measured, doesn't get done." He improved accountability at British Petroleum by turning the company into many small profit centers. Even in a less structured company like Virgin, Richard Branson makes sure that things get measured.

constant comparison with "the best in class" is a good antidote against arrogance

Virgin benchmarks both inside and outside the company, believing that constant comparison with "the best in class" is a good antidote against arrogance.

Authentizotic organizations facilitate innovation because of their people orientation. They provide the "AIR" necessary to forward-looking innovation:

A   They give people a considerable amount of Autonomy to encourage creativity.

I   They encourage Interaction between different parts of the organization to create synergy.

R   They Recognize individual contributions to foster empowerment.

Because of this people orientation, authentizotic organizations are characterized by collaboration, teamwork, and mutual support. They strive for and reward successful interactions between people and departments, thereby building a high level of trust. They seek diversity of gender, race, and age, knowing that breadth of experience enriches decision making and creativity. They encourage constructive risk taking and experimentation, and they accept (and are sometimes persuaded by) contrarian thinking. As a result, candor flourishes. (See Figure 13.1 for an overview of the characteristics that distinguish the authentizotic organization.)

1 A sense of community

2 An orientation toward fun and enjoyment

3 A sense of meaning (both personal and societal)

4 A safe holding environment

5 Selectivity in entry

6 A sense of ownership and empowerment

7 Emphasis on training and development

8 "Flat" hierarchical structure and small units

9 Accessibility of leadership

10 Accountability

11 A people orientation

AIR: Autonomy, interaction, recognition
A team orientation
Trust
Diversity
An emphasis on experimentation
Candor

Figure 13.1 Essential elements of the authentizotic organization

The gender question

Although we can find more women in middle management positions today, and more serving as nonexecutive directors, the number of women in *top* management positions hasn't increased very much over the last few decades.

This situation is ironic when we look at the trends in organizational life. The organizations that are on the rise these days are service oriented and cross-cultural, and women are typically perceived as better than men at applying interpersonal and cross-cultural skills. So where are all the women who should be in senior positions in these organizations? Why are an increasing number of women starting their own organizations? Why do so many women feel uncomfortable in large organizations (Box 13.2)?

Are you a "real" man (or woman)?

Though this quiz is obviously tongue in cheek, the extremes it presents are mirrored, in subtle form, in many businesses throughout the world. Bottom line? Management and interpersonal encounters are typically handled differently by men than by women.

1 Your project team is working overtime to finish a proposal. The deadline is dangerously tight, but obtaining the project is essential if the company is to make it back into the black. To your increasing frustration, one team member – his name is John – keeps coming up with one objection after the other. To keep the project on target, you:

A Suggest a timeout; then, after a few minutes to compose thoughts, have everyone present his or her position and listen carefully to the others, and guide the group to an acceptable compromise.

B Hit John on the mouth.

2 You're walking down the street and pass a bar. A drunk named Pete, a bit too friendly but obviously inoffensive, approaches you and wants to shake your hand. You:

A Shake his hand, wish him a nice day, and walk on.

B Tense up, become anxious, and hit him on the mouth.

Scoring: If you answered B to both questions, you're most likely male.

There are many explanations given for the gender gap in business. Very often they center on the anatomy-is-destiny theme; they assume, in other words, that pregnancy and childrearing throw women off the critical periods of their career trajectory. There is truth to this observation, but is it the *full* truth? The fact that in certain societies men play an active part in childrearing, taking on most of the responsibilities, suggests that other factors are involved.

Another answer given is that women are more concerned than men about keeping a balanced lifestyle and are therefore not prepared to make the kind of sacrifices that top management demands. A further answer is that women are by nature more nurturing than men and therefore choose to focus on the needs of family and friends over career commitments.

A more controversial answer sometimes given is that many men, in their heart of hearts, are scared of women. Some are, certainly. I know quite a few men who feel comfortable only with other men; they can't be at ease in the company of women. Women, contrariwise, are more likely to feel comfortable with both men and women. And although men typically don't mind ordering their secretaries around, being told what to do by a female boss is hard for quite a few men to take. (After all, haven't their mothers been pushing them around long enough?)

many men, in their heart of hearts, are scared of women

To get a better idea of how sexuality complicates the workplace, let's look at mentoring, which I've mentioned frequently in these pages as a necessary form of leadership development. Say a promising young executive – a woman – is looking for someone to show her the ropes, help her avoid making political mistakes, and give constructive feedback. If this woman approaches a gray-haired gentleman with a request for that kind of help, what do you think goes through his mind? What kind of fantasies do you think he has? How about her? What fantasies do *you* have?

Understandably, many men have a hard time taking on that mentoring role. They may be scared of their feelings. They may be concerned about how their wife or partner will react, what their colleagues at the office will think when they make business trips together, and so on. They may even think about cases of sexual harassment. Clearly, then, there's an enormous amount of ambivalence about male–female interaction, and that ambivalence can lead to the subtle discrimination that undergirds the infamous glass ceiling. It's not a conscious conspiracy, certainly (at least not in most firms). But the end effect is that career advancement isn't easy for women. In many instances, they have to be supercompetent before they get the attention they deserve. All too often, they are victims of subtle discrimination.

career advancement isn't easy for women

So what do we do about it? Well, acquiescing to the present state is unacceptable. Discrimination is bad enough on its own, but from a purely economic point of view it's not in the best interests of the company either. Diversity, as I've indicated before, makes for richer decision making and more creative problem solving. In fact, it's a prerequisite of authentizotic organizations. Fortunately, all the authentizotic prerequisites are closely interwoven. Thus as we strive in our organizations to be more community oriented, more empowering, and more open and trusting, we'll progress on the diversity front as well.

14 Final thoughts

I never let my schooling interfere with my education.

MARK TWAIN

Time ripens all things; no man is born wise. MIGUEL DE CERVANTES

Experience is the comb that nature gives us after we are bald. BELGIAN PROVERB

In this book I've commented on the importance of the clinical paradigm in understanding organizations. I've emphasized the significance of emotional intelligence. I've discussed the shadow side of leadership – the various traps into which a leader can fall. I've highlighted traits that make for effective leadership, roles that leaders need to play, and practices they need to engage in. I've also made a plea for authentizotic organizations. Now, in concluding this book, I'd like to make a case for the fool in organizations and offer some final thoughts on leadership.

The fool as necessary truth teller

This fool I'm talking about isn't the leader. He or she is a *foil* for the leader – and every leader needs one. The fool is a very traditional role, the stabilizer of kings and queens (and other leaders) down through the ages. The fool, a guardian of reality, uses antics and humor to prevent the pursuit of foolish action, avoid group-think, show the leader his or her reflection, and remind the leader of the transience of power. This is the fool of King Lear – the *wise* fool, or, as the French say, the *morosophe*.

Let me explain the importance of the fool through an anecdote. A couple goes to a fair. At the fair there's a large, impressive-looking machine. If you put money in this machine, it tells you your age and what kind of person you are. The husband gets quite excited at this prospect and puts in the required coin. Immediately, out comes a ticket.

the fool uses antics and humor to remind the leader of the transience of power

Before the man can take the ticket, his wife grabs it and reads out, "You're intelligent and charming. You're mesmerizing; women fall all over you." Then she turns the ticket over and says, "You know what? They got your age wrong too." All leaders need someone who, like this wife, is willing to tell them how things really are, to show them a mirror in which they can see themselves honestly. Because fools remind leaders of the need for candor, they help leaders confront their true self.

Leaders need to ask themselves whether they have a person (or people) playing the role of fool for them. If the answer is no, they need to determine whether they've created the kind of organization in which a fool would be tolerated, the kind of organization in which people can "talk back" to the boss without negative consequences.

I once had lunch with the president of one of the largest banks in Singapore, and he told me that every leader needs to have a number of good friends who always tell the truth – friends who are willing to confront the leader with things he or she may not want to hear. Once leaders achieve a position of power, they tend to forget that they are, after all, only human. Because of that tendency, there's a need for people who have the courage to point out the feet of clay.

Sometimes these truth tellers come from inside the corporation, perhaps nonexecutive directors or members of the supervisory board. Sometimes they're outsiders, perhaps consultants. (This is a good argument against hiring "hungry" consultants or leadership coaches – they tend to tell their clients what they want to hear.) Wherever truth tellers come from, senior executives need them badly; they need sparring partners with whom they can test reality.

Final thoughts on leadership

Having presented a whirlwind tour of leadership and organizational life, I've probably left you thoroughly confused. I've been all over the organizational map in these chapters. And I've rarely made things simple, largely because my suggestions about leadership and organizations are based on concepts from many different disciplines. The blending of ideas from diverse **the four H's of effective leadership: hope, humanity, humility, and humor** domains such as anthropology, family systems theory, psychotherapy, psychoanalysis (particularly object relations theory), cognitive theory, and management theory results in a certain degree of mystification. Let me try to simplify (*over*simplify!) my message through the use of an acronym.

In this age of acronyms in management, we have the seven-S model of McKinsey, the five-F model of Warren Bennis, the three B's of creativity, and so on. As for me, I've introduced various I's, P's, C's, M's, T's, and D's in these pages. Now I'd like to introduce the four H's of effective leadership: hope, humanity, humility, and humor:

- ❖ **Hope** Leadership starts with the H of hope. Leaders have to create a sense of hope, or both they and their aspirations are lost. Without hope, there's nowhere for leaders to lead or followers to follow.

- ❖ **Humanity** As I mentioned earlier, leaders should never forget that they're human. The humanity of leaders is often best revealed in how they treat people whom they can't benefit from.

- ❖ **Humility** Humility is closely related to humanity, in that it's rooted in accurate self-perception. Good leaders realize that no conquest is theirs alone.

- ❖ **Humor** Effective leaders have a good sense of humor, even in the face of disaster, and they're willing to laugh at their own foibles. Humor is a good indicator of mental health and an asset to any workplace.

As I mentioned in Chapter 1, many of the things I've said in this book aren't new. Many of my observations have been made before, and exemplary leaders through the ages have practiced many of the things I recommend. The question is, Do *you* practice them? For that matter, do you practice the theories that you yourself espouse? Experience has shown me that there's a great difference between what leaders *say* they do and what they *actually* do.

To illustrate the vintage of leadership theory, let me share a perspective on effective leadership that's been around more than a millennium – a perspective that may seem paradoxical in light of the need for strong leadership. In 604 BC, the sage Lao-tzu said, emphasizing the timelessness of "distributed leadership":

> A leader is best
> When people barely know that he exists,
> Not so good when people obey and acclaim him,
> Worst when they despise him.
> Fail to honor people,
> They will fail to honor you.
> But of a good leader, who talks little,
> When his work is done, his aim fulfilled,
> They will all say, "We did it ourselves."

Let me end this book with one final anecdote. A few years ago a very senior executive participated in my leadership seminar at INSEAD. He was not only the oldest in the group, he was far older than the typical participant in any of my sessions. He saw the seminar as an opportunity to prepare for succession and plan his retirement.

This man was responsible for a very large organization: 75,000 people reported to him. When he described his leadership style to the group – remember, the seminar's focus is the "life" case presentation – he confessed that he possessed a rather Machiavellian streak. He said:

> I'm a very good manipulator. Sometimes I have a good idea and
> manage to present it in such a way that others think it's really *their*
> idea. Then they run with it and the idea is implemented. If it turns
> out to be successful, I'm delighted, of course. So I go home, open
> the liquor cabinet in my study, and pour myself a shot of the best

whiskey. I raise my glass in a toast. But a toast to whom? To myself? Is there no more to it? I guess I have to do without the applause.

This person managed his narcissistic disposition well. He was willing to let other people shine even when the victory was his. That's largely why he led his organization so successfully. He made sure that both leadership and credit were distributed throughout the company.

Can the same be said of you? Do you have the self-confidence to place others at center stage? Do you get pleasure from helping others learn and grow? Are you willing to learn yourself, accepting teaching not only from superiors but also from the up-and-comers in your organization? Are you able to keep an open mind and prevent yourself from getting stuck in a psychic prison?

Whether you're a capital-L Leader or a lowercase-l leader aspiring for greater things, these questions should never be forgotten. They'll help you cultivate and retain the four H's of leadership – hope, humanity, humility, and humor – and the all-important sense of "flow" that keeps your enthusiasm alive. The challenge in life is to die young as late as possible. People who meet that challenge head-on ask every day, every hour, *What if?* and *What next?*

the challenge in life is to die young as late as possible

Suggested further reading

For readers who want to go to the sources on which this book is based, this chapter lists first a number of my writings and then a collection of books that have contributed to my reflections on leadership and organizations.

Relevant writings by Kets de Vries

Kets de Vries, M. F. R. (1980) *Organizational Paradoxes: Clinical Approaches to Management*. New York: Routledge.

Kets de Vries, M. F. R. (1989) *Prisoners of Leadership*. New York: Wiley.

Kets de Vries, M. F. R. (1993) *Leaders, Fools, and Impostors*. San Francisco: Jossey-Bass.

Kets de Vries, M. F. R. (1995) *Life and Death in the Executive Fast Lane: Essays on Irrational Organizations and their Leaders*. San Francisco: Jossey-Bass.

Kets de Vries, M. F. R. (1996) *Family Business: Human Dilemmas in the Family Firm*. London: International Thompson Business Press.

Kets de Vries, M. F. R. (2001a) *Struggling with the Demon: Perspectives on Individual and Organizational Irrationality*. Garden City, NJ: Psychosocial Press.

Kets de Vries, M. F. R. (2001b) *Meditations on Happiness*. London: Ebury Press.

Kets de Vries, M. F. R. (2004) *Lessons on Leadership by Terror: Finding Shaka Zulu in the Attic*. Cheltenham: Edward Elgar.

Kets de Vries, M. F. R. (2005) *Global Executive Leadership Inventory: Participant's Guide (& Facilitator's Guide)*. San Francisco: Pfeiffer.

Kets de Vries, M. F. R. (2006) *Leaders on the Couch*. London: Wiley.

Kets de Vries, M. F. R., and Engellau, E. (2004) *Are Leaders Born or Are They Made? The Case of Alexander the Great*. London: Karnac.

Kets de Vries, M. F. R., with Florent-Treacy, E. (1999) *The New Global Leaders, Percy Barnevik, Richard Branson, and David Simon and the Making of the International Corporation.* San Francisco: Jossey-Bass.

Kets de Vries, M. F. R., and Miller, D. (1984) *The Neurotic Organization.* San Francisco: Jossey-Bass.

Kets de Vries, M. F. R., and Miller, D. (1988) *Unstable at the Top.* New York: New American Library.

Kets de Vries, M. F. R., and Perzow, S. (1991) *Handbook of Character Studies.* New York: International University Press.

Kets de Vries, M. F. R., Shekshia, S., Korotov, K., and Florent-Treacy, E. (2004) *The New Russian Business Leaders.* Cheltenham: Edward Elgar.

Relevant writings by other authors

American Psychiatric Association (2000) *Diagnostic and Statistical Manual of the Mental Disorders, DSM-IV-Tr.* 4th edn. Washington, DC: American Psychiatric Association.

Arieti, S. (1976) *Creativity: The Magic Synthesis.* New York: Basic Books.

Bandura, A. (1997) *Self-Efficacy: The Exercise of Control.* New York: Freeman.

Bass, B. M. (1990) *Bass and Stogdill's Handbook of Leadership.* 3rd edn. New York: The Free Press.

Bennis, W., and Nanus, B. (1985) *Leadership.* New York: HarperCollins.

Bettelheim, B. (1976) *The Uses of Enchantment.* New York: Alfred A. Knopf.

Bion, W. R. (1959) *Experiences in Groups.* London: Tavistock.

Bowlby, J. (1969) *Attachment and Loss. Vol. 1: Attachment.* New York: Basic Books.

Chandler, A. D. (1962) *Strategy and Structure: Chapters in the History of the American Enterprise.* Cambridge, MA: MIT Press.

Collins, J. C., and Porras, J. I. (1994) *Build to Last.* New York: HarperBusiness.

Collins, J. C. (2001) *Good to Great.* New York: HarperCollins.

Crozier, M. (1964) *The Bureaucratic Phenomenon.* Chicago, IL: University of Chicago Press.

Csikszentmihalyi, M. (1990) *Flow: The Psychology of Optimal Experience.* New York: Harper & Row.

Davonloo, H. (2000) *Intensive Short-Term Dynamic Psychotherapy.* New York: Wiley.

Dement, W. C. (1999) *The Promise of Sleep.* New York: Random House.

Erikson, E. H. (1963) *Childhood and Society.* New York: W. W. Norton.

Fenichel, O. (1945) *The Psychoanalytic Theory of Neurosis.* New York: W. W. Norton.

Frankl, V. (1962) *Man's Search for Meaning: An Introduction to Logotherapy.* Boston, MA: Beacon Press.

Freud, S. (1921) "Group psychology and the analysis of the ego" in J. Strachey (ed.) *The Standard Edition of the Complete Psychological Works of Sigmund Freud (Vol. 7).* London: Hogarth Press and Institute of Psychoanalysis.

Freud, S. (1929) "Civilization and its discontents" in J. Strachey (ed.) *The Standard Edition of the Complete Psychological Works of Sigmund Freud (Vol. 21).* London: Hogarth Press and the Institute of Psychoanalysis.

Freud, S. (1933) "New introductory lectures" in J. Strachey (ed.) *The Standard Edition of the Complete Psychological Works of Sigmund Freud (Vol. 22).* London: Hogarth Press and the Institute of Psychoanalysis.

Fromm, E. (1951) *The Forgotten Language.* New York: Grove Press.

Gabriel, Y. (1999) *Organizations in Depth.* London: Sage.

Geertz, C. (1973) *The Interpretation of Cultures.* New York: Basic Books.

Goleman, D. (1995) *Emotional Intelligence.* London: Bloomsbury.

Greenberg, J. R., and Mitchell, S. A. (1983) *Object Relations in Psychoanalytic Theory.* Cambridge, MA: Harvard University Press.

Hall, E. T. (1959) *The Silent Language.* Greenwich, CT: Fawcett Publications.

Hofstede, G. (1991) *Culture's Consequences: Software of the Mind.* New York: McGraw-Hill.

Hogan, R. T., Johnson, J., and Briggs, R. (eds) (1997) *Handbook of Personality Psychology.* New York: Morgan Kaufmann.

Jung, C. G. (1973) *C. G. Jung: Psychological Reflections: A New Anthology of His Writings.* Princeton, NJ: Princeton University Press.

Kernberg, O. (1985) *Internal World and External Reality.* New York: Jason Aronson.

Kohut, H. (1971) *The Analysis of the Self.* New York: International Universities Press.

Kotter, J. P. (1982) *The General Managers.* New York: The Free Press.

Kouzes, J. M., and Posner, B. Z. (1995) *The Leadership Challenge.* San Francisco: Jossey-Bass.

Laing, R. D. (1960) *The Divided Self.* London: Tavistock.

Lefcourt, H. M. (1976) *Locus of Control.* New York: Wiley.

Lemma-Wright, A. (1995) *Invitation to Psychodynamic Psychology.* London: Whurr Publishers.

Levinson, D. (1978) *The Seasons of Man's Life.* New York: Alfred A. Knopf.

Levinson, H. (1982) *Executive.* Cambridge, MA: Harvard University Press.

Levinson, H. (2002) *Organizational Assessment.* Washington, DC: American Psychological Association.

Lichtenberg, J. (1989) *Psychoanalysis and Motivation.* Hillsdale, NJ: Analytic Press.

Lorenz, K. (1966) *On Aggression.* London: Methuen.

Luborsky, L., and Crits-Cristophe, P. (1998) *Understanding Transference: The Core Conflictual Relationship Theme Method.* Washington, DC: American Psychological Organization.

Malan, D., and Osimo, F. (1992) *Psychodynamics, Training, and Outcome in Brief Psychotherapy.* Oxford: Butterworth Heinemann.

McAdams, D. P. (1993) *Stories We Live By: Personal Myths and the Making of the Self.* New York: William Morrow.

McCullough Vaillant, L. (1997) *Changing Character.* New York: Basic Books.

McDougall, J. (1985) *Theaters of the Mind.* New York: Basic Books.

Millon, T. (1996) *Disorders of Personality: DSM IV and Beyond.* New York: John Wiley.

Mintzberg, H. (1973) *The Nature of Managerial Work.* New York: Harper & Row.

Mintzberg, H. (1979) *The Structuring of Organizations.* Englewood Cliffs, NJ: Prentice Hall.

Morgan, G. (1986) *Images of Organization.* London: Sage.

Pfeffer, J. (1998) *The Human Equation: Building Profits by Putting People First.* Boston, MA: Harvard Business School Press.

Schein, E. (1985) *Organizational Culture and Leadership.* San Francisco: Jossey-Bass.

Scott Rutan, J., and Stone, W. N. (2001) *Psychodynamic Group Psychotherapy.* New York: The Guilford Press.

Selye, H. (1974) *Stress Without Distress.* New York: New American Library.

Shapiro, D. (1965) *Neurotic Styles.* New York: Basic Books.

Sheehy, G. (1995) *New Passages.* New York: Ballantine Books.

Storr, A. (1979) *The Art of Psychotherapy.* New York: Methuen.

Sullivan, H. S. (1953) *The Interpersonal Theory of Psychiatry.* New York: W. W. Norton.

Tichy, N. M. (1997) *The Leadership Engine.* New York: HarperCollins.

Trompenaars, F. (1993) *Riding the Waves of Culture: Understanding Cultural Diversity in Business.* Avon: The Bath Press.

Vaillant, G. E. (1977) *Adaptation to Life.* Boston, MA: Little, Brown.

Watzlawick, P., Weakland, J., and Frisch, R. (1974) *Change: Principles of Problem Formation and Problem Resolution.* New York: W. W. Norton.

White, R. (1966) *Lives in Progress.* New York: Holt, Rinehart and Winston.

Zaleznik, A. (1966) *Human Dilemmas of Leadership.* New York: HarperCollins.

Zaleznik, A. (1989) *The Managerial Mystique.* New York: Harper & Row.

Index